The Prince
and
The Art of War

NICCOLO MACHIAVELLI

The Prince
and
The Art of War
Two Classic Works of Strategy, Tactics and Politics
by One of the Foremost Proponents

Niccolo Machiavelli

The Prince and The Art of War
Two Classic Works of Strategy, Tactics and Politics by One of the Foremost Proponents
by Niccolo Machiavelli

First published under the titles
The Prince
and
The Art of War

Leonaur is an imprint
of Oakpast Ltd

Copyright in this form © 2012 Oakpast Ltd

ISBN: 978-0-85706-836-1 (hardcover)
ISBN: 978-0-85706-837-8 (softcover)

http://www.leonaur.com

Publisher's Notes

The views expressed in this book are not necessarily
those of the publisher.

Contents

The Prince	7
The Art of War	105

The Prince

Contents

Dedication	13
Of the Various Kinds of Princedoms, and of the Methods in Which They Are Acquired	15
Of Hereditary Princedoms	16
Of Mixed Princedoms	17
Why the Kingdom of Darius,	24
Conquered by Alexander, Did Not, On Alexander's Death, Rebel Against His Successors	24
How to Govern Cities or Princedoms Which Before Their Acquisition Have Lived Under Their Own Laws	27
Of Those New Princedoms Which a Prince Acquires With His Own Arms and by Merit	29
Of New Princedoms Acquired by the Aid of Others and by Good Fortune	33
Of Those Who by Their Crimes Come to be Princes	39
Of the Civil Princedom	43
How the Strength of All Princedoms Should be Measured	47
Of Ecclesiastical Princedoms	49
How Many Different Kinds of Soldiers There Are, and of Mercenaries	52
Of Auxiliary, Mixed, and National Arms	57

Of the Duty of a Prince in Respect of Military Affairs	61
Of the Qualities in Respect of Which Men, and Most of all Princes, are Praised or Blamed	64
Of Liberality and Miserliness	66
Of Cruelty and Clemency, and Whether it is Better to be Loved or Feared	69
How Princes Should Keep Faith	72
That a Prince Should Seek to Avoid Contempt and Hatred	75
Whether Fortresses, and Various Other Expedients to Which Princes Often Have Recourse, are Profitable or Hurtful	84
How a Prince Should Govern Himself so as to Acquire Reputation	88
Of the Secretaries of Princes	92
That Flatterers Should be Shunned	94
Why the Princes of Italy have Lost Their States	96
What Fortune Can Effect in Human Affairs, and How She May be Withstood	98
An Exhortation to Liberate Italy From the Barbarians	101

Inscitia in plerisque et sermonum multitudo. Nisi quod unius tamen Machiavelli ingenium non contemno, acre, subtile, igneum; et qui utinam Principem suum recta duxisset ad templum illud Virtutis et Honoris! Sed nimis saepe deflexit, et dum commodi illas semitas intente sequitur, aberravit a regia hac via.

Justus Lipsius.

Lorenzo Di Piero De' Medici.

Dedication

NICCOLO MACHIAVELLI TO THE MAGNIFICENT
LORENZO DI PIERO DE' MEDICI.

It is customary for such as would gain a prince's favour, to present themselves before him with those of their possessions which they themselves most value, or in which they perceive him chiefly to delight. Accordingly, we often see horses, armour, cloth of gold, precious stones, and such like ornaments offered to princes as worthy of their greatness. Desiring, in like manner, to approach your Magnificence with some token of my devotion, I have found among my possessions none that I so much prize and esteem as a knowledge of the actions of great men, acquired in the course of a long experience of modern affairs and a continual study of antiquity. Which knowledge most carefully and patiently thought out and sifted by me, and now reduced into this little book, I send to your Magnificence. And though I deem the work unworthy of your greatness, I am still bold enough to hope that your courtesy will dispose you to accept it, considering that I can offer you no better gift than the means of mastering in a very brief time, all that I in the course of so many years, and at the cost of so many hardships and dangers, have learned, and know.

This work I have not adorned or amplified with rounded periods, swelling and high-flown language, or any other of those extrinsic attractions and allurements with which many authors are wont to set off and grace their writings. For it is my desire that it should either pass wholly unhonoured, or that the truth of its matter and the importance of its subject should alone recommend it.

Nor would I have it thought presumption that a person of the meanest and humblest station should venture to discourse and lay down rules concerning the government of princes. For as those who make maps of countries place themselves low down in the plains to study the character of mountains and elevated lands, and place themselves high up on the mountains to get a better view of the plains, in like manner to understand the people a man should be a prince, and to have a clear notion of princes he should belong to the people.

Let your Magnificence, then, accept this little gift in the spirit in which I offer it; in which, if you diligently read and study it, you will recognize my extreme desire that you should attain to that eminence which fortune and your own merits promise you. If from the height of your greatness you should some time turn your eyes to these humbler regions, you will become aware how undeservedly I have to bear the great and unremitting malignity of fortune.

CHAPTER 1

Of the Various Kinds of Princedoms, and of the Methods in Which They Are Acquired

All the states and governments by which men are or ever have been ruled, have been and are either republics or princedoms. Princedoms are either hereditary, in which the sovereignty is derived through an ancient line of ancestors, or they are new. New princedoms are either wholly new, as that of Milan to Francesco Sforza; or they are like limbs joined on to the hereditary possessions of the prince who acquires them, as the Kingdom of Naples to the dominions of the King of Spain. The states thus acquired have either been used to live under a prince or have been free; and he who acquires them does so either by his own arms or by the arms of others, and either by good fortune or by merit.

CHAPTER 2

Of Hereditary Princedoms

Of republics I shall not now speak, having elsewhere spoken of them at length. Here I shall treat exclusively of princedoms, and filling in the outline above traced out, shall proceed to examine how such states are to be governed and maintained.

I say, then, that hereditary states, accustomed to the family of their prince, are maintained with far less difficulty than new states, since all that is required is that the prince shall not depart from the usages of his ancestors, trusting for the rest to deal with events as they arise. So that if an hereditary prince be of average address, he will always maintain himself in his princedom, unless deprived of it by some extraordinary and irresistible force; and even if so deprived, will be able to recover it, should any, even the least mishap overtake the usurper.

We have in Italy an example of this in the Duke of Ferrara, who never could have withstood the attacks of the Venetians in 1484, nor those of Pope Julius in 1510, had not his authority in that State been consolidated by time. For since a prince by birth has less cause and fewer occasions to give offence, he ought to be better loved, and will naturally be popular with his subjects unless extraordinary vices make him odious. Moreover, the very antiquity and continuance of his rule will efface the recollections and causes which lead to innovation. For one change always leaves a dovetail into which another will fit.

CHAPTER 3

Of Mixed Princedoms

But in new princedoms difficulties abound. And, first, if the princedom be not wholly new, but joined on to the ancient dominions of the prince, so as to form with them what may be termed a mixed princedom, disturbances will arise from a defect inherent in all new states. For since men, thinking to better their condition, are always ready to change masters, and in this expectation to take up arms against any ruler, they often deceive themselves, and find afterwards by experience that they are worse off than before. This again results naturally and necessarily from the circumstance that it is impossible for the prince to avoid giving offence to his new subjects, either in respect of the troops he quarters on them, or of some other of the numberless vexations attendant on a new acquisition.

And in this way you may find that you have enemies in all those whom you have injured in seizing the princedom, while you are unable to pre. serve the friendship of those who helped you to gain it, since you can neither reward them as they expect, nor yet, being under obligations to them, use violent remedies against them. For however strong you may be in respect of your army, it is essential that in entering a new province you should have the goodwill of the inhabitants.

Hence it happened that Louis XII. of France, speedily gaining possession of Milan, as speedily lost it; and that on the occasion of its first capture, Lodovico Sforza was able with his own forces only to take it from him. For the very people who had opened the gates to the French king, when they found themselves deceived in their expectations and hopes of future benefits, could not put up with the insolence of their new ruler. It is true that when a state rebels, and is again got under, it will not afterwards be lost so easily. For the prince, using the rebellion as a pretext, will not scruple to secure himself by punishing the guilty, bringing the suspected to trial, and otherwise strengthening his position in the points where it was weak.

So that if to recover Milan from the French it was enough on the first occasion that a Duke Lodovico should raise alarms on the frontiers, to wrest it from them a second time the whole world had to be ranged against them, and their armies destroyed and driven out of Italy. And this for the reasons above assigned. And yet, for a second time, Milan was lost to the king. The general causes of its first loss have been shown. It remains to note the causes of the second, and to point out the remedies which the French king had, or which might have been used by another in like circumstances to maintain his conquest more successfully than he did.

I say, then, that those states which, upon their acquisition, are joined on to the ancient dominions of the prince who acquires them, are either of the same race and tongue as the people of these dominions, or they are not. When they are, there is great ease in retaining them, especially when they have not been accustomed to live in freedom. To hold them securely it is enough to have rooted out the line of the reigning prince; because if in other respects the old condition of things be continued, and there be no discordance in their customs, men live peaceably with one another, as we see to have been the case in Brittany, Burgundy, Gascony, and Normandy, which have so long been united to France. For although there be some slight difference in their languages, their customs are similar, and they can easily get on together. He, therefore, who acquires such a state, if he mean to keep it, must attend to two things; first, to destroy the blood of the ancient line of princes; second, to make no change in respect of laws or taxes, for in this way the newly acquired state speedily becomes incorporated with the hereditary.

But when states are acquired in a country differing in language, usages, and laws, difficulties multiply, and great good fortune as well as address are needed to overcome them. One of the best and most efficacious methods for dealing with such a state, is for the prince who acquires it to go and dwell there, since this will tend to make his tenure more secure and lasting. This course has been followed by the Turk in regard to Greece, and had he not, in addition to all his other precautions for securing that province, himself come to live in it, he could never have kept his hold of it Because when you are on the spot, disorders are detected in their beginnings and remedies can be readily applied; but when you are at a distance, they are not heard of until they have gathered strength, and the case is past cure. Moreover, the province in which you take up your abode is not pillaged by your officers, the people are pleased to have a ready recourse to their prince, and have all the more reason if they are well disposed, to love, if disaffected, to fear him. A foreign enemy desiring to attack that state would be cautious how he did so. In short, while the prince resides there in person, it will be extremely difficult to oust him.

Another excellent expedient is to send colonies into one or two places, so that these may become, as it were, the keys of the province; for it is necessary either to do this, or else to keep up a numerous force of men-at-arms and foot soldiers. A prince need not spend much on colonies. He can send them out and support them at little or no charge to himself and the only persons to whom he gives offence are those whom he deprives of their lands and houses to bestow them on the new inhabitants. Those who are thus injured, forming but a small part of the community, and remaining scattered and poor, can never become dangerous.

All others remain, on the one hand, unmolested, and therefore easily quieted, and on the other hand, afraid to make a false move, lest they should share the fate of those who have been deprived of their possessions. In few words, these colonies cost less than soldiers, are more faithful, and give less offence, while those who are offended, being, as I have said, poor and dispersed, cannot hurt. And let it here be noted that men are either to be kindly treated, or utterly crushed, since they can revenge lighter injuries, but not graver. Wherefore the injury we do to a man should be of a kind to leave no fear of reprisals.

But if instead of colonies you send troops, the cost is vastly greater, and the whole revenues of the country are spent in guarding it; so that the gain becomes a loss, and much deeper offence is given; since by shifting the quarters of the soldiers from place to place the whole country suffers hardship, which as all feel, all are made enemies; and enemies who remaining, although vanquished, in their own homes, have power to hurt In every way, therefore, this mode of defence is as disadvantageous as that by colonizing is useful

The prince who establishes himself in a province whose laws and language differ from those of his own people, ought also to make himself the head and protector of his less powerful neighbours, and endeavour to weaken the stronger, and must see that by no accident shall any other stranger as powerful as himself find an entrance there.

For it will always happen that some such person will be called in by those of the province who are discontented either through ambition or fear; as we see of old the Romans brought into Greece by the Etolians, and in every other country which they entered, invited there by its inhabitants.

And the usual course of things is that so soon as a powerful stranger enters a province, all the weaker states side with him, moved thereto by the ill-will they bear towards him who has hitherto kept them in subjection. So that in respect of these lesser powers, no trouble is needed to gain them over, because at once, together, and of their own accord, they throw in their lot with the government of the stranger. The new prince, therefore, has only to see that they do not increase too much in strength, and with his own forces, aided by their good will, can easily subdue any who are powerful, so as to remain supreme in the province. He who does not manage this part of the business well, will soon lose whatever he has gained, and while he retains it will be harassed by countless internal troubles and annoyances.

In dealing with the countries of which they took possession the Romans diligently followed the methods which I have described. They planted colonies, conciliated weaker states without adding to their strength, humbled the great, and never suffered a powerful stranger to acquire influence. A single example will suffice to show this. In Greece the Romans took the Achaians and Etolians into their pay; the Macedonian monarchy was humbled; Antiochus was driven out. But the services of the Achaians and Etolians never obtained for them any addition to their power; no persuasions on the part of Philip could induce the Romans to be his friends on the condition of sparing him humiliation; nor could all the power of Antiochus bring them to consent to his exercising any authority within that province.

And in thus acting the Romans did as all wise rulers should, who have to consider not only present difficulties but also future, against which they must use all diligence to provide; for these, if they be foreseen while yet remote, admit of easy remedy, but if their approach be awaited, are already past cure, the disorder having become hopeless; realizing what the physicians tell us of hectic fever, that in its beginning it is easy to cure, but hard to recognize, but that after a time, not having been detected and treated at the first, it becomes easy to recognize but impossible to cure.

And so it is with state affairs. For the distempers of a state being discovered while yet inchoate, which can only be done by a sagacious ruler, may easily be dealt with; but when, from not being observed, they are suffered to grow until they are obvious to everyone, there is no longer any remedy.

The Romans, therefore, foreseeing evils while they were yet far off, always provided against them, and never suffered them to take their course for the sake of avoiding war, since they knew that war is not so to be avoided, but is only postponed to the advantage of the other side. They chose, therefore, to make war with Philip and Antiochus in Greece, that they might not have to make it with them in Italy, although for a while they might have escaped both. This they did not desire, nor did the maxim *leave it to Time*, which the wise men of our own day have always on their lips, ever recommend itself to them. What they looked to enjoy were the fruits of their own valour and foresight. For Time, driving all things before it, may bring with it evil as well as good.

But let us now go back to France and examine whether she has followed any of these methods of which I have made mention. I shall speak of Louis and not of Charles, because from the former having long held possession of Italy his manner of acting is more plainly seen. You will find, then, that he has done the direct opposite of what he should have done in order to retain a foreign State.

King Louis was brought into Italy by the ambition of the Venetians, who hoped by his coming to gain for themselves a half of the State of Lombardy. I will not blame this coming, nor the part taken by the king, because, desiring to gain a footing in Italy, where he had no friends, but on the contrary, owing to the conduct of Charles, every door was shut against him, he was driven to accept such friendships as he could get. And his designs might easily have succeeded had he not made mistakes in other particulars of conduct.

By the recovery of Lombardy, Louis at once regained the credit which Charles had lost.

Genoa was ready to make terms; the Florentines became his friends; the Marquis of Mantua, the Duke of Ferrara, the Bentivogli, the Countess of Forlì, the Lords of Faenza, Pesaro, Rimini, Camerino and Piombino; the citizens of Lucca, Pisa, and Siena, all came forward offering their friendship. The Venetians, who to obtain possession of a couple of towns in Lombardy had made the French king master of two-thirds of Italy, had now cause to repent the rash game they had played.

Let anyone, therefore, consider how easily the French king might have preserved his authority in Italy had he attended to the rules which I have noticed above, and secured and protected all those friends of his, who being numerous, and weak, and fearful, some of the Church, some of the Venetians, were of necessity obliged to attach themselves to him, and with whose assistance he might easily have made himself safe against any other powerful State. But no sooner was he in Milan than he took a contrary course, in helping Pope Alexander to occupy Romagna; not perceiving that in seconding this enterprise he weakened himself by alienating those friends who had thrown themselves into his arms, while he strengthened the Church by adding great temporal power to the spiritual power which of itself confers so mighty an authority. Making this first mistake, he was forced to follow it up, until at last, in order to curb the ambition of Pope Alexander, and prevent him becoming master of Tuscany, he was obliged to come himself into Italy.

And as though it were not enough for him to have aggrandized the Church and stripped himself of friends, he must needs in his desire to possess the Kingdom of Naples, divide it with the King of Spain, thus bringing into Italy, where before he had been supreme, a rival to whom the ambitious and discontented in that province might have recourse. And whereas he might have left in Naples a king willing to hold as his tributary, he removed him to make way for another powerful enough to effect his expulsion. The wish to acquire is no doubt a natural and common sentiment, and when men attempt things within their power, they will always be praised rather than blamed. But when they persist in attempts which are beyond their power, mishaps and blame ensue. If France, therefore, with her own forces could have attacked Naples, she should have done so. If she could not, she ought not to have divided it And if the partition of Lombardy with the Venetians may be excused as the means whereby a footing was gained in Italy, this other partition is to be condemned as not justified by the like necessity.

Louis, then, had made these five blunders. He had destroyed weaker states, he had strengthened a prince already strong, he had brought into the country a very powerful stranger, he had not come to reside, and he had not sent colonies. And yet all these blunders might not have proved disastrous to him while he lived, had he not added to them a sixth in depriving the Venetians of their dominions. For had he neither aggrandized the Church, nor brought Spain into Italy, it might have been at once reasonable and necessary to humble the Venetians;

but after committing himself to these other courses, he should never have consented to the ruin of Venice. For while the Venetians were powerful they would always have kept others back from any attempt on Lombardy, as well because they never would have agreed to that enterprise on any terms save of themselves being made its masters, as because others would never have desired to take it from France in order to hand it over to them, nor would ever have ventured to defy both.

And if it be said that Louis ceded Romagna to Alexander, and Naples to Spain in order to avoid war, I answer that for the reasons already given, you ought never to suffer your designs to be crossed in order to avoid war, since war is not so to be avoided, but is only deferred to your disadvantage. And if others should allege the king's promise to the Pope to undertake that enterprise on his behalf in return for the dissolution of his marriage, and for the cardinal's hat conferred on d'Amboise, I answer by referring to what I say further on concerning the faith of princes and how it is to be kept.

King Louis, therefore, lost Lombardy from not following any one of the methods pursued by others who have taken provinces with the resolve to keep them. Nor is this anything strange, but only what might reasonably and naturally be looked for. And on this very subject I spoke to d'Amboise at Nantes, at the very time when Duke Valentino, as Cesare Borgia was vulgarly called, was occupying Romagna. For, on the cardinal saying to me that the Italians did not understand war, I answered that the French did not understand state-craft, for had they done so, they never would have allowed the Church to grow so powerful. And the event shows that the aggrandizement of the Church and of Spain in Italy has been brought about by France, and that the ruin of France has been wrought by them. And hence we may draw the general axiom, which never or rarely errs, that he who is the cause of another's greatness is himself undone, since he must work either by address or force, each of which excites distrust in the person raised to power.

CHAPTER 4

Why the Kingdom of Darius, Conquered by Alexander, Did Not, On Alexander's Death, Rebel Against His Successors

Alexander the Great having achieved the conquest of Asia in a few years, and dying before he had well entered on possession, it might have been expected, having regard to the difficulty of preserving newly acquired states, that on his death the whole country would rise in revolt Nevertheless, his successors were able to keep their hold, and found in doing so no other difficulty than arose from their own ambition and mutual jealousies.

If anyone think this strange and ask the cause, I answer, that all the princedoms of which we have record have been governed in one or other of two ways either by a sole prince, all others being his slaves permitted by his grace and favour to assist in governing the kingdom as his ministers; or else, by a prince with his barons who hold their rank, not by the favour of a superior lord, but by antiquity of blood, and who have states and subjects of their own who recognize them as their rulers and entertain for them a natural affection. States governed by a sole prince and by his servants, vest in him a more complete authority; because throughout the land none but he is recognized as sovereign, and if obedience be yielded to any others, it is yielded as to his ministers and officers for whom personally no special love is felt

Of these two forms of government we see examples in our own days in the Turk and the King of France. The whole Turkish empire is governed by a sole prince, all others being his slaves. Dividing his kingdom into *sandjaks*, he sends thither different governors whom he shifts and changes at his pleasure. The King of France, on the other hand, is surrounded by a multitude of nobles of ancient descent, each acknowledged and loved by by subjects of his own, and each asserting a pre-eminence in rank of which the king can deprive him only at his peril.

He, therefore, who considers the different character of these two states, will perceive that it would be difficult to gain possession of that of the Turk, but that once won it might be easily held. The obstacles to its conquest are that the invader cannot be called in by a native nobility, nor expect his enterprise to be aided by the defection of those whom the sovereign has around him. And this for the various reasons already given, namely, that all being slaves and under obligations they are not easily corrupted, or if corrupted can render little assistance, being unable, as I have already explained, to influence the people.

Whoever, therefore, attacks the Turk must reckon on finding a united people, and must trust rather to his own strength than to divisions on the other side. But if his adversary were once overcome and defeated in the field, so as to be unable to repair his armies, no cause for anxiety would remain, except in the family of the prince; which being extirpated, there would be no one else to fear; for since all beside are without credit with the people, the invader, as before his victory he had nothing to hope from them, so after it has nothing to dread.

But the contrary is the case in kingdoms governed like that of France, into which, because men who are discontented and desirous of change are to be found everywhere, you may readily procure an entrance by gaining over some Baron of the Realm. Such persons, for the reasons already given, are able to open the way to you for the invasion of their country and to render its conquest easy. But afterwards the effort to maintain your ground involves you in endless difficulties, as well in respect of those who have helped you, as of those whom you have overthrown. Nor will it be enough to have destroyed the family of the prince, since all those other lords remain to put themselves at the head of new movements; whom being unable either to content or destroy, you will lose the state whenever occasion serves them.

Now, if you examine the nature of the government of Darius, you will find that it resembled that of the Turk, and, consequently, that it was necessary for Alexander, first of all, to defeat him utterly and strip him of his dominions; after which defeat, Darius having died, the country, for the causes above explained, was permanently secured to Alexander. And had his successors continued united they might have enjoyed it undisturbed, since there arose no disorders in that kingdom save those of their own creating.

But kingdoms ordered like that of France cannot be retained with the same ease. Hence the repeated risings of Spain, Gaul and Greece against the Romans, resulting from the number of small princedoms of which these provinces were made up. For while the memory of these lasted, the Romans could never think their tenure secure. But when that memory was worn out by the authority and long continuance of their rule, they gained a secure hold, and were able afterwards in their contests among themselves, each to carry with him some portion of these provinces, according as each had acquired influence there; and this because, on the extinction of the line of their old princes, the people came to recognize no other lords than the Romans.

Bearing all this in mind, no one need wonder at the ease with which Alexander was able to lay a firm hold on Asia, nor that Pyrrhus and many others should have found difficulty in preserving other acquisitions; since this arose, not from the less or greater merit of the conquerors, but from the different character of the states with which they had to deal.

CHAPTER 5

How to Govern Cities or Princedoms Which Before Their Acquisition Have Lived Under Their Own Laws

When a newly-acquired state has been accustomed, as I have said, to live under its own laws and in freedom, there are three methods whereby it may be held. The first is to destroy it; the second, to go and reside there in person; the third, to suffer it to live on under its own laws, while subjecting it to a tribute and entrusting its government to a few of its citizens who will keep the rest your friends. Such a Government, since it is the creature of the new prince, will see that it cannot stand without his protection and support, and must therefore do all it can to maintain him; and a city accustomed to live in freedom, if it is to be preserved, is more easily controlled through its own citizens than in any other way.

We have examples of all these methods in the histories of the Spartans and the Romans. The Spartans held Athens and Thebes by creating oligarchies in these cities, yet lost them in the end. The Romans, to retain Capua, Carthage and Numantia, destroyed them and never lost them. On the other hand, when they thought to hold Greece as the Spartans had held it, leaving it its freedom, and allowing it to be governed by its own laws, they failed, and had to destroy many cities of that province before they could secure it. For, in truth, there is no sure way of holding other than by destroying, and whoever becomes master of a city accustomed to live in freedom and does not destroy it, may reckon on being destroyed by it.

For if it should rebel, it can always screen itself under the name of liberty and its ancient laws, which no length of time, nor any benefits conferred will ever cause it to forget; and do what you will, and take what care you may, unless the inhabitants be scattered and dispersed, this name, and the old order of things, will never cease to be remembered, but will at once be turned against you whenever misfortune overtakes you, as when Pisa rose against the Florentines after a hundred years of servitude.

If, however, the newly acquired city or province has been accustomed to live under a prince, and his line is extirpated, it will be impossible for its inhabitants, used, on the one hand, to obey, and deprived, on the other, of their old ruler, to agree to choose a leader from among themselves; and as they know not how to live as freemen, and are therefore slow to take up arms, a stranger may readily gain them over and attach them to his cause. But in Republics there is a stronger vitality, a fiercer hatred, a keener thirst for revenge. The memory of their former freedom will not let them rest; so that the safest plan is to destroy them, or to go and live there.

CHAPTER 6

Of Those New Princedoms Which a Prince Acquires With His Own Arms and by Merit

Let no man marvel if in what I am about to say concerning princedoms wholly new, both as regards the prince and the form of government, I cite the highest examples. For since men for the most part follow in the footsteps and imitate the actions of others, and yet are unable to adhere exactly to those paths which others have taken, or arrive at the excellence of those whom they would resemble, the wise man should always follow such roads as have been trodden by the great, and imitate those who have most excelled, so that if he cannot reach their perfection, he may at least acquire something of its savour. Acting in this like the skilful archer, who perceiving that the object which he would hit is distant, and knowing the range of his bow, takes aim much above the destined mark; not designing that his arrow should strike so high, but that flying high it may alight at the point intended.

I say, then, that in entirely new princedoms where the prince himself is new, the difficulty of maintaining possession varies with the greater or less merit of him who acquires possession. And, because the mere fact of a private person rising to be a prince presupposes either merit or good fortune, it will be seen that the presence of one or other of these two things lessens, to some extent, many difficulties. And yet, he who is less beholden to Fortune has often in the end the better success; and it may be for the advantage of a prince that, through having no other territories, he is constrained to reside in person in the state which he has acquired.

Looking first to those who have become princes by their merit and not by their good fortune, I say that the most excellent among them are Moses, Cyrus, Romulus, Theseus and the like. And although perhaps I ought not to name Moses, he being merely an instrument for carrying out the Divine commands, he is still to be admired for these qualities which made him worthy to converse with God. But if we consider Cyrus and those others like him who have founded kingdoms, they will all be seen to be admirable. And if their actions and the particular institutions of which they were the authors be studied, they will be found not to differ from those of Moses, instructed though he was by so great a teacher.

Moreover, on examining their lives and achievements, we see that they were debtors to fortune for nothing beyond the opportunity which enabled them to shape things as they pleased, without which the force of their spirit would have been spent in vain; as on the other hand, opportunity would have offered itself in vain, had the capacity for turning it to account been wanting. It was necessary, therefore, that Moses should find the children of Israel in bondage in Egypt and oppressed by the Egyptians, in order that they might be disposed to follow him, and so escape from their servitude.

It was fortunate for Romulus that he was not received in Alba, but was exposed at the time of his birth, to the end that he might become king and founder of the city of Rome. It was necessary that Cyrus should find the Persians discontented with the rule of the Medes, and the Medes enervated and effeminate from a prolonged peace. Nor could Theseus have displayed his great qualities had he not found the Athenians disunited and dispersed. But while it was their opportunities which made these men fortunate, it was their own merit which enabled them to recognize these opportunities and turn them to account, to the glory and prosperity of their country.

They who become princes, as these did, by virtuous paths, acquire their princedoms with difficulty, but keep them with ease. The difficulties which they have in acquiring arise mainly from the new laws and institutions which they are forced to introduce in founding and securing their government. For, let it be noted, that there is no more delicate matter to take in hand, nor more dangerous to conduct, nor more doubtful in its success, than to set up as a leader in the introduction of changes. Because he who innovates will have for his enemies all those who are well off under the existing order of things, and lukewarm supporters in those who might be better off under the new. This lukewarm temper arises partly from the fear of adversaries who have the laws on their side, and partly from the incredulity of mankind, who will never believe in the truth of anything until they have seen it proved by the event. The result, however, is that whenever the enemies of change make an attack, they do so with all the zeal of partisans, while the others defend themselves so feebly as to endanger both themselves and their cause.

But to get a clearer understanding of this part of our subject, we must look whether these innovators can stand alone, or whether they depend for aid upon others; in other words, whether to carry out their ends they must resort to entreaty, or can prevail by force. In the former case they always fare badly and bring nothing to a successful issue; but when they depend upon their own resources and can employ force, they seldom fail. Hence it comes that all armed prophets have been victorious, and all unarmed prophets have been destroyed.

For, besides what has been said, it should be borne in mind that the temper of the multitude is fickle, and that while it is easy to persuade them of a thing, it is difficult to fix them in that persuasion. Wherefore, matters should be so ordered that when men no longer believe of their own accord, they may be compelled to believe by force; Moses, Cyrus, Theseus, and Romulus could never have made their ordinances to be observed for any length of time had they been unarmed, as was the case, in our own days, with the Friar Girolamo Savonarola, whose new institutions came to nothing so soon as the multitude began to waver in their faith, since he had not the means to keep those who had been believers steadfast in their belief, or to make unbelievers believe.

Such persons, therefore, have great difficulty in carrying out their designs; but all their difficulties are on the road, and may be overcome by courage. Having conquered these, and coming to be held in reverence, and having destroyed all who are jealous of their influence, they remain powerful, safe, honoured, and prosperous.

To the great examples cited above, I would add one other, of less note indeed, but assuredly bearing some proportion to them, and which may stand for all others of a like character. I mean the example of Hiero the Syracusan. He from a private station rose to be Prince of Syracuse, and he too was indebted to fortune only for his opportunity. For the Syracusans being oppressed, chose him for their captain, which office he so discharged as deservedly to be made their king. For even while a private citizen his merit was so remarkable, that he who writes of him says, he lacked nothing which a king should have except a kingdom. He did away with the old army, organized a new one, abandoned existing alliances and assumed new allies, and with an army and allies of his own, was able on that foundation to rear whatever superstructure he pleased; having trouble enough in acquiring, but none in preserving what he had acquired.

Chapter 7

Of New Princedoms Acquired by the Aid of Others and by Good Fortune

They who from a private station become princes by mere good fortune, do so with little trouble, but have much trouble to maintain themselves. They meet with no obstruction on their road, being carried as it were on wings to their destination, but all their difficulties overtake them when they alight. I speak of those on whom states are conferred either in return for money, or through the favour of him who confers them; as it happened to many in the Greek cities of Ionia and the Hellespont to be made princes by Darius, that they might hold these cities for his honour and glory; and as happened in the case of those emperors who, from privacy, attained the Imperial dignity by corrupting the army.

Such men are wholly dependent on the favour and fortunes of those who have made them great, than which two supports, none could be less stable or secure; and they lack both the knowledge and the power which would enable them to maintain their position. They lack the knowledge, because unless they have great parts and force of character, it is not to be expected that having always lived in a private station they should have learned how to command. They lack the power, since they cannot have the support of attached and faithful troops.

Moreover, states suddenly acquired, like everything else which is produced and grows up rapidly, can never have such root or firm hold as that the first storm which strikes them shall not overthrow them; unless, indeed, as I have said already, those who thus suddenly become princes have a capacity for learning quickly how to defend what fortune has placed in their lap, and know how to lay these foundations after their rise which by others are laid before.

Of each of these methods of becoming a prince, namely, by merit and by good fortune, of some part of them; and this became easy for him when he found that the Venetians, moved by other causes, were plotting to bring the French once more into Italy. This design he accordingly did not oppose, but facilitated by annulling the old marriage of the French king. King Louis therefore came into Italy at the instance of the Venetians, and with the consent of Alexander, and no sooner was he in Milan than the Pope obtained men from him for the invasion of Romagna, which province, influenced by the reputation of the king, at once submitted. After thus obtaining possession of Romagna, and after quelling the Colonnesi, Duke Valentino was desirous to maintain and extend his conquests.

Two causes, however, held him back, namely, the doubtful fidelity of his own forces, and the opposition of France. For he feared that the Orsini, of whose arms he had made use, might fail him, and not merely prove a hindrance to further acquisitions, but take from him what he had gained, and that the king might serve him the same turn. How little he could count on the Orsini was made plain when, after the capture of Faenza, he turned his arms against Bologna, and saw how reluctantly they took part in that enterprise. The king's mind he understood, when, after seizing on the Dukedom of Urbino, he was moving forward to attack Tuscany, from which design Louis compelled him to desist Whereupon the duke resolved to depend no longer on the fortunes or the arms of others. His first step, therefore, was to weaken the factions of the Orsini and Colonnesi in Rome. Those of the latter following who were of good birth, he gained over by making them his own gentlemen, assigning them a liberal provision, and conferring upon them commands and appointments suited to their rank, so that in a few months, party ties being completely broken up, they became devoted to his interest.

Having succeeded in dividing the Colonnesi, he next watched for an occasion to crush the Orsini, and a good opportunity soon presenting itself, he turned it to the best account. For when the Orsini came at last to see that the greatness of the duke and the Church involved their ruin, they assembled a council at Magione in the Perugian territory, from which resulted the revolt of Urbino, the commotions in Romagna, and an infinity of dangers to the Duke, all of which he overcame with the help of France.

His credit being thus restored, he resolved to trust no more to the French, or to any other foreign aid, but that he might not have to confront them openly, he had recourse to stratagem, and was so well able to dissemble his designs, that the Orsini (through the mediation of Signor Paolo, whom the duke failed not to secure by every friendly attention, furnishing him with clothes, money, and horses) were so won over as to be drawn in their simplicity into his hands at Sinigaglia. When these leaders were got rid of, and their followers made his friends, the duke had laid sufficiently good foundations for his future power, since he held the whole of Romagna, together with the Dukedom of Urbino, and had ingratiated himself with the entire population of these states, who now began to see that they were well off.

And since this part of his conduct merits both attention and imitation, I shall not pass it over in silence. After the duke had taken Romagna, finding that it had been ruled by feeble lords, who thought more of plundering than correcting their subjects, and gave them more cause for division than for union, so that the country was overrun with robbery, tumult, and every kind of outrage, he judged it necessary, with a view to render it peaceful and obedient to his authority, to provide it with a good government Wherefore he set over it Messer Remiro d'Orco, a stern and unscrupulous ruler, who being entrusted with the fullest powers, in a very short time, and with much credit to himself, restored it to tranquillity and order.

But afterwards apprehending that such unlimited authority might become odious, the duke decided that it was no longer needed, and established in the centre of the province a civil tribunal, with an excellent president, in which every town was represented by its advocate. And knowing that past severities had generated ill feeling against himself, in order to purge the minds of the people and gain their goodwill, he sought to show them that any cruelty which had been done had not originated with him, but in the harsh disposition of his minister. Availing himself of the pretext which this afforded, he one morning caused Remiro to be beheaded, and exposed in the market place of Cesena with a block and bloody axe by his side. The barbarity of this spectacle at once confounded and satisfied the populace.

But, returning to the point whence we diverged, I say that the duke, finding himself sufficiently strong and in a measure secured against present dangers, being furnished with arms of his own forging and having to a great extent destroyed those which his neighbours might have turned against him, had to consider, if he desired to follow up his conquests, how he was to deal with France, since he knew that he could expect no further support from the French king, whose eyes were at last opened to his mistake. He therefore began to look out for new alliances, and to waver in his adherence to the French, then occupied with their expedition into the kingdom of Naples against the Spaniards who at that time were laying siege to Gaeta; his object being to secure himself against France, in which he would certainly have succeeded had Alexander lived.

Such were his arrangements with regard to the existing state of affairs. As regards the future, he had to apprehend that a new head of the Church might not be his friend, and might even seek to deprive him of what his father had given. This he thought to provide against in four ways. First, by exterminating the families of all those lords whom he had despoiled of their possessions, that they might not become instruments in the hands of a new Pope. Second, by gaining over all the Roman nobles, so as to be able with their help to put a bridle, as the saying is, in the Pope's mouth. Third, by bringing the College of Cardinals, so far as he could, under his control. And fourth, by establishing his authority so firmly before his father's death, as to be able by himself to withstand the shock of a first onset

Of these measures, at the time when Alexander died, he had already effected three, and had almost carried out the fourth. For of the Lords whose possessions he had usurped, he had put to death all whom he could reach, and very few had escaped. He had gained over the Roman nobility, and had the majority in the College of Cardinals on his side.

As to further acquisitions, he had laid his plans for becoming master of Tuscany. He was already in possession of Perugia and Piombino, and had assumed the protectorship of Pisa, on which city he was preparing to spring; taking no heed of France, as indeed he no longer had occasion, since the French had been deprived of the kingdom of Naples by the Spaniards under circumstances which made it necessary for both of them to buy his friendship. Had he got possession of Pisa, Lucca and Siena must at once have yielded, partly through jealousy of Florence, partly through fear, and the position of the Florentines would then have been desperate.

Had he therefore succeeded in these designs, as he was succeeding in that very year in which Alexander died, he would have acquired such power and reputation that he might afterwards have stood alone, relying on his own strength and resources, without being beholden to the power and fortune of others. But Alexander died five years from the time when he first unsheathed the sword, leaving his son with the State of Romagna alone consolidated, with all the rest unsettled, between two powerful hostile armies, and sick almost to death. But in the duke there was such fire and courage, he knew so well that men must either be conciliated or crushed, and so solid were the foundations he had laid in that short period, that had these armies not been upon his back, or had he been in sound health, he must have surmounted every difficulty.

How strong his foundations were may be seen from this, that Romagna waited for him for more than a month, and that although half dead, he remained in safety in Rome, where though the Baglioni, the Vitelli, and the Orsini came to attack him they met with no success. Moreover, since he was able if not to make whom he liked Pope, at least to prevent the election of any one whom he did not like, had he been in health at the time when Alexander died, all would have been easy for him. But he told me himself on the day on which Julius II. was created, that he had foreseen and provided for everything else that could happen on his father's death, but had never anticipated that when his father died his own life would be in danger.

Taking all these actions of the duke together, I can find no fault with him; nay, it seems to me reasonable to put him forward, as I have done, as the pattern of all such as have risen to power by good fortune and the help of others. For with his great spirit and high ambition he could not act otherwise than he did, and nothing but the shortness of his father's life and his own illness prevented the success of his designs. Whoever, therefore, on entering a new princedom, sees it to be necessary to secure himself against enemies, to conciliate friends, to prevail by force or by address, to make himself loved and feared by his subjects, respected and obeyed by his soldiers, to crush those who can or ought to injure him, to introduce changes in the old order of things, to be at once severe and affable, magnanimous and liberal, to rid himself of a mutinous army and create a new one, to maintain relations with kings and princes on such a footing that they must see it to be for their interest to aid him, and dangerous to offend, can find no more brilliant example than in the actions of this prince.

The one thing for which he may be blamed was the creation of Pope Julius II., in respect of whom he chose badly. Because, as I have said already, though unable to secure the election he desired, he could have prevented any other, and he should never have consented to the creation of any one of those cardinals whom he had injured, or who on becoming Pope would have reason to fear him; for fear is as dangerous an enemy as resentment Those whom he had offended were, among others, S. Pietro ad Vincula, Colonna, S. Giorgio, Ascanio; all the rest, excepting d'Amboise and the Spanish Cardinals (the latter from their connection and obligations, the former from the power which he derived through his relations with France), would on assuming the Pontificate have had reason to fear him.

The duke, therefore, ought, in the first place, to have laboured for the creation of a Spanish Pope; failing in which, he should have agreed to the election of d'Amboise, but never to that of S. Pietro ad Vincula. And he deceives himself who believes that with the great, recent benefits cause old wrongs to be forgotten.

The duke, therefore, erred in the part he took in this election; and his error was the cause of his ultimate downfall.

CHAPTER 8

Of Those Who by Their Crimes Come to be Princes

But since from privacy a man may also rise to be a prince in one of two ways which cannot be referred wholly either to merit or to fortune, it is fit that I notice them here, though one of them may fall to be discussed more fully in treating of republics.

The ways I speak of are, first, when the ascent to power is made by paths of wickedness and crime; and second, when a citizen becomes ruler of his country by the favour of his fellow-citizens. The former method I shall make clear by two examples, one ancient, the other modern, without otherwise entering on the merits of the matter, for these, I think, should be enough for anyone who is driven to follow them.

Agathocles the Sicilian came, not merely from a private station, but from the very dregs of the people, to be King of Syracuse. Son of a potter, through all the stages of his fortunes he led an evil life. His vices, however, were conjoined with so great vigour both of mind and body, that becoming a soldier, he rose through the various grades of the service to be *praetor* of Syracuse. Once established in that post, he resolved to make himself prince, and to hold by violence and without obligation to others the authority which had been spontaneously entrusted to him. Accordingly, after imparting his design to Hamilcar, who with the Carthaginian armies was at that time waging war in Sicily, he one morning assembled the people and senate of Syracuse as though to consult with them on matters of public moment, and on a preconcerted signal caused his soldiers to put to death all the senators, and the wealthiest of the citizens.

These being thus got rid of, he assumed and retained possession of the sovereignty without opposition on the part of the people; and although twice defeated by the Carthaginians, and afterwards besieged, not only was he able to defend his city, but leaving a part of his forces for its protection, to invade Africa with the remainder, and so in a short time to raise the siege of Syracuse, reducing the Carthaginians to the utmost extremities, and compelling them to make terms whereby they abandoned Sicily to him and confined themselves to Africa.

Whoever examines this man's actions and achievements will discover little or nothing in them which can be ascribed to Fortune, seeing, as has already been said, that it was not through the favour of any, but by the regular steps of the military service, gained at the cost of a thousand hardships and hazards, that the supremacy was reached which he afterwards maintained by so many daring and dangerous enterprises. Still, to slaughter fellow-citizens, to betray friends, to be devoid of honour, pity, and religion, cannot be counted as merits, since these are means which may lead to power, but which confer no glory. Wherefore, if in respect of the courage with which he encountered and extricated himself from difficulties, and the constancy of his spirit in supporting and conquering adverse fortune, there seem no reason to judge him inferior to the greatest captains who have ever lived, his unbridled cruelty and inhumanity, joined with his other countless crimes, forbid us to number him with the greatest men; but, at any rate, we cannot attribute to Fortune or to merit that which he accomplished without either.

In our own times, during the papacy of Alexander VI., Oliverotto of Fermo, who some years before had been left an orphan, and had been brought up by his maternal uncle Giovanni Fogliani, was sent while still a lad to serve under Paolo Vitelli, in the expectation that a thorough training under that commander might qualify him for high rank as a soldier. After the death of Paolo, he served under his brother Vitellozzo, and in a very short time, being of a quick wit, hardy and resolute, he became one of the first soldiers of his company. But thinking it beneath him to serve under others, he, with the countenance of the Vitelleschi and with the connivance of certain citizens of Fermo who preferred the slavery to the freedom of their country, formed the design to seize on that town.

He accordingly wrote to Giovanni Fogliani that after many years of absence from home, he desired to see him and his native city once more, and to look a little into the condition of his patrimony; and as his one endeavour had been to acquire reputation, in order that his fellow-citizens might see that his time had not been misspent, he proposed to return honourably attended by a hundred horsemen from among his own friends and followers; and he begged Giovanni graciously to arrange for his reception by the citizens of Fermo with corresponding marks of distinction, as this would be creditable not only to himself, but also to the uncle who had brought him up.

Giovanni, accordingly, did not fail in any proper attention to his nephew, but caused him to be splendidly received by his fellow-citizens, and lodged him in his house; where Oliverotto having passed some days, and having made the necessary arrangements for carrying out his wickedness, gave a formal banquet, to which he invited his uncle and all the first men of Fermo. When the repast and the other entertainments proper to such an occasion had come to an end, Oliverotto artfully turned the conversation to matters of grave interest, by speaking of the greatness of Pope Alexander and his son, and of their enterprises; and when Giovanni and the others were replying to what he said, he suddenly rose up, observing that these were matters to be discussed in a more private place, and so withdrew to another chamber, whither his uncle and all the other citizens followed him, and where they had no sooner seated themselves, than soldiers rushing out from places of concealment put Giovanni and all the rest to death.

After this butchery Oliverotto mounted his horse, rode through the streets, and besieged the palace of the chief magistrate, so that all were constrained by fear to yield obedience and accept a government of which he made himself the head. And all who from their being displeased were likely to stand in his way, he put to death, while he strengthened himself with new ordinances, civil and military, to such purpose, that for the space of a year during which he retained the Princedom, he not merely kept a firm hold of the city, but became formidable to all his neighbours. And it would have been as impossible to unseat him as it was to unseat Agathocles, had he not allowed himself to be overreached by Cesare Borgia on the occasion when, as has already been, told, the Orsini and Vitelli were entrapped at Sinigaglia; where he too being taken, one year after the commission of his parricidal crime, was strangled along with Vitellozzo, whom he had assumed for his master in villany as well as in valour.

It may be asked how Agathocles and some like him, after numberless acts of treachery and cruelty, have been able to live long in their native country in safety, and to defend themselves from foreign enemies, without being plotted against by their fellow-citizens, whereas, many others, by reason of their cruelty, have been unable to maintain their position even in peaceful times, not to speak of the perilous times of war. I believe that this results from cruelty being well or ill employed. Those cruelties we may say are well employed, if it be permitted to speak well of things evil, which are done once for all under the necessity of self-preservation, and are not afterwards persisted in, but so far as possible modified to the advantage of the governed. Ill employed cruelties, on the other hand, are those which from small beginnings increase rather than diminish with time. They who follow the first of these methods, may, by the grace of God and man, find, as did Agathocles, that their condition is not desperate. But the others can by no possibility maintain themselves.

From which we may learn the lesson that on seizing a state, the usurper should make haste to inflict what injuries he must, at a stroke, so that he may not have to renew them daily, but be enabled by their discontinuance to reassure men's minds, and afterwards win them over by benefits. He who, either through timidity or from following bad counsels, adopts a contrary course, must keep the sword always drawn, and can put no trust in his subjects, who, while they suffer from continual and constantly renewed severities, can never yield him their confidence. Injuries should, therefore, be inflicted all at once, that their ill savour being less lasting may the less offend; whereas, benefits should be conferred little by little in order that they may be the more fully relished.

But, before all things, a prince should so live with his subjects that no vicissitude of good or evil fortune shall oblige him to alter his behaviour; because, if a need to change come through adversity, it is then too late to resort to severity; while any leniency you may then use will be thrown away, since it will be seen to be compulsory and gain you no thanks.

CHAPTER 9

Of the Civil Princedom

I come now to the second case, namely, of the leading citizen who, not through wickedness or other prevailing force, but by the favour of his fellow-citizens, is made Prince of his country. This may be called a Civil Princedom, and its attainment depends not wholly on merit, nor wholly on good fortune, but rather on what may be termed a *fortunate astuteness*, I say then that the road to this princedom lies either through the favour of the people or of the nobles. For in every city are to be found these two opposed factions having their origin in this, that the people desire not to be domineered over or oppressed by the nobles, while the nobles desire to oppress and domineer over the people. And from these two contrary desires there arises in cities one of three results, a princedom, or liberty, or licence.

A princedom is created either by the people or by the nobles, according as one or other of these factions has occasion for it For when the nobles perceive that they are unable to withstand the people, they set to work to magnify the reputation of one of their number, and make him their prince, to the end that under his protection they may be enabled to gratify their desires. The people, on the other hand, when they see that they cannot make head against the nobles, invest a single citizen with all their influence and make him prince, that they may have the shelter of his authority.

He who is made prince by the favour of the nobles, has greater difficulty to maintain himself than he who comes to the princedom by the aid of the people, since he finds many about him who think themselves as good as he, and whom, on that account, he cannot guide or govern as he would. But he who reaches the princedom by the popular support, finds himself alone, with none, or but a very few about him who are not ready to obey. Moreover, the demands of the nobles cannot be gratified with credit to the prince, nor without injury to others, while those of the people may, the aim of the people being more honourable than that of the nobles, the latter seeking to oppress, the former not to be oppressed.

Add to this, that a prince can never secure himself against a disaffected people, their number being too great, while he may against a disaffected nobility, since their number is small The worst that a prince need fear from a disaffected people is, that they may desert him, whereas when the nobles are his enemies he has to fear not only that they may desert him, but also that they may turn against him; because, as they have greater penetration and foresight, they always choose their time to suit their safety, and seek favour with the side which they think will win. Again, a prince must always live with the same people, but need not always live with the same nobles, being able to make and unmake these from day to day, and to give and take away their authority at his pleasure.

But to make this part of the matter clearer, I say that the nobles are to be looked at chiefly in two lights. They either so govern their conduct as to bind themselves wholly to your fortunes, or they do not Those who so bind themselves, and who are not grasping, deserve to be esteemed and honoured. Those who do not, are influenced for the most part by pusillanimity and a natural defect of courage, in which case you should make use of them, and of those among them more especially who are prudent, for they will do you honour in prosperity, and in adversity give you no cause for fear. But where they abstain from attaching themselves to you of set purpose and for ambitious ends, it is a sign that they are thinking more of themselves than of you, and against such men a prince should be on his guard, and treat them as though they were declared enemies, since in his adversity they will always help to ruin him.

He who becomes a prince through the favour of the people ought always to keep on good terms with them; which it is easy for him to do, since all that they ask is not to be oppressed. But he who against the will of the people is made a prince by the favour of the nobles, must, above all things, seek to conciliate the people, which he readily may, by taking them under his protection. For since men who are well treated by one whom they expected to treat them ill, fed the more beholden to their benefactor, the people will at once become better disposed to such a prince when he protects them, than if he owed his princedom to them.

There are many ways in which a prince may gain the goodwill of his subjects, but, since these vary with circumstances, no certain rule can be laid down respecting them, and I shall, therefore, say no more about them. But this is the sum of the matter, that it is essential for a prince to be on a friendly footing with his people, since, otherwise, he will have no resource in adversity. Nabis, Prince of Sparta, was attacked by the whole hosts of Greece and by a Roman army flushed with victory, and defended his country and crown against them; and when danger approached, there were few of his subjects against whom he needed to guard himself, whereas had the people been hostile, this would not have been enough.

And what I affirm let no one controvert by citing the old saw that '*he who builds on the people builds on mire*,' for that may be true of a private citizen who presumes on his favour with the people, and counts on being rescued by them when overpowered by his enemies or by the magistrates. In such cases a man may often find himself deceived, as happened to the Gracchi in Rome, and in Florence to Messer Giorgio Scali. But when he who builds on the people is a prince capable of command, of a spirit not to be cast down by ill-fortune, and who, while he animates the whole community by his courage and bearing, neglects no prudent precaution, he will not find himself betrayed by the people, but will be seen to have laid his foundations well.

The most critical juncture for princedoms of this kind, is at the moment when they are about to pass from the popular to the absolute form of government: and as these princes exercise their authority either directly or through the agency of the magistrates, in the latter case their position is weaker and more hazardous, since they are wholly in the power of those citizens to whom the magistracies are entrusted, who can, and especially in difficult times, with the greatest ease deprive them of their authority, either by opposing, or by not obeying them.

And in times of danger it is too late for a prince to assume to himself an absolute authority, for the citizens and subjects who are accustomed to take their orders from the magistrates, will not consent at such a moment to take them from the prince, and in seasons of doubt there must always be very few in whom he can trust such princes, therefore, must not build on what they see in tranquil times when the citizens fed the need of the state. For then everyone is ready to run, to promise, and, danger of death being remote, even to die for the state. But in evil times, when the state has need of its citizens, few of them are to be found. And the risk of the experiment is the greater in that it can only be made once. Wherefore, a wise prince should devise means whereby his subjects may at all times, whether favourable or adverse, feel the need of the state and of him, and then they will always be faithful to him.

Chapter 10
How the Strength of All Princedoms Should be Measured

In examining the character of these princedoms another circumstance has to be considered, namely, whether the prince is strong enough, if occasion demands, to maintain himself, or whether he stands in need of continual help from others. To make the matter clearer, I pronounce those to be capable of maintaining themselves who, with the men and money at their disposal, can get together an army fit to take the field against any assailant; and, conversely, I judge those to stand in constant need of help who are unable to take the field against their enemies, but are obliged to retire behind their walls, and to defend themselves there.

Of the former I have already spoken, and shall speak again as occasion may require. As to the latter there is nothing to be said, except to exhort such princes to strengthen and fortify the towns in which they dwell, and take no heed of the country outsider For whoever has thoroughly fortified his town, and has placed himself on such a footing with his subjects as I have already indicated and shall hereafter speak of, will always be attacked with much circumspection; because men are always averse to those enterprises which axe attended with difficulty, and it is impossible not to foresee difficulties in attacking a prince whose town is strongly defended and who is not hated by his subjects.

The towns of Germany enjoy great freedom. Having little territory, they render obedience to the emperor only when so disposed, fearing neither him nor any other neighbouring power. For they are so fortified that it is plain to everyone that it would be a difficult and dangerous task to reduce them, all of them being protected by moats and suitable ramparts, well supplied with artillery, and having their public magazines constantly stored with victual, drink and fuel, enough to last them for a year. Besides which, in order to support the poorer class of citizens without public loss, they lay in a common stock of materials for these to work on in the handicrafts which are the life and sinews of such cities, and by the exercise of which the common people live. Moreover, they esteem military exercises and have many regulations for their maintenance.

A prince, therefore, who has a strong city, and who does not make himself hated, is not likely to be attacked, and should he be so, his assailant may expect to come badly off; since human affairs are so unstable that it is next to impossible for an invader to maintain a beleaguering army for a whole year without interruption of some sort It may be objected that if the citizens have possessions outside the town, and see them burned, they will lose patience, and that self-interest, together with the hardships of a protracted siege, will cause them to forget their loyalty. I answer that a capable and courageous prince will always overcome these difficulties, now, by holding out hopes to his subjects that the evil will not be of long continuance, now, by exciting their fears of the enemy's cruelty, and, again, by dexterously silencing those who seem to him too forward in their complaints.

Moreover, it is to be expected that the enemy will burn and lay waste the country immediately on their arrival, at a time when men's minds are still heated and resolute for defence. And for this very reason the prince ought the less to hesitate, because after a few days, when the first ardour has cooled down, the injury is already done and suffered, and cannot be undone; and the people, then, all the more readily, make common cause with their prince from his seeming to be under obligations to them, their houses having been burned and their lands wasted in his defence. For it is the nature of men to incur obligation as much by the benefits they render as by those they receive. Wherefore, if the whole matter be well considered, it ought not to be difficult for a prudent prince, both at the outset and afterwards, to maintain the spirits of his subjects during a siege; provided always that victuals and the other means of defence do not run short.

Chapter 11

Of Ecclesiastical Princedoms

It now only remains for me to treat of Ecclesiastical Princedoms, all the difficulties in respect of which precede their acquisition. For they are acquired by merit or good fortune, but are maintained without either; being upheld by the venerable ordinances of religion, which are in themselves of such a nature and influence that they secure the authority of their princes in whatever way they may act or live. These princes alone have territories which they do not defend, and subjects whom they do not govern, and their territories are not taken from them through not being defended, nor are their subjects concerned at not being governed, or led to think of throwing off their allegiance; nor is it in their power to do so. Wherefore these princedoms alone are secure and happy. But inasmuch as they are sustained by agencies of a higher nature than the mind of man can reach, I forbear to speak of them: for since they are supported and exalted by God himself, he would be a rash and presumptuous man who should venture to discuss them.

Nevertheless, should any one ask me how it comes about that the temporal power of the Church, which before the time of Alexander was looked on with contempt by all the potentates of Italy, and not only by those so styling themselves, but by every baron and lordling however insignificant, has now reached such a pitch of greatness that the King of France trembles before it, and that it has been able to drive him out of Italy and to crush the Venetians; though the causes be known, it seems to me not superfluous to call them in some measure to recollection.

Before Charles of France passed into Italy, that country was under the control of the Pope, the Venetians, the King of Naples, the Duke of Milan, and the Florentines. Two chief objects had to be kept in view by all these powers; first, that no armed foreigner should be allowed to invade Italy; second, that no one of their own number should be suffered to extend his territory. Those whom it was especially needed to guard against, were the Pope and the Venetians. To hold back the Venetians it was necessary that all the other states should combine, as was done for the defence of Ferrara; while to restrain the Pope, use was made of the Roman barons, who being divided into two factions, the Orsini and Colonnesi, were at constant feud with one another, and standing with arms in their hands under the very eyes of the pontiff, kept the Popedom feeble and insecure.

And although there arose, from time to time, a courageous Pope like Sixtus, neither his prudence nor his good fortune was able to relieve him from these embarrassments, the cause of which was the shortness of the lives of the Popes. For in the ten years, which was the average duration of a Pope's life, he could barely succeed in humbling one of these factions; so that if, for example, one Pope had almost exterminated the Colonnesi, he was followed by another, who, being the enemy of the Orsini, had no time to rid himself of them, but so far from completing the destruction of the Colonnesi, restored them to life. This led to the temporal authority of the Popes being little esteemed in Italy.

Then came Alexander VI., who more than any of his predecessors showed what a Pope could effect with money and troops, achieving by the instrumentality of Duke Valentino, and by taking advantage of the coming of the French into Italy, all those successes which I have already noticed in speaking of the actions of the duke. And although his object was to aggrandize, not the Church, but the duke, what he did turned to the advantage of the Church, which after his death, and after the duke had been put out of the way, became the heir of his labours.

After him came Pope Julius, who found the Church strengthened by the possession of the whole of Romagna, and the Roman barons exhausted and their factions shattered under the blows of Pope Alexander. He found also a way opened for the accumulation of wealth, which before the time of Alexander no one had followed. These advantages Julius not only used but added to. He undertook the conquest of Bologna, the overthrow of the Venetians, and the expulsion of the French from Italy; in all which enterprises he succeeded, and with the greater glory to himself in that whatever he did, was done to strengthen the Church and not to aggrandize any private person.

He succeeded, moreover, in keeping the factions of the Orsini and Colonnesi within the same limits as he found them; and, although some seeds of insubordination may still have been left among them, two causes operated to keep them in check; first, the great power of the Church, which overawed them, and, second, their being without cardinals, who had been the cause of all their disorders. For these factions while they have cardinals among them can never be at rest, since it is they who foment dissension both in Rome and out of it, in which the barons are forced to take part, the ambition of the prelates thus giving rise to tumult and discord among the barons.

His Holiness, Pope Leo, has consequently found the papacy most powerful; and from him we may hope, that as his predecessors made it great with arms, he will render it still greater and more venerable by his goodness and other countless virtues.

CHAPTER 12

How Many Different Kinds of Soldiers There Are, and of Mercenaries

Having spoken particularly of all the various kinds of Princedoms of which at the outset I proposed to treat, considered to what extent the elements of strength and weakness exist in each, and pointed out the ways by which men commonly seek to acquire them, it now remains that I should discourse generally concerning the methods of attack and defence of which each of these different kinds of princedom may make use.

I have already said that a prince must lay solid foundations, since otherwise he will inevitably be destroyed. Now the main foundations of all states, whether new, old, or mixed, are good laws and good soldiers. But since you cannot have the former without the latter, and where you have the latter, are likely to have the former, I shall here omit all discussion on the subject of laws, and speak only of soldiers.

I say then that the soldiers with whom a prince defends his state are either his own subjects, or they are mercenaries, or they are auxiliaries, or they are partly one and partly another. Mercenaries and auxiliaries are at once useless and dangerous, and he who holds his state by means of mercenary troops can never be solidly or securely seated. For such troops are disunited, ambitious, insubordinate, treacherous, insolent among friends and cowardly before foes. Without fear of God or faith with man, whenever they fight they are sure to be beaten; so that in peace you are plundered by them, in war by your enemies. The cause of which is that they have no tie or motive to keep them in the field beyond their paltry pay, in return for which it would be too much to expect them to give their lives. They are ready enough, therefore, to be your soldiers while you are at peace, but when war is declared they make off and disappear.

I ought to have little difficulty in persuading people of this, for the present ruin of Italy results from no other cause than from her having for many years relied on mercenaries, who though they may have helped to aggrandize individuals, and presented an appearance of strength when matched with one another, have always shown themselves in their true colours so soon as foreign enemies appeared. Hence it was that Charles of France was suffered to conquer Italy with chalk; and whoever said our sins were the cause, said truly, though it was not the sins he meant, but those which I have noticed. And as these were the sins of princes, they it is who have paid the penalty.

But I desire to show still more clearly the untoward character of these forces. Captains of mercenaries are either able men or they are not. If they are, you cannot trust them, since they will always seek their own aggrandizement, either by overthrowing you who are their master, or by the overthrow of others contrary to your desire. On the other hand, if the commanders be not courageous, you are ruined again. If it should be urged that all generals will do the same, whether mercenaries or others, I would answer, that all war is managed either by a prince or republic.

The prince is obliged to go in person, and perform the office of general himself; the republic must depute some one of her choice citizens, who is to be changed if he carries himself ill; if he behaves himself well he is to be continued, but so straitened and circumscribed by his commission that he may not transgress. And indeed experience tells us that princes alone, and commonwealths alone, with their own private forces have performed great things, whereas mercenaries do nothing but hurt. Besides, a martial common wealth that stands upon its own legs and maintains itself by its own prowess is not easily usurped, and falls not so readily under the obedience of one of their fellow-citizens as where all the forces are foreign. Rome and Sparta maintained their own liberty for many years together by their own forces and arms. The Swiss are more martial than their neighbours, and by consequence more free.

Of mercenary arms in ancient times you have an example in the Carthaginians, who at the close of their first war with Rome, were almost ruined by their hired troops, although their own citizens commanded them.

After the death of Epaminondas the Thebans made Philip of Macedon their general, who defeated their enemies and enslaved themselves. Upon the death of Duke Philip the Milanese entertained Francesco Sforza against the Venetians, and Francesco, having worsted the enemy at Caravaggio, joined himself with him, with design to have mastered his masters. Francesco's father was formerly in the service of Joan, Queen of Naples, and on a sudden marched away from her with his army and left her utterly destitute, so that she was constrained to throw herself under the protection of the King of Arragon; and though the Venetians and Florentines both have lately enlarged their dominion by employing these forces, and their generals have rather advanced than enslaved them, I answer that the Florentines may impute it to their good fortune, because of such of their generals as they might have rationally feared some had no victories to encourage them, others were obstructed, and others turned their ambition another way.

He that was not victorious was Giovanni Acuto, whose fidelity could not be known because he had no opportunity to break it, but everybody knows, had he succeeded, the Florentines had been all at his mercy. Sforza had always the Braccheschi in opposition, and they were reciprocally an impediment the one to the other. Francesco turned his ambition upon Lombardy, Braccio upon the Church and the kingdom of Naples. But to speak of more modern occurrences. The Florentines made Paul Vitelli their general, a wise man, and one who from a private fortune had raised himself to a great reputation. Had Paul taken Pisa, nobody can be insensible how the Florentines must have comported with him; for should he have quitted their service and taken pay of their enemy they had been lost without remedy, and to have continued him in that power had been in time to have made him their master.

If the progress of the Venetians be considered, they will be found to have acted securely and honourably, whilst their affairs were managed by their own forces (which was before they attempted anything upon the *terra firma*); then all was done by the gentlemen and common people of that city. But when they took to making war by land, they forsook those methods in which they excelled and were content to follow the customs of Italy.

At first, indeed, in extending their possessions on the mainland, having as yet but little territory and being held in high repute, they had not much to fear from their captains; but when their territories increased, which they did under Carmagnola, they were taught their mistake. For as they had found him a most valiant and skilful leader when, under his command, they defeated the Duke of Milan, and, on the other hand, saw him slack in carrying on the war, they made up their minds that no further victories were to be had under him; and because, through fear of losing what they had gained, they neither could nor would discharge him, to make sure of him they were forced to put him to death.

After him they have had for captains, Bartolommeo of Bergamo, Roberto of San Severino, the Count of Pitigliano, and the like, under whom their danger has not been from victories, but from defeats; as, for instance, at Vaila, where they lost in a single day what it had taken the efforts of eight hundred years to acquire. For the gains resulting from mercenary arms are slow, and late, and inconsiderable, but the losses sudden and astounding.

And since these examples have led me back to Italy, which for many years past has been defended by mercenary arms, I desire to go somewhat deeper into the matter, in order that the causes which led to the adoption of these arms being seen, they may the more readily be corrected. You are to understand, then, that when in these later times the Imperial control began to be rejected by Italy, and the temporal power of the Pope to be held in higher esteem, Italy suddenly split up into a number of separate states. For many of the larger cities took up arms against their nobles, who, before, relying on the favour of the emperor, had kept them in subjection, and were supported by the Church with a view to add to her temporal authority: while in many others of these cities, private citizens became rulers. Hence Italy, having passed almost entirely into the hands of the Church and of certain republics, the former made up of priests the latter of citizens unfamiliar with arms, began to take foreigners into her pay.

The first who gave reputation to this service was Alberigo of Conio in Romagna, from whose school of warlike training descended, among others, Braccio and Sforza, who in their time were supreme in Italy; after whom came all those others who down to the present hour have held similar commands, and to whose merits we owe it that our country has been overrun by Charles, plundered by Louis, wasted by Ferdinand, and insulted by the Swiss.

The object of these mercenaries has been to bring foot soldiers into disrepute, in order to enhance the merit of their own followers; and this they have done, because lacking territory of their own and depending on their profession for their support, a few foot soldiers gave them no importance, while for a large number they were unable to provide. For these reasons they had recourse to horsemen, a less number of whom was thought to confer distinction and enabled them to maintain themselves. And the matter went to such a length, that in an army of twenty thousand men, not two thousand foot soldiers were to be found.

Moreover, they spared no endeavour to relieve themselves and their men from fatigue and danger, not killing one another in battle, but making prisoners who were afterwards released without ransom. They would attack no town by night; those in towns would make no sortie by night against a besieging army. Their camps were without rampart or trench. They had no winter campaigns. All which arrangements were sanctioned by their military rules, contrived by them, as I have said already, to escape fatigue and danger; but the result of which has been to bring Italy into servitude and contempt.

CHAPTER 13

Of Auxiliary, Mixed, and National Arms

The second sort of unprofitable troops are auxiliaries, by whom I mean, troops brought to help and protect you by a potentate whom you summon to your aid; as was done in recent times by Pope Julius II., who, observing the pitiful behaviour of his mercenaries at the enterprise of Ferrara, had recourse to auxiliaries, and obtained an engagement from Ferdinand of Spain to supply him with horse and foot soldiers.

Auxiliaries may be excellent and useful soldiers for themselves, but are always hurtful to him who calls them in; for if they are defeated, he is undone, if victorious, he becomes their prisoner. Ancient histories abound with instances of this, but I shall not pass from the example of Pope Julius, which is still fresh in men's minds. It was the height of rashness for him, in his eagerness to gain Ferrara, to throw himself without reserve into the arms of a stranger. Nevertheless, his good fortune came to his rescue, and he had not to reap the fruits of his ill-considered conduct For after his auxiliaries were defeated at Ravenna, the Swiss suddenly descended and swept the victors out of the country, so that, contrary to his own expectation and that of everyone else, he neither remained a prisoner with his enemies, they having been routed, nor with his auxiliaries, because the victory was won by other arms than theirs.

The Florentines being wholly without soldiers of their own, brought ten thousand French men-at-arms to the siege of Pisa, whereby they incurred greater peril than at any previous time of trouble. To protect himself from his neighbours, the Emperor of Constantinople summoned ten thousand Turkish soldiers into Greece, who, when the war was over, refused to leave, and this was the beginning of the servitude of Greece to the Infidels. Let him, therefore, who would deprive himself of every chance of success, have recourse to auxiliaries, since they are far more dangerous than mercenary arms, bringing ruin with them ready made.

For they are united and wholly under the control of their own officers; whereas mercenaries, even when victorious, require longer time and exceptional opportunities before they can do you hurt; because, as they are made up of separate companies, and are supported and paid by you, the person whom you place in command cannot at once acquire such authority over them as will be injurious to you. In short, with mercenaries your greatest danger is from their cowardice, with auxiliaries from their valour. Wise princes, therefore, have always eschewed these arms, and trusted rather to their own, and have preferred defeat with the latter to victory with the former, counting it no true victory which is gained by foreign aid.

I shall never hesitate to cite the example of Cesare Borgia and his actions. He entered Romagna with a force of auxiliaries entirely composed of French men-at-arms, with whose assistance he took Imola and Forli. But afterwards, perceiving that these troops could not be trusted, he had recourse to mercenaries, from whom he thought there would be less danger, and took the Orsini and Vitelli into his pay. But finding these likewise while under his command to be fickle, false, and treacherous, he destroyed them, and fell back on troops raised within his own dominions. And we may readily discern the difference between these various kinds of arms, by observing the different degrees of reputation in which the duke stood while he depended upon the French alone, when he took the Orsini and Vitelli into his pay, and when he fell back on his own troops and his own resources; for we find that reputation always increasing, and that he was never so well thought of as when everyone perceived him to be sole master of his own forces.

I am unwilling to leave these examples, drawn from what has taken place in Italy and in recent times; and yet I must not omit to notice the case of Hiero of Syracuse, who is one of those whom I have already named. He, as I have before related, being made by the Syracusans captain of their armies, saw at once that a force of mercenary soldiers, supplied by men like our Italian *condotterri*, was not serviceable; and as he would not retain and could not disband them, he caused them all to be cut to pieces, and afterwards made war with native soldiers only, without other aid.

And here I would call to mind a figure of the Old Testament, as bearing on this point. When David offered himself to Saul to go forth and fight Goliath the Philistine champion, Saul to encourage him armed him with his own armour, which David, so soon as he had put it on, rejected, saying that with these weapons he could not prevail, and that he chose rather to meet his enemy with only his sling and his sword. In a word, the armour of others is too wide, or too strait for us; it falls off us, or it weighs us down.

Charles VII., the father of Louis XI., who by his good fortune and valour freed France from the English, saw the necessity of strengthening himself with a national army, and drew up ordinances regulating the service both of men-at-arms and of foot soldiers throughout his kingdom. But afterwards his son, King Louis, abolished the national infantry, and began to hire Swiss mercenaries. Which blunder having been followed by subsequent princes, has been the cause, as the result shows, of the dangers into which the kingdom of France has fallen; because, by enhancing the reputation of the Swiss, the whole of the national troops of France have been deteriorated. For from their infantry being done away with, their men-at-arms are made wholly dependent on foreign assistance, and being accustomed to co-operate with the Swiss, have grown to think that they can do nothing without them. Hence the French are no match for the Swiss, and without them cannot succeed against others.

The armies of France, then, are mixed, being partly national and partly mercenary. Armies thus composed are far superior to mere mercenaries or mere auxiliaries, but far inferior to forces purely national. And this example is in itself conclusive, for the realm of France would be invincible if the military ordinances of Charles VII. had been retained and extended. But from want of foresight men introduce changes which relishing well at first do not betray their hidden venom, as I have already observed respecting hectic fever. Nevertheless, the ruler is not truly wise who cannot discern evils before they develop themselves, and this faculty is given to few.

If we look for the causes which led to the overthrow of the Roman Empire, they will be found to have had their origin in the employment of Gothic mercenaries, for from that hour the strength of the Romans began to wane, and all the virtue which went from them passed to the Goths. And, to be brief, I say that without national arms no princedom is safe, but on the contrary is wholly dependent on fortune, being without the strength which could defend it in adversity. And it has always been the deliberate opinion of the wise, that nothing is so infirm and fleeting as a reputation for power not founded upon a national army, by which I mean one composed of subjects, citizens, and dependants, all others being mercenary or auxiliary.

The methods to be followed in organising a national army may readily be ascertained, if the rules elsewhere laid down by me, and by which I allude, be considered, and attention be given to the manner in which Philip, father of Alexander the Great, and many other princes and republics have armed and disposed their forces.

CHAPTER 14

Of the Duty of a Prince in Respect of Military Affairs

A prince, therefore, should have no care or thought but for war, and for the regulations and training which it requires, and should devote himself exclusively to this as his peculiar province; for war is the sole art looked for in one who rules, and is of such efficacy that it not merely maintains those who are born princes, but often enables men to rise to that rank from a private station; while, on the other hand, we often see that when princes devote themselves more to pleasure than to arms, they lose their dominions. And as neglect of this art is the prime cause of such calamities, so to be a proficient in it is the surest way to acquire power. Francesco Sforza, from his renown in arms, rose from privacy to be Duke of Milan, while his sons, seeking to avoid the hardships and fatigues of military life, from being princes became private citizens. For among other causes of misfortune resulting from your not being armed, is this, that it renders you contemptible, which is one of those reproaches against which, as shall presently be explained, a prince ought most carefully to guard.

Between an armed and an unarmed man no proportion holds, and it is contrary to reason to expect that the armed man should voluntarily submit to him who is unarmed, or that the unarmed man should stand in safety among armed retainers. For with contempt on one side, and distrust on the other, it is impossible that men should act harmoniously together. Wherefore, as has already been said, a prince who is ignorant of military affairs, in addition to his other disadvantages, can neither be respected by his soldiers, nor can he trust them. A prince, therefore, ought never to allow his attention to be diverted from warlike pursuits, and should devote himself to them even more in peace than in war. This he can do in two ways, practically or theoretically.

As to the practice, he ought, besides keeping his soldiers well trained and disciplined, to be constantly engaged in the chase, so as to inure his body to hardships and fatigue, and at the same time gain a knowledge of places, by observing how the mountains slope, the valleys open, and the plains spread; acquainting himself with the characters of rivers and marshes, and giving the greatest attention to this subject Such knowledge is useful to him in two ways; for first, he learns to know his own country, and to understand better how it may be defended; and next, from his familiar acquaintance with its localities, he readily comprehends the character of another district when obliged to observe it for the first time. For the hills, valleys, plains, rivers, and marshes of Tuscany, for example, have a certain resemblance to those elsewhere; so that from a knowledge of the natural features of that province, similar knowledge in respect of other provinces may readily be gained.

The prince who is wanting in this kind of knowledge, is wanting in the first qualification of a good captain, for by it he is taught how to surprise an enemy, how to choose an encampment, how to array his army for battle, and how to dispose it to the best advantage for a siege.

Among the commendations which Philopoemon, Prince of the Achidans, has received from historians is this—that in times of peace he was always thinking of methods of warfare, so that when walking in the country with his friends he would often stop and talk with them on the subject "If the enemy," he would say, "were posted on that hill, and we found ourselves here with our army, which of us would have the better position? How could we most safely and in the best order advance to meet them? If we had to retreat, what direction should we take? If they retired, how should we pursue?" In this way he put to his friends, as he went along, all the contingencies which can befall an army. He listened to their opinions, stated his own, and supported them with reasons; and from his being constantly occupied with such meditations, it resulted, that when in actual command no complication could ever arise with which he was not prepared to deal.

As to the mental training of which we have spoken, a prince should read histories, and in these should note the actions of great men, observe how they conducted themselves in their wars, and examine the causes of their victories and defeats, so as to avoid the latter and imitate them in the former. And above all, he should, as many great men of past ages have done, assume for his models such persons as before his time have been renowned and celebrated, whose deeds and achievements he should constantly keep in mind, as it is related that Alexander the Great sought to resemble Achilles, Caesar Alexander, and Scipio Cyrus. And whoever reads the life of this last-named hero, written by Xenophon, recognises afterwards in the life of Scipio, how much this imitation was the source of his glory, and how nearly in his chastity, affability, humanity, and generosity, he conformed to the character of Cyrus as Xenophon describes it.

A wise prince, therefore, should pursue such methods as these, never resting idle in times of peace, but strenuously seeking to turn them to account, so that he may derive strength from them in the hour of danger, and find himself ready, should fortune turn against him, to resist her blows.

CHAPTER 15

Of the Qualities in Respect of Which Men, and Most of all Princes, are Praised or Blamed

It now remains for us to consider what ought to be the conduct and behaviour of a prince in relation to his subjects and friends. And since I know that many have written on this subject, I fear it may be thought presumptuous in me to write of it also; and the more so, because in my treatment of it I depart from the views which others have held.

But since it is my object to write what shall be useful to whoever understands it, it seems to me better to follow the real truth of things than an imaginary view of them. For many republics and princedoms have been imagined which were never seen or known to exist in reality. And the manner in which we live, and that in which we ought to live, are things so wide asunder, that he who quits the one to betake himself to the other is more likely to destroy than to save himself; since he who proposes to himself to act up to a perfect standard of goodness among all men alike, must be ruined among so many who are not good.

It is necessary, therefore, for a prince who desires to maintain his position, to use or not to use his goodness as occasion may require. Laying aside, therefore, all fanciful notions concerning a prince, and considering those only which are true, I say that all men when they are spoken of, and princes more than others from their being set so high, are characterised by some one of those qualities which attach either praise or blame. Thus one is accounted liberal, another miserly (which word I use, rather than *avaricious*, to denote the man who is too sparing of what is his own, *avarice* being the disposition to take wrongfully what is another's); one is generous, another greedy; one cruel, another tender-hearted; one is faithless, another true to his word; one effeminate and cowardly, another high-spirited and courageous; one is courteous, another haughty; one impure, another chaste; one simple, another crafty; one serious, another frivolous; one devout, another unbelieving; and the like.

Every one, I know, will admit that it would be most laudable for a prince to be endowed with all of the above qualities which are reckoned good; but since it is impossible for him to possess, or constantly practise them all, the conditions of human nature not allowing it, he must be prudent enough to know how to avoid the infamy of those vices which would deprive him of his government, and, if possible, be on his guard also against those which might not deprive him of it; but if unable wholly to restrain himself he may with less scruple indulge in the latter. He need never hesitate, however, to incur the infamy of those vices without which his authority can hardly be preserved; for if he well considers the whole matter, he will find that there may be a line of conduct having the appearance of virtue, to follow which would be his ruin, and that there may be another course having the appearance of vice, by following which his safety and well-being are secured.

CHAPTER 16

Of Liberality and Miserliness

Beginning, then, with the first of the qualities above noticed, I say that it may be a good thing to be reputed liberal, but, nevertheless, that liberality without the reputation of it is hurtful; because, however worthily and rightly it be employed, if it be not known, you do not escape the infamy of its opposite vice. Hence, to have credit for liberality with the world at large, you must neglect no circumstance of sumptuous display; the result of which is, that a prince of a liberal disposition will consume his whole substance in things of this sort, and, after all, will be obliged, if he desire to maintain his reputation for liberality, to burden his subjects with extraordinary taxes, and to resort to confiscations and all the other shifts whereby money may be raised. In this way he becomes hateful to his subjects, and growing impoverished is held in little esteem by any. So that in the end, having by his liberality offended many and obliged few, he is worse off than when he began, and is exposed to all his original dangers. Recognizing this, and endeavouring to retrace his steps, he at once incurs the infamy of miserliness.

A prince, therefore, being unable without injury to himself to practise the virtue of liberality so that it may be known, will not, if he be wise, greatly concern himself if he be called miserly. Because in time he will come to be regarded as more and more liberal, when it is seen that through his parsimony his revenues are sufficient; that he is able to defend himself against anyone who makes war on him; that he can engage in enterprises against others without burdening his subjects; and in this way exercise liberality towards all those from whom he does not take, whose number is infinite, while he is miserly in respect of those only to whom he does not give, whose number is few.

In our own times we have seen no princes accomplish great results save those who have been accounted miserly. All others have been ruined. Pope Julius II. after availing himself of his reputation for liberality to obtain the Popedom, made no effort to preserve that reputation when making war on the King of France, but carried on all his numerous campaigns without levying from his subjects a single extraordinary tax, providing for the increased expenditure out of his long-continued savings. Had the present King of Spain been accounted liberal, he never could have engaged or succeeded in so many enterprises.

A prince, therefore, if he is enabled thereby to forbear from plundering his subjects, to defend himself, to escape poverty and contempt, and the necessity of becoming rapacious, ought to care little though he incur the reproach of miserliness, for this is one of those vices which enable him to reign.

And if any should object that Caesar by his liberality rose to power, and that many others have been advanced to the highest dignities from then: having been liberal and so reputed; I reply, "Either you are already a prince, or you are seeking to become one; in the former case liberality is hurtful, in the latter it is very necessary that you should be thought liberal; Caesar was one of those who desired to obtain the sovereignty of Rome; but if after obtaining it he had lived on, and had not retrenched his expenditure, he must have ruined the Empire." And if anyone should insist that many princes reputed to have been most liberal, have achieved great things with their armies; I answer that a prince spends either what belongs to himself and his subjects, or what belongs to others; in the former case he ought to be sparing, but in the latter he ought not to refrain from any kind of liberality.

And for a prince who accompanies his armies and maintains them by plunder, pillage, and forced contributions, dealing as he does with the property of others, this liberality is necessary, since otherwise he would not be followed by his soldiers. Of what does not belong to you or to your subjects, you should, therefore, be a lavish giver, as were Cyrus, Caesar, and Alexander, for to be liberal the property of others does not hurt your reputation, but adds to it. What injures you is to give away what is your own. And there is nothing so self-destructive as liberality; for while you practise it you lose the means whereby it can be practised, and become poor and contemptible, or else to avoid poverty, you become rapacious and hated. For liberality leads to one or other of these two results, against which, beyond all others, a prince should guard.

Wherefore it is wiser to put up with the name of being miserly, which breeds ignominy but without hate, than to be obliged, from the desire to be reckoned liberal, to incur the reproach of rapacity which breeds hate as well as ignominy.

CHAPTER 17

Of Cruelty and Clemency, and Whether it is Better to be Loved or Feared

Passing to others of the qualities above enumerated, I say that every prince should desire to be accounted merciful and not cruel Nevertheless, he should be on his guard against the abuse of this quality of mercy. Cesare Borgia was reputed cruel, and yet his cruelty restored Romagna, gave it solidity, and reduced it to order and obedience; so that if we look at things in a true light, it will be seen that he was in fact far more merciful than the people of Florence, who, to avoid the reputation of cruelty, suffered Pistoja to be torn to pieces by factions.

A prince should therefore disregard the infamy of being thought cruel where it enables him to keep his subjects united and obedient. For he who quells disorder by a very few signal examples, will in the end be more merciful than he who from too great leniency permits things to take their course and so to result in rapine and bloodshed. For these hurt the whole state, whereas the severities of the prince injure individuals only.

And for a new prince, more than any other, it is impossible to escape the reproach of cruelty, since new states are full of dangers. Wherefore Virgil, by the mouth of Dido, excuses the inhumanity of her reign on the plea that it was new, saying:—

Res dura et regni novitas me talia cogunt
Moliri, et late fines custode tueri.

Nevertheless, the new prince should not be too ready of belief, nor too easily set in motion; nor should he himself be the first to raise alarms; but should so temper prudence with humanity that too great confidence in others shall not throw him off his guard, nor groundless distrust render him insupportable.

And here arises the question whether it is better to be loved rather than feared, or feared rather than loved. It might perhaps be answered that both are best; but since love and fear can hardly exist together, if we must choose between them, it is far safer to be feared than loved. For of men it may in general be affirmed that they are thankless, fickle, false, studious to avoid danger, greedy of gain, devoted to you while you are able to confer benefits upon them, and ready, as I said before, while danger is distant, to shed their blood, and to sacrifice their property, their lives, and their children for you; but in the hour of need they forsake you. The prince, therefore, who has built wholly on their professions leaving himself bare of other preparation is undone. For those friendships which we buy with a price, and do not gain by greatness and nobility of character, though they be fairly earned are not made good, but fail us when we have occasion to use them.

Moreover men are less careful how they offend him who makes himself loved than him who makes himself feared. For love is held by the tie of obligation, which, since men are scoundrels, is broken on every whisper of private interest; but fear is bound by the apprehension of punishment which never relaxes its grasp.

Nevertheless a prince should inspire fear in such a fashion, that if he do not win love he may escape hate. For a man may very well be feared and yet not hated, and this will be the case so long as he does not meddle with the property or with the women of his citizens and subjects. And if compelled to put any to death, he should do so only when there is manifest cause or reasonable justification. But, above all, he must abstain from the property of others. For men will sooner forget the death of their father than the loss of their patrimony. Moreover, pretexts for confiscation are never to seek, and he who has once begun to live by rapine has always excellent reasons for taking what is not his; whereas reasons for shedding blood are harder to find and sooner exhausted.

But when a prince is with his army and has many soldiers under his command, he must needs disregard the reproach of cruelty, for without such a reputation in its captain, no army can be held together or kept under any kind of control Among the things remarkable in Hannibal this has been noted, that having a very great army, made up of men of many different nations and brought to fight in a foreign country, no dissension ever arose among the soldiers themselves, nor any mutiny against their leader, either in his good or in his evil fortune. This we can only ascribe to the transcendent cruelty, which, united with numberless great qualities, rendered him at once venerable and terrible in the eyes of his soldiers. And without this reputation for cruelty these other virtues would not have produced the like results.

Unreflecting writers, indeed, while they praise his achievements, have condemned the chief cause of them; but that his other merits would not by themselves have been so efficacious, we may see from the case of Scipio, one of the greatest captains, not merely of his own time but of all times of which we have record, whose armies rose against him in Spain, from no other cause than his too great leniency in indulging them with a freedom inconsistent with military strictness. With which weakness Fabius Maximus taxed him in the Senate House, calling him the corrupter of the Roman soldiery.

Again, when the Locrians were shamefully treated by one of his lieutenants, he neither avenged them nor punished the insolence of his officer; and this from the natural easiness of his disposition. So that it was said in the Senate by one who sought to excuse him, that there were many who knew better how to refrain from doing wrong themselves, than how to correct the wrongdoing of others. This temper, however, must in time have marred the fame and reputation even of Scipio, had he continued in it, and had he been an absolute prince. But living, as he did, under the control of the Senate, this hurtful quality was not merely disguised but came to be regarded as a glory.

But returning to the question of being loved or feared, I sum up by saying, that since his being loved depends upon his subjects, while his being feared depends upon himself, a wise Prince should build on what is his own and not on what rests with others. Only, as I have said, he must endeavour to escape hatred.

CHAPTER 18

How Princes Should Keep Faith

Everyone understands how praiseworthy it is in a prince to keep faith, and to live uprightly and not craftily. Nevertheless, we see from what has taken place in our own days, that princes who have set little store by their word, but have known how to overreach men by their cunning, have accomplished great things, and in the end have got the better of .those who have relied upon honest dealing.

Be it known, then, that there are two ways of contending, one in accordance with the laws, the other by force; the first of which is proper to men, the second to beasts. But since the first method is often ineffectual, it becomes necessary to resort to the second. A prince should, therefore, understand how to use well both the man and the beast. And this lesson has been covertly taught by the ancient writers, who relate how Achilles and many others of these old princes were given over to be brought up and trained by Chiron the centaur; since the only meaning of their having for instructor one who was half man and half beast is, that it is necessary for a prince to know how to use both natures, and that the one without the other has no stability.

But since a prince should know how to use the beast's nature wisely, he ought of beasts to choose both the lion and the fox; for while the lion knows not how to guard himself from the toils, the fox is unable to defend himself from wolves. He must therefore be a fox to discern toils, and a lion to keep off wolves.

To rely wholly on the lion is unwise; and for this reason a prudent prince neither can nor ought to keep his word, when to keep it is hurtful, and the causes which led him to pledge it are removed. If all men were good, this would not be good advice, but since they are wicked and do not keep faith with you, you, in return, need not keep faith with them; and no prince need ever be at a loss for plausible reasons to cloak a breach of faith. Of this, numberless recent instances might be given, and it might be shown how many solemn treaties and engagements have been rendered inoperative and idle by want of faith in princes, and that he who has best known to play the fox has had the best success.

It is necessary, indeed, to put a good colour on this nature, and to be skilful in simulating and dissembling. But men are so simple, and governed so absolutely by their present needs, that he who wishes to deceive will never fail in finding willing dupes. One recent example I will not omit. Alexander VI. had no care or thought but how to deceive, and always found material to work on. No man ever had a more effective manner of asseverating, or made promises with more solemn protestations, or observed them less. And yet, because he understood this side of human nature, his frauds always succeeded.

It is not essential, therefore, that a prince should have all the good qualities which I have enumerated above, but it is most essential that he should seem to have them. I will even venture to affirm that if he has and invariably practises them all, they are hurtful, while the appearance of having them is useful. Thus, it is well to seem merciful, faithful, humane, religious, and upright, and even to be so; but the mind should remain so balanced that if it were needful not to be so; you should be able and know how to change to the contrary.

And you are to understand that a prince, and most of all a new prince, cannot observe all those roles of conduct in respect of which men are accounted good, being frequently obliged, in order to preserve his princedom, to act in opposition to good faith, charity, humanity, and religion. He must therefore keep his mind ready to shift as the winds and tides of fortune turn, and, as I have already said, he ought not to quit good courses if he can help it, but should know how to follow evil courses if he must.

A prince should therefore be very careful that nothing ever escapes his lips which is not replete with the five qualities above named, so that to see and hear him, one would think him the embodiment of mercy, good faith, integrity, humanity, and religion. And there is no virtue which it is more necessary for him to seem to possess than this last; because men in general judge rather by the eye than by the hand, for everyone can see but few can touch. Everyone sees what you seem, but few know what you are, and these few dare not oppose themselves to the opinion of the many who have the majesty of the state to back them up.

Moreover, in the actions of all men, and most of all of princes, where there is no tribunal to which we can appeal, we look to results. Wherefore if a prince succeeds in establishing and maintaining his authority, the means will always be judged honourable and be approved by everyone. For the vulgar are always taken by appearances and by results, and the world is made up of the vulgar, the few only finding room when the many have no longer ground to stand on.

A certain prince of our own days, whose name it is as well not to mention, is always preaching peace and good faith, although the inveterate enemy of both; and both, had he practised as he preaches, would, oftener than once, have lost him his kingdom and authority.

CHAPTER 19

That a Prince Should Seek to Avoid Contempt and Hatred

Haying now spoken of the chief of the qualities above enumerated, the rest I shall dispose of briefly with these general remarks, that a prince, as has already been said, should consider how he may avoid such courses as tend to make him hated or despised; and that whenever he succeeds in keeping dear of these, he has performed his part, and runs no risk though he incur other infamies. And, as I have said before, a prince sooner becomes hated by being rapacious and by interfering with the property and with the women of his subjects, than in any other way. From these, therefore, he should abstain. For so long as neither their property nor their honour is touched, the mass of mankind live contentedly, and the prince has only to cope with the ambition of a few, which can in many ways and easily be kept within bounds.

A prince is despised when he is seen to be fickle, frivolous, effeminate, pusillanimous, or irresolute, against which defects he ought, therefore, most carefully to guard, striving so to bear himself that greatness, courage, wisdom, and strength may appear in all his actions. In his private dealings with his subjects his decisions should be irrevocable, and his reputation such that no one would dream of over-reaching or cajoling him.

The prince who inspires such an opinion of himself is greatly esteemed, and against one who is greatly esteemed conspiracy is difficult; because, when a prince is understood to be good and to be held in reverence by his subjects, it is not easy to attack him. For a prince is exposed to two dangers, from within in respect of his subjects, from without in respect of foreign powers. Against the latter he will defend himself with good soldiers and good allies, and if he have good soldiers he will always have good allies; and when things are settled abroad, they will always be settled at home, unless disturbed by conspiracies; and even if there should be hostility from without, if he has taken those measures, and has lived in the way I have recommended, and if he never abandons hope, he will resist every attack, as I have related of Nabis the Spartan.

But as to his own subjects, when affairs are quiet abroad, he has to fear that they may engage in secret plots; against which a prince best secures himself when he escapes being hated or despised, and keeps on good terms with his people, and this, as I have already shown at length, it is essential that he should do. Not to be hated or despised by the body of his subjects, is one of the strongest safeguards which a prince can have against conspiracy; for he who conspires always reckons on pleasing the people by putting the prince to death; but when he sees that instead of pleasing he will offend them, he cannot summon courage to carry out his design. For the difficulties which attend conspirators are infinite, and we know from experience that while there have been many conspiracies, few of them have succeeded.

He who conspires cannot do so alone, nor can he assume as his companions any save those whom he believes to be discontented; but so soon as you impart your design to a discontented man, you furnish him with the means of removing his discontent, since by betraying you he can procure for himself every advantage; so that seeing on the one hand certain gain, and on the other a doubtful and dangerous risk, he must either be a rare friend to you, or an inveterate enemy of his Prince, if he keep your secret.

To bring the matter into narrow compass, I say that on the side of the conspirator there is distrust, jealousy, and dread of punishment to deter him, while on the side of the prince there is the majesty of the throne, the laws, the protection of friends and of the government to defend him; to which if the general goodwill of the people be added, it is hardly possible that any one should be rash enough to conspire. For while, in ordinary cases, the conspirator has ground for fear only before the execution of his villany, in this case he has also cause to fear after the crime has been committed, since he has the people for his enemy, and is thus cut off from every hope of shelter.

Of this many instances might be given, but I shall content myself with one which happened within the recollection of our fathers. Messer Annibale Bentivoglio, Lord of Bologna and grandfather of the present Messer Annibale, was conspired against and murdered by the Canneschi, leaving behind none belonging to him save Messer Giovanni, then an infant in arms. Immediately upon the murder the people rose and put all the Canneschi to death. This resulted from the general esteem in which the House of the Bentivogli were then held in Bologna; which feeling was so strong, that when upon the death of Messer Annibale, no one was left who could govern the state, there being reason to believe that an illegitimate descendant of the family was living in Florence, who up to that time had been thought to be the son of a smith, the citizens of Bologna came for him to Florence, and entrusted him with the government of their city, which he retained until Messer Giovanni was old enough to govern.

To be brief; a prince has little to fear from conspiracies when his subjects are well disposed towards him; but when they are hostile and hold him in detestation, he has then reason to fear everything and everyone. And well ordered states and wise princes have provided with extreme care that the nobility shall not be driven to desperation, and that the commons shall be kept satisfied and contented; for this is one of the most important matters that a prince has to look to.

Among the well ordered and governed kingdoms of our day is that of France, wherein we find an infinite number of wise institutions, upon which depend the liberty and security of the king, and of which the most important are the Parliament and its authority. For he who gave its constitution to this realm, knowing the ambition and turbulence of the nobles, and judging it necessary to bridle and restrain them, and on the other hand knowing the hatred, originating in fear, entertained against the nobles by the people, and desiring that these last should be safe, was unwilling that the responsibility for this should rest on the king; and to relieve him of the ill-will which he might incur with the nobles by favouring the people, or with the people by favouring the nobles, appointed a third party to be arbitrator, who without committing the king, might depress the nobles and uphold the people.

Nor could there be any better, wiser, or surer safeguard for the king and the kingdom. And from this we may draw another notable lesson, namely, that princes should throw on others those offices which entail responsibility, and reserve to themselves those which gain them favour. And I say again that a prince should esteem the great, but must not make himself odious to the people.

To some it may perhaps appear, that if the lives and deaths of many of the Roman emperors be considered, they offer examples opposed to the views expressed by me; since we find that some among them who had always lived good lives, and shewn themselves possessed of great qualities, were nevertheless deposed and even put to death by their subjects who had conspired against them.

In answer to such objections, I shall examine the characters of several emperors, and show that the causes of their downfall have been in no way different from those which I have already noticed. In doing this I shall submit for consideration such matters only as must strike everyone who reads the history of these times; and it will be enough for my purpose to take those emperors who reigned from the time of Marcus the Philosopher to the time of Maximinus, who were, inclusively, Marcus, Commodus his son, Pertinax, Julian, Severus, Antoninus Caracalla his son, Macrinus, Heliogabalus, Alexander, and Maximinus.

In the first place, then, we have to note that while in other princedoms the prince has only to contend with the ambition of the nobles and the insubordination of the people, the Roman emperors had a further difficulty to encounter in the cruelty and rapacity of their soldiers, which were so distracting as to cause the ruin of many of these princes. For it was hardly possible for them to satisfy both the soldiers and the people; since the latter loved peace and therefore preferred temperate princes, while the former preferred a Prince of a warlike spirit, however harsh, haughty, or rapacious, being willing that he should exercise these qualities against the people, as the means of procuring for themselves double pay and indulging their greed and cruelty.

Whence it followed that those emperors who had not inherited or made fort themselves such influence as enabled them to keep both people and soldiers in check, were always ruined. The most of them, and those especially who came to the Empire new and without experience, seeing the difficulty of dealing with these conflicting interests, set themselves to satisfy the soldiers, and made little account of offending the people. And for them this was a necessary course to take; for as princes cannot escape being hated by some, they should, in the first instance, endeavour not to be hated by a class; failing in which, they must use every effort to escape the hatred of that class which is the stronger. Wherefore those emperors who, by reason of their newness, stood in need of extraordinary support, sided with the soldiery rather than with the people, a course which turned out advantageous or otherwise, according as the prince knew, or did not know, how to maintain his authority over them.

From the causes indicated it resulted that Marcus, Pertinax, and Alexander, being princes of a temperate disposition, lovers of justice, enemies of cruelty, humane, and kindly, had all, save Marcus, an unhappy end. Marcus alone lived and died honoured in the highest degree; and this because he had succeeded to the Empire by right of inheritance, and not through the favour either of the soldiery or the people; and also because, being endowed with many virtues which made him revered, he kept, while he lived, both factions within bounds, and was never either hated or despised.

But Pertinax was chosen emperor against the will of the soldiery, who being accustomed to a licentious life under Commodus, could not tolerate the decent manner of living to which his successor sought to bring them back. And having thus made himself hated, and being at the same time despised by reason of his advanced age, he was ruined at the very outset of his reign.

And here it is to be noted that hatred is incurred as well on account of good actions as of bad; for which reason, as I have already said, a prince who is resolved to maintain his authority is often compelled to be other than good. For when the class, be it the people, the soldiers, or the nobles, on whom you judge it necessary to rely for your support, is corrupt, you must needs adapt yourself to its humours, and satisfy them, in which case virtuous conduct will only prejudice you.

Let us now come to Alexander, who was so just a ruler that among the praises ascribed to him it is recorded, that during the fourteen years he held the Empire, no man was ever put to death by him without trial. Nevertheless, being accounted effeminate, and thought to be governed by his mother, he fell into contempt, and the army conspiring against him, slew him.

If we next turn to consider the characters of Commodus, Severus, and Antoninus Caracalla, we shall find them to have been most cruel and rapacious princes, who to satisfy the soldiery, scrupled not to inflict every kind of wrong upon the people. And all of them, except Severus, came to a bad end. But in Severus there was such strength of character, that, keeping the soldiers his friends, he was able, although he oppressed the people, to reign on prosperously to the last; because his great qualities rendered him so admirable in the eyes both of the people and the soldiers, that the former remained in a manner awestruck and confounded, while the latter were respectful and contented.

And because his actions, for one who was a new prince, were thus remarkable, I will point out shortly how well he understood to use both the lion and the fox, each of which natures, as I have observed before, a prince should know how to assume.

Knowing the slothful nature of the Emperor Julianus, Severus persuaded the army which he commanded in Illyria that it was their duty to go to Rome to avenge the death of Pertinax, who had been slain by the Pretorian guards. Under this pretext, and without disclosing his design on the Empire, he put his army in march, and reached Italy before it was known that he had set out. On his arrival in Rome, the Senate, through fear, elected him emperor and put Julianus to death. After taking this first step, two obstacles still remained to his becoming sole master of the Empire; one in Asia, where Niger who commanded the armies of the East had caused himself to be proclaimed emperor; the other in the West, where Albinos, who also had designs on the Empire, was in command. And as Severus judged it dangerous to declare open war against both, he resolved to proceed against Niger by arms, and against Albinus by artifice.

To the latter, accordingly, he wrote, that having been chosen emperor by the Senate, he desired to share the dignity with him; that he therefore sent him the title of Caesar, and in accordance with a resolution of the Senate, assumed him as his colleague. All which statements Albinus accepted as true. But so soon as Severus had defeated and slain Niger, and had restored tranquillity in the East, returning to Rome he complained in the Senate that Albinus, wholly unmindful of the favours which he had received from him, had treacherously sought to destroy him; for which cause he was compelled to go and punish his ingratitude. Whereupon he set forth to seek Albinus in Gaul, where he at once deprived him of his dignities and his life.

Whoever, therefore, examines carefully the actions of this emperor, will find in him all the fierceness of the lion and all the craft of the fox, and will remark how he was feared and respected by the people, and yet not hated by the army, and will not be surprised that, although a new man, he was able to maintain his hold of so great an Empire. For the splendour of his reputation always shielded him from the odium which the people might otherwise have conceived against him by reason of his cruelty and rapacity.

Antoninus Caracalla, his son, was likewise a man of great parts, and endowed with qualities which made him admirable in the sight of the people and endeared him to the army, being of a warlike spirit, most patient of fatigue, an enemy to luxury in food and to every other effeminacy. Nevertheless, his ferocity and cruelty were so extravagant and unheard of, he having put to death a large number of the inhabitants of Rome at different times, and the whole of those of Alexandria at a stroke, that he came to be detested by all the world, and so feared even by those whom he had about him, that at the last he was killed by a centurion in the midst of his army.

And here let it be noted that deaths like this which are the result of a deliberate and fixed resolve, cannot be escaped by princes, since anyone who disregards his own life can effect them. A prince, however, need the less fear them as they are extremely uncommon. The only precaution he can take is to avoid doing grave wrong to any of those who serve him, or whom he has near him as officers of his court, a precaution which Antoninus neglected in putting to a shameful death the brother of this centurion, and in using daily threats against the man himself, whom he nevertheless retained as one of his bodyguard. This, as the event showed, was a rash and fatal course.

We come next to Commodus, who, as he took the Empire by hereditary right, ought to have held it with much ease. For being the son of Marcus, he had only to follow in his father's footsteps to content both the people and the soldiery. But being of a cruel and brutal nature, to gratify his rapacity at the expense of the people, he had recourse to the army, and indulged them in every kind of excess. On the other hand, by an utter disregard of his dignity, in frequently appearing in the arena to fight with gladiators, and by other base acts wholly unworthy of the Imperial station, he became despicable in the eyes of the soldiery; and being on the one hand hated, on the other despised, he was at last conspired against and murdered.

The character of Maximinus remains to be described. He was of a very warlike disposition, and on the death of Alexander, of whom we have already spoken, was chosen emperor by the army who had been displeased with the effeminacy of that prince. But this dignity he did not long enjoy, since two causes concurred to render him at once odious and contemptible; the one the baseness of his origin, he having at one time herded sheep in Thrace, a fact well known to all, and which led all to look on him with disdain; the other that on being proclaimed emperor, delaying to repair to Rome and enter on possession of the Imperial throne, he incurred the reputation of excessive cruelty from having, through his prefects in Rome and other parts of the Empire, perpetrated many atrocities.

The result was that the whole world, stirred at once with scorn of his mean birth and with the hatred which the dread of his ferocity inspired, combined against him, Africa leading the way, the Senate and people of Rome and the whole of Italy following. In which conspiracy his own army joined. For they, being engaged in the siege of Aquileja and finding difficulty in reducing it, disgusted with his cruelty, and less afraid of him when they saw so many against him, put him to death.

I need say nothing of Heliogabalus, Macrinus, or Julianus, all of whom being utterly despicable, came to a speedy downfall, but shall conclude these remarks by observing, that the princes of our own days are less troubled with the difficulty of having to make extraordinary efforts to keep their soldiers in good humour. For although they must treat them with some indulgence, it need not be continually shewn, since none of these princes possess standing armies which, like the armies of the Roman Empire, have strengthened with the growth of their government and the administration of their states. And if it was then necessary to satisfy the soldiers rather than the people, it was because the soldiers were more powerful than the people, whereas now it is more necessary for all princes, except the Turk and the *soldan*, to satisfy the people rather than the soldiery, since the former are more powerful than the latter.

I except the Turk because he has always about him some twelve thousand foot soldiers and fifteen thousand horse, on whom depend the security and strength of his kingdom, and with whom he must needs keep on good terms, all considerations of the people being subordinate. The government of the *soldan* is similar, for as he is wholly in their hands, he too must keep well with his soldiers without regard to the people.

And here it may be observed that the state of the *soldan*, while it is unlike all other princedoms, resembles the Christian Pontificate in this, that it can neither be classed as a new, nor as an hereditary princedom. For the sons of a *soldan* who dies do not succeed to the kingdom as his heirs, but he who is elected to the post by those who have authority to make such elections. And this being the ancient and established order of things, the princedom cannot not be accounted new, since none of the difficulties which attend new princedoms are found in it For although the prince, be new, the institutions of the state are old, and are so contrived that the elected prince is accepted as though he were an hereditary sovereign.

But to return to our subject, I say that whoever reflects on the above reasoning will see, that either hatred or contempt was the ruin of those Emperors whom I have named; and will likewise understand how it happened that some taking one way and some the opposite, one only came to a happy, and all the rest to an unhappy end. For as to Pertinax and Alexander, they being new princes, it was useless and disadvantageous for them to endeavour to imitate Marcus, who was an hereditary prince; and similarly for Caracalla, Commodus, and Maximinus it was a fatal error to imitate Severus, since they lacked the qualities which would have enabled them to walk in his footsteps.

In short, a prince new to the princedom cannot imitate the actions of Marcus, nor is it necessary for him to imitate those of Severus; but he should borrow from Severus those parts of his conduct which are needed to serve as a foundation for his government, and from Marcus those which are suited to maintain it, and render it glorious when once it has been established.

CHAPTER 20

Whether Fortresses, and Various Other Expedients to Which Princes Often Have Recourse, are Profitable or Hurtful

To hold their states more securely some princes have disarmed their subjects, others have kept the towns subject to them divided into factions; some have fostered hostility to themselves, others have set themselves to gain over those who at the beginning of their reign were looked on with suspicion; some have built fortresses, others have dismantled and destroyed them; and although no definite judgment can be pronounced respecting any of these methods, without regard to the particular circumstances of the state to which it is proposed to apply them, I shall nevertheless speak of them in as comprehensive a way as the nature of the subject will admit.

It has never chanced that any new prince has disarmed his subjects. On the contrary, when he has found them unarmed he has always armed them. For the arms thus provided become yours, those whom you suspected grow faithful, while those who were faithful at the first, continue so, and from your subjects become your partisans. And although all your subjects cannot be armed, still, since those of them whom you arm are benefited, you can deal more securely with the rest For the difference which those whom you furnish with arms perceive in their treatment, binds them to you, while the others excuse you, recognising that those who incur greater risk and responsibility merit greater rewards.

But by disarming, you at once give offence, since you show your subjects that you distrust them, either as doubting their courage, or as doubting their fidelity, each of which imputations begets hatred against you. Moreover, as you cannot remain unarmed, you must have recourse to mercenary troops. What these are I have already shown, but even if they were good, they could never be strong enough to defend you, at once, against powerful enemies abroad and against subjects whom you suspect Wherefore as I have said already, new princes in new princedoms have always provided for their being armed; and of instances of this history is full.

But when a prince acquires a new state, which thus becomes joined on like a limb to his ancient dominions, he must disarm its inhabitants, except such of them as have taken part with him while he was acquiring it; and even these, as time and occasion serve, he should endeavour to render soft and effeminate; and he must so manage matters that all the arms of the new state shall be in the hands of his own soldiers who have served under him in his ancient dominions.

Our forefathers, even such among them as were esteemed wise, were wont to say that *Pistoja was to be held by feuds, and Pisa by fortresses*, and on this principle they used to promote dissensions in various subject towns with a view to retain them with less effort. At a time when Italy was in some measure in equilibrium, this may have been a prudent course to follow; but at the present day it seems impossible to recommend it as a general rule of policy. For I do not believe that divisions can ever lead to good; on the contrary, when an enemy approaches, divided cities are lost at once, since the weaker faction will always side with the invader, and the other will not be able to stand alone.

The Venetians, influenced as I believe by the reasons above mentioned, maintained the factions of Guelf and Ghibelline in the cities subject to them; and although they did not suffer blood to be shed, they nevertheless fomented their disputes, in order that the citizens having their minds occupied with these contests might not unite against them. But this, as we see, did not turn out to their advantage, for after their defeat at Vaila, one of the two factions, suddenly taking courage, deprived them of the whole of their territory.

Moreover, methods like these betray weakness in a prince, for under a strong government such divisions would never be tolerated, since they are only useful in time of peace as an expedient whereby subjects may be more easily managed, whereas on war breaking out their mistake is demonstrated.

Doubtless, princes become great by vanquishing difficulties and opposition, and Fortune, on that account, when she desires to aggrandize a new prince, who has more need than an hereditary prince to win reputation, causes enemies to rise up, and urges them on to attack him, to the end that he may have opportunities to overcome them, and make his ascent by the very ladder which they have planted. For which reason, many are of the opinion that a wise prince, when he has the occasion, ought dexterously to promote hostility to himself in certain quarters that his greatness may be enhanced by crushing it.

Princes, and new princes especially, have found greater fidelity and helpfulness in those men who, at the beginning of their reign, have been held in suspicion, than in those who at the outset have enjoyed their confidence; and Pandolfo Petrucci, Lord of Siena, governed his state by the instrumentality of those whom he had at one time distrusted, in preference to all others. But on this point it is impossible to lay down any general rule, since the course to be followed varies with the circumstances. I shall only say this, that those men who at the commencement of a reign have been hostile, if of a sort to require support in order to maintain them, may always be gained over by the prince with much ease, and are the more bound to serve him faithfully because they know that they have to efface by their actions the unfavourable impression he had formed of them; and in this way a prince always obtains better help from them than from those who, serving him in too complete security, neglect his affairs.

And since the occasion suggests it, I must not fail to remind the prince who acquires a new state through the favour of its inhabitants, to weigh well what were the causes which led those who favoured him to do so; and if it be seen that they have acted not from any natural affection for him, but merely out of discontent with the existing condition of things, that he will find the greatest difficulty in keeping them his friends, since it will be impossible for him to content them. Carefully considering the cause of this, with the aid of examples taken from ancient and modern events, he will perceive that it is far easier to gain the friendship of those who were satisfied with things as they stood, and for that very reason were his enemies, than of those who became his friends only because they were discontented, and on that account assisted him in his usurpation.

It has been customary for princes, with a view to hold their dominions more securely, to build fortresses which might serve as a curb and restraint on such as have designs against them, and as a safe refuge against a first onset I approve this custom, because it has been followed from the earliest times. Nevertheless, in our own days, Messer Niccolo Vitelli thought it advisable to dismantle two fortresses in Città di Castello in order to secure that town: and Guido Ubaldo, Duke of Urbino, on returning to his dominions, whence he had been driven out by Cesare Borgia, razed to their foundations the fortresses throughout the Dukedom, judging that if these were removed, it would not again be so easily lost The same course was followed by the Bentivogli on their return to Bologna.

Fortresses, therefore, are useful or no, according to circumstances, and if in one way they benefit, in another they injure you. We may state the case thus: the prince who is more afraid of his subjects than of strangers ought to build fortresses, while he who is more afraid of strangers than of his subjects, should leave them alone. The citadel built in Milan by Francesco Sforza has been, and will hereafter prove to be, more dangerous to the House of Sforza than any other disorder of that state. So that, on the whole, the best fortress you can have, is in not being hated by your subjects. If they hate you no fortress will save you; for when once the people take up arms, foreigners are never wanting to assist them.

Within our own time it does not appear that fortresses have been of service to any prince, unless to the Countess of Forli after her husband Count Girolamo was murdered; for by this means she was able to escape the first onset of the insurgents, and awaiting succour from Milan, to recover her state; the circumstances of the times being such that no foreigner was able to lend assistance to the people. But afterwards, when Cesare Borgia attacked her, and the people, out of hostility to her, took part with the invader, her fortresses were of little avail. So that, everything considered, both on this and on the former occasion, it would have been safer for her to have been without fortresses than to be hated by her subjects.

All which considerations being taken into account, I shall applaud him who builds fortresses, and him who does not; but I shall blame him who trusting in them, counts it a light thing to be held in hatred by his people.

CHAPTER 21

How a Prince Should Govern Himself so as to Acquire Reputation

Nothing makes a prince so well thought of as to undertake great enterprises and give striking proofs of his capacity.

Among the princes of our time Ferdinand of Aragon, the present King of Spain, (as at time of first publication), may almost be accounted a new prince, since from one of the weakest he has become, through the fame and glory of his achievements, the foremost King in Christendom. And if you consider his actions you will find them all great, and some extraordinary.

In the beginning of his reign he made war on Granada, which enterprise was the foundation of his power. At first he carried on the war at his ease, without fear of interruption, and kept the attention and thoughts of the barons of Castile so completely occupied with it, that they had no time to think of changes at home. By these means he insensibly acquired reputation among them and authority over them. With the money of the Church and of his subjects he was able to maintain his armies, and during the prolonged contest to lay the foundations of that military system for which he afterwards became so famous.

Moreover, to enable him to engage in still greater undertakings, always covering himself with the cloak of religion, he had recourse to what may be called *pious cruelty*, in driving out and clearing his kingdom of the Moors; than which exploit none could be more wonderful or uncommon. Using the same pretext, he made war on Africa, undertook an expedition into Italy, and finally attacked France; and being thus constantly engaged in planning and executing vast designs, he kept the minds of his subjects in suspense and admiration, and occupied with the results of his actions, which arose one out of another in such close succession as left neither time nor opportunity to oppose them.

It is likewise very advantageous for a prince to follow striking methods in administering the internal government of his state, such as those related of Messer Bernabò of Milan, whenever the remarkable actions of any one in civil life, whether for good or for evil, afford him occasion; and to choose such ways of rewarding and punishing as cannot fail to be much spoken of. But above all, he should strive by all his actions to inspire a sense of his greatness and goodness.

A prince is also esteemed who is a staunch friend and a thorough foe, that is to say, who without reserve openly declares for one against another, because this is always a more advantageous course than to stand neutral For supposing two of your powerful neighbours come to blows, it must either be that you will, or that you will not, have reason to fear him who comes off victorious. In either case it will always be well for you to declare yourself, and join in frankly with one side or other. For should you fail to do so, in the former of the cases put, you are certain to become the prey of the victor to the satisfaction and delight of the vanquished, and no reason or circumstance which you may plead will be of any avail to shield or shelter you. For the victor dislikes doubtful friends, and such as will not help him at a pinch; and the vanquished will have nothing to say to you, since yon would not share his fortunes sword in hand.

When Antiochus passed into Greece, at the invitation of the Etolians, in order to drive out the Romans, he sent envoys to the Achaians, who were friendly to the Romans, exhorting them to stand neutral. The Romans, on the other hand, urged them to take up arms on their behalf. The matter coming to be discussed in the Council of the Achaians, the legate of Antiochus again urged neutrality, whereupon the Roman envoy answered—"Nothing can be more to your disadvantage than the course which has been described as the best and most useful for your state, namely, to refrain from taking any part in our war, for by standing aloof you will gain neither favour nor fame, but remain the prize of the victor."

And it will always happen that he who is not your friend will invite you to neutrality, while he who is your friend will call on you to declare yourself openly in arms. Irresolute princes, to escape immediate danger, commonly follow the neutral path, in most instances to their destruction. But when you pronounce valiantly in favour of one side or other, if he to him you give your adherence conquers, although he be powerful and you are at his mercy, still he is under obligations to you, and has become your friend; and none are so lost to shame as to destroy with ostentatious ingratitude one who has helped them. Besides which, victories are never so complete that the victor can afford to disregard all considerations whatever, more especially considerations of justice. On the other hand, if he with whom you take part should lose, you will always be favourably regarded by him; while he can he will aid you, and you become his companion in a cause which may recover.

In the second case put, namely, when both combatants are of such limited strength, that whichever wins you have no cause to fear, it is all the more prudent for you to take a side, for you will then be ruining the one with the help of the other, who were he wise would endeavour to save him. If he whom you help conquers, he remains in your power, and with your aid he cannot but conquer.

And here let it be noted that a prince should be careful not to join with one stronger than himself in attacking others, unless, as we have said, he be driven to it by necessity. For if he whom you join prevails, you are at his mercy; and princes, so far as in them lies, should avoid placing themselves in the power of others. The Venetians, although they might have declined the alliance, joined with France against the Duke of Milan, which brought about their ruin. But when an alliance cannot be avoided, as was the case with the Florentines when the Pope and Spain led their armies to attack Lombardy, a prince, for the reasons given, must take a side. Nor let it be supposed that any state can select for itself a perfectly safe line of policy. On the contrary, it must reckon on every course which it may take being doubtful; for it happens in all human affairs that we never seek to escape from one mischief without falling into another. Prudence therefore consists in knowing how to distinguish degrees of disadvantage, and in accepting a less evil as a good.

Again, a prince should show himself a patron of merit, and should honour those who excel in every art. He ought accordingly to encourage his subjects by enabling them to pursue their callings, whether mercantile, agricultural, or any other, in security, so that this man shall not be deterred from beautifying his possessions from the apprehension that they may be taken from him, or that other refrain from opening a trade through fear of taxes; and he should provide rewards for those who desire so to employ themselves, and consider how and in what ways he can add to the greatness of his city or state.

He ought, moreover, at suitable seasons of the year to entertain the people with festivals and shows. And because all cities are divided into guilds and companies, he ought to show attention to these corporations, and sometimes take part in their meetings; offering an example of courtesy and magnificence, but never compromising the dignity of his station, which must under no circumstances be lost sight of.

CHAPTER 22

Of the Secretaries of Princes

The choice of ministers is a matter of no small moment to a prince. Whether they shall be good or otherwise depends on his prudence, so that the readiest conjecture we can form of the sagacity and character of a prince is from seeing what sort of men he has about him. When they are at once capable and faithful, we may always count him wise, since he has known to recognize the competent and to retain their fidelity. But if they be otherwise, we must pronounce unfavourably of him, since he has committed a first fault in making this selection.

There was none who knew Messer Antonio of Venafro as Minister of Pandolfo Petrucci, Lord of Siena, but pronounced Pandolfo a most prudent ruler in having secured his services. And since there are three scales of intelligence, one which understands by itself, a second which understands what is shown it by others, and a third which neither understands by itself nor on the showing of others, the first of which is most excellent, the second good, but the third worthless, we must needs admit that if Pandolfo was not in the first of these degrees, he was in the second; because whenever a man has the judgement to discern between the good and evil which another does or says, however devoid he may be of the faculty of invention, he is able to recognize the merit or demerit of his minister, and will commend the former, while he corrects the latter. The minister can have no hope to deceive such a prince, and will continue virtuous.

As to how a prince is to know his minister, this unerring rule may be laid down. When you see a minister thinking more of himself than of you, and in all his actions seeking his own ends, that man can never be a good minister or one that you can trust. For he who has the charge of the state committed to him, ought never to think of himself but only of his prince, and should never bring to the notice of the latter what does not directly concern him. On the other hand, the prince, in order to keep his minister good, ought to be considerate of him, dignifying, enriching, binding him to himself by benefits, and sharing with him the honours as well as the burthens of the state, so that the great honours and wealth bestowed upon him may divert him from seeking these at the hands of others; while the great responsibilities with which he is charged may lead him to dread change, knowing that he cannot stand alone without his master's support When prince and minister are upon this footing they can mutually trust one another; but when the contrary is the case, the result will always be calamitous for one or other of them.

CHAPTER 23

That Flatterers Should be Shunned

One error into which princes, unless very prudent or very fortunate in their choice of friends, are apt to fall, is of such importance that I must not pass it over. I mean in respect of flatterers. These abound in courts, because men take such pleasure in their own concerns, and so deceive themselves with regard to them, that they can hardly escape this plague; while even in the attempt to escape it there is risk of their incurring contempt.

For there is no way to guard against flattery but by letting it be understood that you take no offence in hearing the truth: but when everyone is free to tell you the truth, respect falls short. Wherefore a prudent prince should follow a middle course, by choosing certain wise men of his dominions and allowing them free leave to speak their minds on any matter on which he asks their opinion, and on none other. But he ought to ask their opinion on everything, and after hearing them should reflect and judge for himself. And with these counsellors collectively, and with each of them separately, his bearing should be such, that each and all of them may know that the more openly they speak their minds the better they will be liked. Besides these, the prince should listen to no others, but proceed at once to make up his mind, and afterwards adhere firmly to his resolves. Whoever acts otherwise is either undone by flatterers, or from continually vacillating as opinions vary, comes to be held of slight esteem.

In reference to this matter, I shall cite a recent instance. Father Luke, who is attached to the court of the present Emperor Maximilian, in speaking of his Majesty told me, that he took advice from no man, yet never had his own way; and this from his following a course contrary to that above described. For being of a reserved disposition, he never discloses his intentions to any, nor asks their opinion; and it is only when his plans are to be carried out that they begin to be known and understood, and at the same time they begin to be thwarted by those he has about him, when he being facile gives way. Hence it happens that what he wishes or designs to do is never fully ascertained, and that it is impossible to build on his resolves.

A prince, therefore, ought always to take counsel, but at such times and seasons only as he himself pleases, and not when it pleases others; on the contrary, he should discourage everyone from obtruding advice on matters on which it is not sought. But he ought to be free in asking advice, and afterwards, in respect of the matters on which he has asked it, a patient hearer of the truth, and even displeased should he perceive that any one, from whatever motive, keeps it back.

But those who think that every prince who has a name for prudence owes it to the wise counsellors he has around him, and not to any merit of his own, are certainly mistaken; since it is an unerring rule and of universal application that a prince who is not wise himself cannot be well advised by others, unless by chance he surrenders himself to be wholly governed by someone adviser who happens to be supremely prudent; in which case he may, indeed, be well advised, but not for long, since such an adviser will soon deprive him of his Government. If he listen to a multitude of advisers, the prince who is not wise will never have consistent counsels, nor will he know of himself how to reconcile them. Each of his counsellors will study his own advantage, and the prince will be unable to detect or correct them. And this cannot be otherwise, for men will always grow bad on your hands unless they find themselves under a necessity to be good.

Hence it follows that good counsels, whencesoever they come, have their origin in the prudence of the prince, and not the prudence of the prince in wise counsels.

CHAPTER 24

Why the Princes of Italy have Lost Their States

The lessons above taught if prudently followed will cause a new prince to be regarded with the same feelings as an hereditary one, and will at once establish him in his place more firmly and securely than if his authority had the sanction of time. For the actions of a new prince are watched much more closely than those of an hereditary prince; and when seen to be virtuous are far more effectual than antiquity of blood in gaining men over and attaching them to his cause. For men are more nearly touched by things present than by things past, and when they find themselves well off as they are, enjoy their felicity and seek no further; nay, are ready in every way to defend the existing state of things, provided the prince be not wanting to himself in other respects. In this way there accrues to the new prince a double glory, in having laid the foundations of the new princedom, and in haring strengthened and adorned it with good laws and good arms, with faithful friends and great deeds; as, on the other hand, there is a double disgrace in one who has been born to a princedom losing it by his own want of wisdom.

And if we contemplate those lords who in our own times have lost their dominions in Italy, such as the King of Naples, the Duke of Milan, and others, we shall see, in the first place, that in respect of arms they have, for reasons already dwelt on, been all alike defective; and next, that some of them have either had the people against them, or if they have had the people with them, have not known how to secure the favour of their nobles. For without such inherent defects, states which are powerful enough to keep an army in the field are never overthrown.

Philip of Macedon, not the father of Alexander the Great, but he who was defeated by Titus Quintius, had no great state as compared with the strength of the Romans and Greeks who attacked him. Nevertheless, being a prince of a warlike spirit, and skilful in gaining the goodwill of the people and in securing the adherence of the nobles, he for many years maintained himself against his assailants, and in the end, although he lost some towns, he succeeded in saving his kingdom.

Let those princes of ours, therefore, who have lost their dominions after holding them for so many years, accuse not fortune but their own inertness. For never having reflected in tranquil times that there might come a change, and it is human nature when the sea is calm not to think of storms, when adversity overtook them, they thought not of defence but only of escape, trusting that their people, disgusted with the insolence of the conqueror, would someday recall them.

This course may be a good one when all others fail, but it is the height of folly, trusting to it, to abandon all other precautions, since none would wish to fall on the chance of another being found to lift him up. It may not happen that you are recalled by your people, or if it happen, it gives you no security. It is an ignoble resource, since it does not depend on you for its success; and those modes of defence are alone good, certain, and lasting, which depend upon yourself and your own worth.

CHAPTER 25

What Fortune Can Effect in Human Affairs, and How She May be Withstood

I am not ignorant that many have been and are of the opinion that human affairs are so governed by fortune and by God, that men cannot alter them by any prudence of theirs, and indeed have no remedy against them; and for this reason have come to think that it is not worth their while to labour much about anything, but that they must leave everything to be determined by chance.

Having often reflected on the matter, I am in part inclined to agree with this opinion, which has had the readier acceptance in our own times from the very great changes in things which we have seen, and every day see happen contrary to all human expectation. Nevertheless, since our free will is not destroyed, I think it may be the case that fortune is the mistress of one half of our actions, and yet leaves the control of the other half, or a little less, to ourselves. And I would liken her to one of those destructive torrents which, when angry, overflow the plains, sweep away trees and houses, and carry off soil from one bank to throw it down upon the other. Everyone flees before them, and yields to their fury without the least power to resist.

And yet, though this be their nature, it does not follow that in seasons of fair weather, men cannot take such precautions by constructing weirs and moles, as will cause them when again in flood to pass off by some artificial channel, or at least prevent their course from being so uncontrolled and destructive. And so it is with Fortune, who displays her might where there is no organised strength to resist her, and directs her onset where she knows that there is neither barrier nor embankment to confine her.

And if you look at Italy, which has been once the seat of these changes and their cause, you will perceive that it is a field without embankment or barrier. For if, like Germany, France, and Spain, it had been guarded with sufficient skill, this inundation, if it took place at all, would never have wrought the violent changes which we have witnessed.

This I think enough to say generally on the subject of resistance to fortune. But confining myself more strictly to the matter in hand, I observe that one day we see a prince prospering and the next day overthrown, without detecting any change in his nature or character. This, I believe, arises chiefly from a cause which has already been dwelt upon, namely, that a prince who rests wholly on fortune is ruined when she changes. Moreover, I believe that he will be most prosperous whose mode of acting adapts itself best to the character of the times; and in like manner that he will be unprosperous, with whose mode of acting the times do not accord. For we see that men in these matters which lead to the end which each has before him, namely, glory and wealth, proceed by different ways, one with caution, another with impetuosity, one with violence, another with artifice, one with patience, another with its contrary; and by one or other of these different courses each may succeed.

Again, of two who act cautiously, you shall find that one attains his end, the other not, and similarly that two of different temperament, the one being cautious, the other impetuous, are equally successful All which happens from no other cause than that the character of the times harmonizes or does not harmonize with their methods of acting. And hence it comes, as I have already said, that two operating differently arrive at the same result, and two operating similarly, the one succeeds and the other not On this likewise depend the vicissitudes of fortune. For if to one who conducts himself with caution and patience, time and circumstances are propitious, so that his method of acting is good, he goes on prospering; but if these change he is ruined, because he does not change his method of acting.

For no man is found so prudent as to know how to adapt himself to these changes, both because he cannot deviate from the course to which nature inclines him, and because, having always prospered while adhering to one path, he cannot be persuaded that it would be well for him to forsake it And so when occasion requires the cautious man to act impetuously, he cannot do so and is undone: whereas, had he changed his nature with time and circumstances, his fortune would have been unchanged.

Pope Julius II. proceeded with impetuosity in all his undertaking, and found time and circumstances in such accord with his mode of acting that he always obtained a happy result. Witness his first expedition against Bologna, when Messer Giovanni Bentivogli was still living. The Venetians were not favourable to the enterprise. Negotiations respecting it between the kings of France and Spain were still open. Nevertheless, the Pope with his wonted fierceness and hardihood marched in person on the expedition, and by this movement brought the King of Spain and the Venetians to a check, the latter through fear, the former from his desire to recover the entire Kingdom of Naples; while, at the same time, he secured the co-operation of the King of France, who seeing him in motion, and being anxious to secure his friendship with the view to humble the Venetians, concluded that he could not refuse him his soldiers without openly breaking with him.

By the impetuosity of his movements, therefore, Julius effected what no other pontiff endowed with the highest human prudence could. For had he, as any other Pope would have done, delayed his departure from Rome until terms had been settled and everything duly arranged, he never would have succeeded. For the King of France would have found a thousand pretexts to delay him, and the others would have menaced him with a thousand alarms. I shall not touch upon his other actions, which were all of a like character, and all of which had a happy issue, since the shortness of his life did not allow him to experience reverses. But if times had overtaken him, rendering a cautious line of conduct necessary, his ruin must have ensued, since he could never have departed from those methods to which nature inclined him.

To be brief, I say that since fortune changes, and men stand fixed in their old ways, they are prosperous so long as there is congruity between them, and the reverse when there is not. Of this, however, I am thoroughly persuaded, that it is better to be impetuous than cautious. For Fortune is a woman who to be kept under must be beaten and roughly handled; and we see that she suffers herself to be more readily mastered by those who so treat her than by those who are more timid in their approaches. And always, like a woman, she favours the young, because they are less scrupulous and fiercer, and command her with greater audacity.

CHAPTER 26

An Exhortation to Liberate Italy From the Barbarians

To me, turning over in my mind all the matters which have above been considered, and debating with myself whether in Italy at the present hour the time has come in which a new prince might hope to gain honour, and whether those circumstances now exist which to a person of prudence and courage hold out the opportunity for introducing changes glorious to himself and beneficial to the whole Italian people, it seems that so many conditions combine to further such an enterprise, that I know of no time so favourable to it as the present

And if, as I have said, it was necessary in order to display the valour of Moses that the children of Israel should be slaves in Egypt, and to know the greatness and courage of Cyrus that the Persians should be oppressed by the Medes, and to illustrate the excellence of Theseus that the Athenians should be scattered and divided, so at this hour, to prove the worth of some Italian hero, it was required that Italy should be brought to her present abject condition, so as to be more a slave than the Hebrew, more oppressed than the Persian, more disunited than the Athenian, without a head, without order, beaten, spoiled, torn in pieces, over-run and abandoned to destruction in every shape.

For although, heretofore, glimmerings may have been discerned in this man or that, from which it might be conjectured that they were ordained by God for her redemption, nevertheless it has afterwards been seen in the further course of their actions that fortune has disowned them; so that our country, left almost without life, waits to know who it is that is to heal her bruises, to put an end to the devastation and plunder of Lombardy, to the pillage and imposts of Naples and Tuscany, and to close those wounds of hers which neglect has changed into running sores.

We see how she prays God to send someone to deliver her from these barbarous cruelties and oppressions. We see how ready and eager she is to follow any standard were there only someone to raise it. But at present we see no one except in your Illustrious House (pre-eminent by its virtues and good fortune, and favoured by God and by the Church whose headship it now holds), who could undertake the part of a deliverer.

But for you this will not be too hard a task, if you keep before your eyes the lives and actions of those whom I have named above. For although these men were singular and extraordinary, after all they were but men, not one of whom had so great an opportunity as now presents itself to you. For their undertakings were not more just than this, nor more easy, nor was God more their friend than yours. The justice of the cause is conspicuous; for that war is just which is necessary, and those arms are sacred from which we derive our only hope. Everywhere there is the strongest disposition to engage in this cause; and where the disposition is strong the difficulty cannot be great, provided you follow the methods observed by those whom I have set before you as models.

But further, we see here extraordinary and unexampled proofs of Divine favour. The sea has been divided; the cloud has attended you on your way; the rock has flowed with water; the manna has rained from heaven; everything has concurred to promote your greatness. What remains to be done must be done by you; since in order not to deprive us of our free will and such share of credit as belongs to us, God will not do everything himself.

And it is not to be marvelled at if none of these Italians I have named has been able to effect what we hope to see effected by your illustrious House; or that amid so many revolutions and so many warlike movements it should always appear as though the military virtues of Italy were spent; for this comes from her old system being defective and from no one being found among us capable to invent a new. Nothing confers such honour on the reformer of a State, as do the new laws and institutions which he devises; for these when they stand on a solid basis and have a greatness in their design make him admired and venerated.

And in Italy material is not wanting for improvement in every form. If the head be weak the limbs are strong, and we see daily in single combats, or where few are engaged, how superior are the strength, dexterity, and intelligence of Italians. But in a pitched battle they are nowhere, and this from no other reason than the weakness of their leaders. For those who are skilful in arms will not obey, and everyone thinks himself skilful, since hitherto we have had none among us so raised by merit or by fortune over his fellows that they should yield him the palm. And hence it happens that for the long period of twenty years, during which so many wars have taken place, whenever there has been an army purely Italian it has always been beaten. And to this testify, first Taro, then Alessandria, Capua, Genoa, Vaila, Bologna, Mestri.

If then your illustrious House should seek to rival the conduct of those great men who have delivered their country in past ages, it is before all things necessary, as the true foundation of every such attempt, to be provided with national troops, since you can have no braver or more faithful soldiers; and although every single man of them be good, collectively they will be better, seeing themselves commanded by their own prince, and honoured and esteemed by him. That you may be able, therefore, to defend yourself against the foreigner with Italian valour, the first step is to provide yourself with an army such as this.

And although the Swiss and the Spanish infantry are each esteemed formidable, there are yet defects in both, by reason of which, troops trained on a different system might not merely withstand them, but be sure of defeating them. For the Spaniards cannot resist cavalry, and the Swiss will give way before infantry if they find them as resolute as themselves at close quarters. Whence it has been seen, and may be seen again, that the Spaniards are unable to withstand the onset of the French men-at-arms, and that the Swiss are thrown into confusion by the Spanish foot. And although of this last we have no complete instance, we have yet an indication of it in the battle of Ravenna, where the Spanish infantry confronted the German companies, who have the same discipline as the Swiss; on which occasion the Spaniards by their agility and with the aid of their bucklers forced their way over the pikes, and stood in safety and ready to close with the Germans, who were no longer in a position to defend themselves; and had they not been charged by cavalry, they would have cut the Germans to pieces.

Knowing, then, the defects of each of these kinds of troops, you can train your men on some different system, to withstand cavalry and not to fear infantry. To effect this, will not require the creation of any new forces, but simply a change in the management of the old. And these are matters in reforming which the new prince acquires reputation and importance.

This opportunity then, for Italy at last to look on her deliverer, ought not to be allowed to pass away. With what love he would be received in all those provinces which have suffered from the foreign inundation; with what thirst for vengeance; with what fixed fidelity, with what devotion, and what tears, no words of mine can express. What gates would be closed against him? What people would refuse him obedience? What jealousy would stand in his way? What Italian but would yield him homage?

This barbarian tyranny stinks in all nostrils.

Let your illustrious House therefore take upon itself this enterprise with all the courage and all the hopes with which a just cause is undertaken; so that under your standard this our country may be ennobled, and under your auspices be fulfilled the words of Petrarch:—

> *Brief will be the strife*
> *When valour arms against barbaric rage;*
> *For the bold spirit of the bygone age*
> *Still warms Italian hearts with life.*

The Art of War

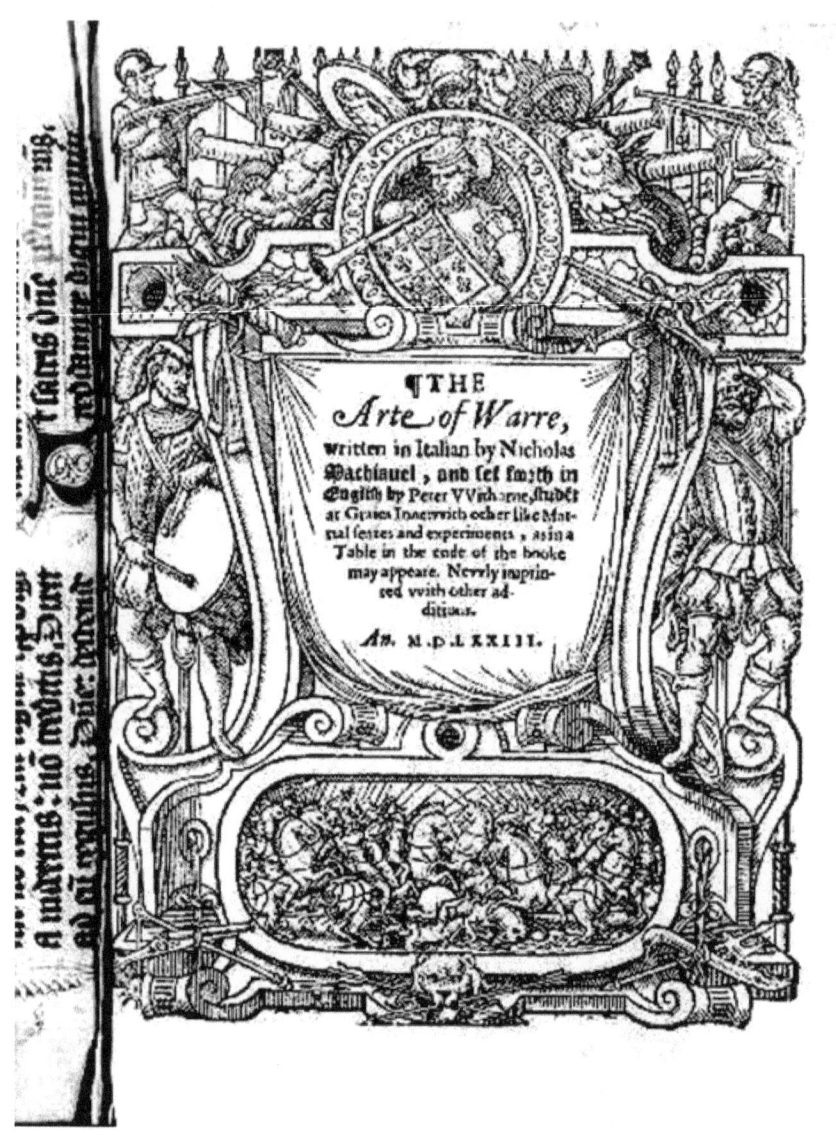

Peter Whitehorne's translation of The Art of War

Contents

The French Translator's Advertisement to the Reader	109
The Author's Preface	115
Book 1	119
Book 2	147
Book 3	179
Book 4	201
Book 5	217
Book 6	233
Book 7	260

The French Translator's Advertisement to the Reader

Although the manner of making war is very different at present from what it was in Machiavel's days, his treatise, or rather dialogues, upon that subject may still be of great use. For in the first place, they are written by a genius of the highest rank, and founded upon some general principles which will always hold good: and in the next, (besides the pleasure of seeing what alteration is made in this science by time) they may furnish other men of parts and abilities with some useful and improvable hints; especially those that follow the profession of arms.

There are further many judicious reflexions in the course of this work, which cannot fail of being very agreeable to connoisseurs: and towards the end of the second book, the author launches out into a digression, in which he shews with great perspicuity to what causes it is chiefly owing, that the number of eminent commanders is greater or less in different times and places.

N. B. The rest of this advertisement is wholly taken up in elucidating some military terms and phrases, which shall be explained in their proper places hereafter.

But as there was an old English translation of Machiavel's *Art of War*, published in the year 1588, by one Peter Whitehorne, who calls himself Student of Gray's Inn, I shall take the liberty of presenting the reader with his dedication of it to Queen Elizabeth: for though the language is now grown obsolete and uncouth, yet the sentiments are just and worthy of observation. The translation indeed is a very bad one, and not intelligible at present: the dedication is as follows.

To the most high and excellent Princes Elizabeth, by the grace of God Queene of England, Fraunce, and Ireland, defender of the Faith, and of the Church of England, and Ireland, on earth next under God, the supreme Governour.

Although commonly every man, most worthy and renommed soveraigne, seeketh specially to commende and extoll the thing, whereunto he feeleth himselfe naturally bent and inclined, yet all such partialitie and private affection laid aside, it is to be thought (that for the defence, maintenance, and advauncement of a kingdom, or common weale, or for the good and due observation of peace, and administration of justice in the same) no one thing can be more profitable, necessarie, or more honourable, than the knowledge of service in warre, and deeds of armes, because considering the ambition of the world, it is impossible for any realme or dominion long to continue free in quietnes and savegard, where the defence of the sword is not alwaies in a readinesse.

For like as the Greekes, being occupied about trifling matters, taking pleasure in refiting of comedies, and such other vaine things altogether neglecting martiall feats, gave occasion to Philip King of Macedonia, father to Alexander the great, to oppresse and to bring them in servitude under his subjection: even so undoubtedly, libertie will not be kept, but men shall be troden under foote, and brought to most horrible miserie and calamitie, if they giving themselves to pastimes and pleasure, forsake the just regard of their own defence, and savegard of their countrie, which in temporall regiment, chiefly consisteth in warlike skilfulnes.

And therefore the aunciet captaines and mightie conquerours, so long as they florished, did devise with most great diligence, all manner of wayes to bring their men to the perfect knowledge of what so ever thing appertained to the warre, as manifestly appeareth by the warlike games, which in olde times the Princes of Grecia ordained upon the mount Olimpus, and also by the orders and exercises, that the auncient Romanes used in sundrie places, and especially in Campo Martio, and in their wonderfull sumptuous theaters, which chiefly they builded to that purpose. Whereby they not onely made their souldiours so expert, that they obtained with a few, in fighting against a great huge multitude of enemies, such marvailous victories, as in many credible histories are mentioned, but also by the same meanes, their unarmed rascall people that followed their campes, got such understanding in the feats of warre, that they in the day of battail, being left destitute of succour, were able without any other helpe to set themselves in good order, for their defence against the enemie, that would seeke to hurt them, and in such dangerous times, have done their countrie so good service, that verie often by their helpe, the adverfaries have beene put to flight, and fieldes most happily wonne.

So that the antiquitie esteemed nothing more happy in a common weale, then to have in the same many men skilfull in warlike affaires: by meanes whereof their Empire continually inlarged, and most wonderfully and triumphantly prospered. For so long as men for their valiauntnes, were then rewarded and had in estimation, glad was he that could finde occasion to venter, yea and spend his life to benefite his countrie: as by the manly actes that Marcus Curtius, Oratius Cocles, and Gaius Mucius did for the savegard of Rome, and also by other innumerable examples, doth plainly appeare. But when through long and continual peace, they began to be altogether given to pleasure and delicatenes, litle regarding martial feats, nor such as were expert in the practise thereof, their dominion and estates did not so much before increase and prosper, as then by such meanes and oversight, they sodainly fell into decay and utter ruine.

For such truly is the nature and condicion, both of peace and warre, that where in government there is not had equall consideracion of them both, the one in fine doth worke and induce the other's oblivion, and utter abbolicion. Wherefore, sith the necessitie of the science of warres is so great, and also the necessarie use thereof so manifest, that even Ladie Peace hir selfe, doth in manner from thence crave hir chiefe defence and preservacion, and the worthinesse moreover and honour of the same so great, that as by proofe wee see, the perfect glorie thereof, cannot easilie finde roote, but in the hearts of most noble, courageous, and manlike personages.

I thought most excellent princes, I could not either to the special gratefying of your highness, the universal delight of al studious gentlemen, or the common utilitie of the publique wealth, imploy my laboures more profitable in accomplishing of my dutie and good will, then in setting forth something, that might induce to the augmenting and increase of the knowledge thereof; and especially the example of your highnesses most politike government over us, giving plaine testimonie of the wonderfull prudent desire that is in you, to have your people instructed in this kind of service, as well for the better defence of your Highnes, themselves, and their countrie, as also to discourage thereby, and be able to refill the malignitie of the enemie, who otherwise would seeke paradventure to invade this noble realme or kingdome.

When therefore, about ten yeares past, in the Emperour's warre's against the Mores and certain Turkes, being, in Barbarie: at the siege and winning of Calibbia, Monesterio, and Affrica, I had as well for my further instruction in those affaires, as also the better to acquaint mee with the Italian tongue, reduced into English, the book called *The arte of Warre*, of the famous and excellent Nicholas Machiavel, which in times past, he being a counsailour, and secretairie of the noble citie of Florence, not without his great laud and praise did write: and having lately againe, somewhat perused the same, the which in such continuall broyles, and unquietnes, was by me translated, I determined with my selfe, by publishing thereof, to bellow as great a gift (since greater I was not able) amongst my countrie men, not expert in the Italian tongue, as in like works I had seene before mee, the Frenchmen, Dutchmen, Spaniardes, and other forreine nacions, most lovingly to have bestowed among theirs: the rather undoubtedly, that as by private reading of the same booke.

I then felt my selfe, in that knowledge marvailously holpen and increased, so by communicating the same to many, our Englishmen finding out the ordering and disposing of exploites of warre therein contained, the aide and direction of these plaine and briefe precepts, might no lesse in knowledge of warres become incomparable, then in prooves also and exercise of the same altogether invincible: which my translacion, most gracious Soveraigne, together with such other thinges, as by mee hath bene gathered, and thought good to adde thereunto, I have presumed to dedicate unto your highness, not onely because the whole charge and furniture of warlike counsailes and preparations, being determined by the arbitremen of governours and princes, the treatise also of like effect should in like manner as of right depend upon the protection of a most worthy and noble patronesse, but also that the discourse itselfe, and the worke of a foraine author, under the pasport and safe conduite of your highnes most noble name, might by speciall authoritie of the same, winne amongst your Majesties subjectes, much better credite and estimacion.

And if, most mighty Queene, in this kinde of philosophie, (if I may so terme it) grave and sage counsailes, learned and wittie precepts, or pollitike and prudent admonicions, ought not to be accounted the lead and bases jewells of weale publike; then dare I boldly affirme, that of many straungers, which from forreine countries, have heretofore in this your Majesties realme arrived, there is none in comparison to be preferred, before this worthy Florentine and Italian, who having freelye without any gaine of exchaunge (as after some acquaintaunce and familiaritie will better appear) brought with him most ritch, rare and plentifull treasure, shall deserve, I trust of all good English hearts, most lovingly and friendly to bee intertained, imbraced and cherished; whose new English apparel, how so ever it shall seeme by mee, after a grosse fashion, more fitly appointed to the campe, then in nice termes atired to the carpet, and in course clothing rather put foorth to battaile, then in any brave shew prepared to the banket; neverthelesse my goodwill I trust, shall of your grace be taken in good part, having fashioned the phraise of my rude stile, even according to the purpose of my travaile, which was rather to profite the desirous man of warre, then to delight the ears of the fine Rethorician, or daintie curious scholeman. Most humbly beseeching your highnes, so to accept my labour herein, as the first frutes of a poore souldiour's studie, who to the uttermost of his smal power, in the service of your most gratious majeftie, and of his countrie, will at all times, according to his boundent dutie and allegeaunce, promptly yeeld himselfe to any labour, travaile or daunger, whatso ever shall happen. Praying in the meane season the aimightie God, to give your highnes in a long prosperous raigne, perfect health, desired tranquilitie, and against all your enemies, lucky and joyful victorie. Your humble subject and dayly

Oratour, Peter Whitehorne

The Author's Preface
Addressed to
Lorenzo Strozzi, Nobleman of Florence

Many are now of opinion, My Dear Lorenzo, that no two things are more discordant and incongruous than a civil and a military life. Hence we see daily, that when a man: goes into the army, he presently changes, not only his dress, but his behaviour, his company, his air, his manner of speaking, and affects to throw off all appearance of anything that may look like common life and conversation. For a man that is to be ready equipped for any sort of violence, despises the formal garb of a citizen, and thinks no dress fit for his purpose but a suit of armour: and as to civility and politeness, how can we expect to find any such thing in one who imagines it would make him look effeminate, and rather be a hindrance to his preferment than otherwise, especially when he thinks it his duty, instead of talking and looking like other men, to fright everybody he meets with a volley of oaths, and a terrible pair of whiskers? This indeed gives some countenance to such an opinion, and makes people look upon a soldier as a different sort of a creature from all other men.

But if we consider the nature of government, and the institutions of the ancients, we shall find a very strict and intimate relation betwixt these two conditions; and that they are not only compatible and consistent with each other, but necessarily connected and united together. For all the arts and sciences which have been introduced into society for the common benefit of mankind, and all the ordinances that have been established to make them live in the fear of God, and obedience to human laws, would be vain and insignificant, if not supported and defended by a military force; which, when properly conducted and applied, will maintain those ordinances and keep up their authority, though perhaps they may not be altogether perfect and without flaw or defect in themselves.

But the best ordinances in the world will be despised and trampled underfoot, if not upheld as they ought to be by a military power; like a magnificent palace that is uncovered at the top, which though full of jewels and costly furniture, must soon moulder into ruin, as it has nothing but its splendour and riches to defend it from the injuries of the weather. The ancient lawgivers and governors of kingdoms and republics took great care therefore to inspire all their subjects, but particularly their soldiers, with fidelity, love of peace, and the fear of God. For who ought to be more faithful than a man that is entrusted with the safety of his country, and has sworn to defend it to the last drop of his blood? Who ought to be fonder of peace than those that suffer by nothing but war? Who is under greater obligations to worship God than soldiers, who are daily exposed to innumerable dangers, and have most occasion for his protection?

These things being well considered by those who governed states and modelled armies in former times, and strongly enforced upon others that were under their command, had such an effect upon their conduct and behaviour, that the life of a soldier was edifying and served as a pattern for others. But since our discipline is now depraved to such a degree, that it is totally different from what it anciently was, it is no wonder that men have so bad an opinion of a military life, and endeavour, as much as they can, to avoid the company and conversation of all such as follow the profession of arms.

As I am of opinion, therefore, from what I have both seen and read, that it is not even yet impossible to revive the discipline of our ancestors, and in some measure to retrieve the reputation of our soldiery, I have written the following treatise concerning the Art of War, as well for the improvements of others who are desirous to imitate the ancients in warlike exploits, as for my own private satisfaction, and to avoid the imputation of spending my leisure in idleness. Now, though perhaps it may seem a presumptuous undertaking to treat of an art which I never professed; yet I cannot help thinking myself more excusable than some other people, who have taken upon them the actual exercise of it: for an error in my writings may easily be corrected, without prejudice to anybody; but an error in their practice may ruin a whole state.

Consider the nature of this work then, good Lorenzo, and freely bestow either your censure or commendation upon it, as you think it justly deserves. I inscribe it to you, not only as a testimony of my gratitude, (though conscious to myself how small a return it is for the favours I have received from you) but because it is usual to address things of this nature to persons who are distinguished by their nobility, their riches, their great parts, or munificence; and I know very well that in birth and fortune you have not many equals, still fewer in parts, and in generosity and liberality, none at all.

Book 1

Fabrizio Colonna refreshing himself in Cosimo Rucellai's gardens at Florence, enters into a conversation concerning the Art of War, That an honest man ought not to make war his only profession. That no prince or republic should suffer any of their subjects to make war their only occupation. In what countries the best soldiers are to be raised. Whether it is better to take them out of towns , or out of the country. The conveniences and inconveniencies of trained bands, or a settled militia. Of what sort of men an army ought to be composed. How the Romans raised their legions. Whether a militia should be numerous, or not. How to prevent the inconveniencies to which a militia is subject. Of raising and paying cavalry.

Since it is allowable, I think, to speak well of any man after he is dead, because there can then be no longer any imputation or suspicion of flattery, I willingly take this opportunity of doing justice to the memory of my dear deceased friend Cosimo Rucellai, whose name I never remember without tears; as I knew him to be possessed of every quality that his friends and country could wish for in a worthy man and a good citizen. For I am very certain he would cheerfully have sacrificed all that he had in the world, and even life itself, for his friends; and that there was no enterprise how difficult and dangerous so ever, which he would not have undertaken for the good of his country.

And I must acknowledge, that amongst all the men I ever was acquainted with, I never met with anyone whose heart was more disposed to great and generous actions. The only thing that he lamented at his death, was, that it should be his fate to die so young, and in his own house, without honour, or the satisfaction of having served any man in so effectual a manner as he passionately desired to have done; so that he was afraid (as he told his familiar acquaintance) nothing more could be said of him after he was dead, than that they had lost a good friend. But as his actions are sunk in oblivion, and scarce any of his acquaintance remaining, I think it proper to give this testimony of his virtues, and many amiable accomplishments.

Time indeed has spared some small specimens of the sprightless of his genius, consisting chiefly of love sonnets, which (though he was not of an amorous turn) he composed at vacant hours in his youth, to avoid being altogether idle, and to entertain himself as well as others, till he should find it necessary to employ his thoughts upon subjects of a higher and more serious nature. But even from these little samples, it appears how happy he was in expressing his conceptions, and what a figure he might have made in poetry, if he had thought it worth his while to give himself wholly up to it.

Since fortune therefore has deprived us of so valuable a friend, the only remedy we have left, is to console ourselves as well as we can with the remembrance of his company, and the recollection of such things, whether of a pleasant or serious cast, as we have often admired in him whilst he lived. And because the conversation that happened not long ago in his gardens, betwixt him and Fabrizio Colonna, concerning the Art of War (at which I and some other friends were present) is the freshest upon my memory, I will endeavour to recollect what I can of it, and commit it to writing: for as Fabrizio laid open the mysteries of that art with great perspicuity on one side, and several pertinent questions were proposed, many objections started, and divers arguments supported with no less strength of reason by Cosimo on the other; a summary account of that conference may serve not only to revive the remembrance of his abilities in the minds of such friends as were then met together, but to make those that were absent regret they were not there, and to recapitulate to others the substance of various topics (no less useful in a civil than a military life) at that time handled in a very masterly manner, by a great and experienced man. But to our purpose.

Fabrizio Colonna returning, from the wars in Lombardy, where he had commanded his Catholic Majesty's forces a considerable time with great reputation, took Florence in his way, with a design to repose himself a few days in that city, and to visit the duke and some other gentlemen there, with whom he was acquainted. Cosimo Rucellai therefore invited him to spend a day with him in his gardens; not merely to gratify his natural turn to hospitality and politeness, but in hopes likewise of being indulged in a long conversation with him concerning several things he wanted to know, and of which he thought he could not have a better opportunity of informing himself, than from the mouth of so great a man.

The invitation being freely accepted by Fabrizio, he came to the gardens at the time appointed, where he was received by Cosimo, and some of his most intimate friends, amongst whom were Zanobi Buondelmonti, Battista dalla Palla, and Luigi Alamanni, (all young men, very dear to him, of the same disposition, and engaged in the same studies) whose virtues and good qualities are so well known to everybody, that it would be altogether unnecessary to say anything here in praise of them.—To be as brief as I can, Fabrizio was regaled there with all possible demonstrations of honour and respect: but after the entertainment and usual formalities were over (which generally are few and short amongst men of sense, who are more desirous of gratifying the rational appetite) the days being long, and the weather intensely hot, Cosimo, under a pretence of avoiding the heat, took his guests into the most retired and shady part of the gardens; and being all sat down, some upon the grass (which was very green and pleasant) and some upon seats placed under the trees; Fabrizio said it was a most delightful garden, and looking earnestly at some of the trees, seemed not to know the names of them; but Cosimo being aware of it, immediately said, "perhaps you may not be acquainted with this sort of trees; and indeed I am not at all surprised at it, for they are very old ones, and were much more in vogue amongst our ancestors than they are at present."

Having then told him the names of them, and that they were planted by his Grandfather Bernardo, who was fond of such amusements: "I thought so," replied Fabrizio; "and both the place and the trees put me in mind of some Princes in the Kingdom of Naples, who took much delight in planting groves and shady arbours, to shelter them from the heat."—Here he stopped short, and after he had paused a little while, proceeded in this manner.—"If I was not afraid of giving offence, I would tell you my opinion of these things: and yet I think none of you will be affronted at what is said amongst friends in free conversation; not with any design to vilify or depreciate such a taste, but for the sake of a little innocent argumentation. How much better then would those princes have done (I speak it without intending to reflect upon their memories) if they had endeavoured to imitate the ancients in bearing hardships, instead of giving themselves up to ease and indolence, in doing such actions as are performed in the sunshine, and not in the shade; in following their example whilst they continued hardy and honest, and not when they became delicate and corrupt; for after that our country soon fell into ruin and diffraction.—"

"You have now introduced a subject," said Cosimo (but to avoid the frequent and tiresome repetition of "such a one said, such a one answered, and such a one replied," I shall hereafter only prefix the name of the several speakers, to what they laid in the course of this conversation) you have now introduced a subject which I have long wished to hear thoroughly discussed, and therefore should take it as a particular favour, if you would speak your sentiments of it freely, and without reserve, or fear of offending anyone here: for my own part, I will take the liberty of proposing some questions and doubts to you, in which I should be glad to be satisfied; but if I shall seem either to impeach or excuse anyone's conduct in my questions or replies, it will not be for the sake of blaming or defending them, but for better information, if I should mistake in my judgement"

Fabrizio. It will be a great pleasure to me, I can assure you, on the other hand, to give you all the satisfaction I can in such questions as you shall think fit to propose to me; but I will not pretend to obtrude my opinions upon you as decisive and infallible; when you have heard them, I beg you will judge for yourself: perhaps I may now and then ask you a question too in my turn, and make no doubt but I shall receive as much satisfaction at least, in your answers, as you will do in mine: for it often happens that a pertinent question puts a man upon considering some things, and gives him light into many others, which otherwise he would never have thought of or known.

Cosimo. Let us return then, if you please, to what you said of my grandfather and some others, who you think would have done better to have imitated the example of the ancients in a hardy and active manner of living, than in making such provisions for ease and luxury. As for my grandfather, I shall make some sort of apology for him; and leave the others to be dealt with as you please: for I do not believe there was any man of his time, who detested a soft and delicate way of life more than he did, or was a greater friend to toil and labour. Nevertheless, he found it impossible either for himself or his sons to practise what he most approved; for such was the corruption of the age he lived in, that if anyone had spirit enough to deviate ever so little from the common customs and manner of living in those times, he would have been laughed at and ridiculed by everybody.

So that if a man should have exposed himself naked upon a sandy beach to the heat of a noonday sun in the middle of summer, or rolled himself in snow in the depth of winter, as Diogenes did, he would have been looked upon as a madman: if anyone had brought up his children, like the Spartans in cottages or farmhouses; if he had accustomed them to sleep in the open air, to go barehead and barefoot, to bathe in the coldest streams, in order not only to make them bear hardships the better, but to despise both life and death, he would have been accounted a beast rather than a man: if, lastly, he had lived upon pulse and roots and such sort of things, if he had made no account of money, like Frabricius of old, he might perhaps have been admired by some few, but he would have been followed by nobody. My grandfather therefore was discouraged from imitating the example of the ancients, in those things, by the general practice of the times, and forced to content himself with doing it in others, which did not lay him so open to the charge of affecting singularity.

Fabrizio. You have made a very handsome apology for your grandfather in that particular, Sir; and there is indeed much truth and reason in it. But in what I said of imitating the ancients in their manner of living, I did not mean to carry matters to such extremities as you seem to think, but to propose some other things of a gentler and more practicable nature, and such as would be more suitable to the present times; which I think might very well be established, if they were introduced and countenanced by some man of authority in the state. And if we consider the practice and institutions observed by the old Romans (whose example I am always fond of recommending) we shall find many things worthy of imitation, which may easily be transplanted into any other state, if it is not become totally corrupt,

Cosimo. Pray what things are those?

Fabrizio. To honour and reward virtue; not to despise poverty; to keep up good order and discipline in their armies; to oblige their fellow-citizens and subjects to love one another; to decline faction; to prefer the good of the public to any private interest; and other such things which would be compatible enough with these times, and may easily be introduced if due means were taken for that purpose: because they appear so reasonable in themselves, and the expediency of them is so obvious to common sense, that nobody could gainsay or oppose them; and he that takes this course, plants trees under the shade of which he may enjoy himself with equal pleasure, and perhaps more security, than we do here.

Cosimo. What you have said of this matter admits of no contradiction, and therefore I shall leave it to the confederation of those whom it most concerns; but should be glad to know, why you, who blame others for not imitating the ancients in weighty and important concerns, have not thought fit in any wise to copy them yourself in their military discipline, and the Art of War, which is your profession, and in which you have gained so much reputation.

Fabrizio. You are now come to the point I expected: for what I said, must naturally lead you to ask such a question; and, for my own part, I shall most willingly give you what satisfaction I can. And though I could make a short and ready excuse for my conduct in this respect, yet since we have so much leisure, and so convenient a place for it, I shall discuss the matter at large; especially as it will give me great pleasure to inform you thoroughly of what you seem so desirous to know.—Men who have any great design in hand must first make all necessary preparations, that their plan, when a proper opportunity offers, may be ready to be put in execution. Now when these preparations are made with caution and privacy, they are not known or talked of; so that a man cannot be blamed for negligence or omission in that respect, except some accident happens which shews that he has either not made due preparations for the executions of his design, or never thought of it at all: and therefore, as I never yet had any such opportunity of mewing what preparations I have made to revive the military discipline of the ancients amongst us, nobody can reasonably blame me for not doing it. This might serve for a sufficient answer to your charge.

Cosimo. It might so indeed, if I was sure you never had such an opportunity.

Fabrizio. Since you seem to doubt of that, I will shew you at large (if you will have patience to hear me) what preparations are necessary for that purpose; what sort of opportunity is requisite; what impediments may obstruct the preparations, and prevent those opportunities from happening; and lastly, (which seems a contradiction in terms) that it is at the same time the easiest and most difficult thing in the word to accomplish such a purpose.

Cosimo. You cannot oblige us more: and if you are not tired with speaking, you may assure yourself we shall never be tired of hearing you. But as the subject is copious and much to be laid upon it, I must beg leave to call in the assistance of these friends now and then: and both they and I hope you will not be offended if we should now and then happen to interrupt you with any question that may seem unnecessary or unreasonable.

Fabrizio. You are all heartily welcome to ask what questions you think fit; for I see the ardour and ingenuity of youth incline you to have a favourable opinion of my profession, and to listen to what I have to say concerning the duties of it: but when men are grown grey-headed, and their blood is frozen in their veins, they generally either hate the very name of a soldier, or become so positive that they can never be argued out of their opinions. Ask freely then and without reserve: for that will give me an opportunity of breathing a little sometimes, as well as satisfaction of answering your questions in such a manner as may leave no doubt or scruple remaining upon your minds.——To begin then with what you said yourself, that in the Art of War (which is my profession) I have not imitated the ancients in any respect whatsoever, I answer, that war being an occupation by which a man cannot support himself with honour at all times, ought not to be followed as a business by any but princes or governors of Commonwealths, and that if they are wise men they will not suffer any of their subjects or citizens to make that their only profession.

Indeed no good man ever did: for surely he cannot be called a good man, who exercises an employment that obliges him to be rapacious, fraudulent, and cruel at all times, in order to support himself; as all those must be of course (of what rank so ever they are) who make a trade of war; because it will not maintain them in time of peace: upon which account, they are under a necessity either of endeavouring to prevent a peace, or of taking all means to make such provisions for themselves in time of war, that they may not want sustenance when it is over. But neither of these courses is confident with common honesty: for whoever resolves to heap as much in time of war as will support him for ever after, must be guilty of robbery, murder, and many other acts of violence upon his friends as well as his enemies: and in endeavouring to prevent a peace, commanders must have recourse to many pitiful tricks and artifices to deceive those that employ them.

But if they fail in their designs, and find they cannot prevent a peace, as soon as their pay is stopped, and they can live no longer in the licentious manner they used to do, they set up for soldiers of fortune, and having got a parcel of their disbanded men together, make no scruple of plundering a whole country without mercy or distinction. You must have heard that when the late wars were over in Italy and the country full of disbanded soldiers, they formed themselves into several bands, and went about plundering some towns and laying others under contribution. You must likewise have read how the Carthaginian soldiers (after the first war was ended in which they had been engaged with the Romans) assembled together under the banners of Matho and Spendius (two officers whom they had chosen in a tumultuary manner to command them) and made a more dangerous war upon their own country, than that which had been just concluded.

In the days of our ancestors, Francisco Sforza, in order to support himself in splendour and magnificence in time of peace, not only betrayed the Milanese who had employed him in their service, but deprived them of their liberties and made himself their sovereign. All the rest of our Italian soldiers, who made war their only occupation acted the same part in those times: and if they did not succeed in their villainies like Sforza, they were not less blameable; for if we consider their conduct, we shall find their designs were altogether as iniquitous as his. Sforza, the father of Francisco, obliged Jane, Queen of Naples, to throw herself into the arms of the King of Arragon, by suddenly quitting her service and leaving her disarmed, as it were, in the midst of her enemies, with an intention either to deprive her of her kingdom, or at least to extort a great sum of money from her.

Braccio da Montone endeavoured by the same arts to have made himself King of Naples; and if he had not been routed and killed at Aquila, he would certainly have accomplished his design. Such evils, and others of the like nature, are owing to men who make war their only occupation; according to the proverb, *War makes thieves, and Peace hangs them*: for those that know not how to get their bread any other way, when they are disbanded, finding nobody that has occasion for their service, and disdaining the thoughts of living in poverty and obscurity, are forced to have recourse to such ways of supporting themselves as generally bring them to the gallows.

Cosimo. I confess, I thought the profession of a soldier the most honourable of all others; but you have let it in such a light, that I am now so much out of conceit with it, that if you have not a great deal more to say in favour of it, you will leave a doubt upon my mind: for if what you have said be true, how comes it to pass that the memories of Julius Caesar, Pompey, Scipio, Marcellus, and many other Roman Generals are immortalized?

Fabrizio. I have not yet finished what I proposed to say concerning the two points I mentioned a little while ago, *viz.* that a good man could not make war his only profession; and that no wise prince or governor of a Commonwealth ought to suffer any of their subjects or citizens to do it. As to the first, I have done with it; and will now proceed to the discussion of the second: in which I shall take an opportunity of answering your last question.—I say then, that Caesar and Pompey, and almost all the Roman generals who lived after the second Punic war, owed their reputation to their abilities, rather than their virtue: but those that lived before that time acquired their glory by being virtuous as well as able men: for the former made war their sole occupation, but the latter did not.

Whilst the Roman Republic continued incorrupt, no citizen, how powerful so ever he might be, ever presumed to avail himself of that profession in time of peace, in such a manner as to trample upon the laws, to plunder provinces, or to turn tyrant, and enslave his country: nor did any private soldier dare to violate his oath, to enter into faction and cabals, to throw off his allegiance to the Senate, or to support any tyrannical attempt upon the liberties of the Commonwealth, in order to enable himself to live by the profession of arms at all times. The commanders, on the contrary, contenting themselves with the honour of a triumph, returned with eagerness to their former manner of living; and the private men laid down their arms when a war was over, with much more pleasure than they had taken them up, and resumed the calling by which they had got their bread before, without any hopes of advancing themselves by plunder and rapine.

Of this we have a remarkable and evident proof in the example of Attilius Regulus, who being commander in chief of the Roman armies in Africa, and having in a manner subdued the Carthaginians, lent to desire leave of the Senate to return home, that he might put his little farm in order again, which had been neglected by his servants: from whence it plainly appears, that if war had been his only occupation, and he had designed to have made his fortune by it, he would not have desired leave to return to the care of his little estate, when he had so many provinces at his mercy, and might daily have gained more by plundering them than his whole patrimony was worth. But as good men who make not war their sole occupation, expect no other reward but glory and honour for their services; so when they have obtained that, they cheerfully return to their former way of life.

As for the common soldiers, we see that they likewise were of the same disposition: for though they entered voluntarily into the service when it was necessary, they were not less glad to return to their families when they were no longer wanted: the truth of which is manifest from many circumstances; particularly from the privilege which the Roman citizens enjoyed, of not being forced into the army against their inclination. So that whilst that republic continued well governed (which was till the time of the Gracchi) there never was any soldier who made war alone his occupation: from whence it came to pals that few of them were dissolute and licentious; and those that were so were severely punished. Every well governed Commonwealth therefore should take care that this art of war should be practised in time of peace only as an exercise; and in time of war, merely out of necessity, and for the acquisition of glory; referring it (when considered as a constant business and employment) to be prosecuted by the public alone: for if any citizen has any other end or design in following this profession, he is not a good man: and if any Commonwealth acts otherwise it is ill governed.

Cosimo. I am thoroughly satisfied of the reasonableness of what you have hitherto said concerning this matter, and admit the conclusion you have drawn to be very just as far as it relates to a Commonwealth: but I cannot tell whether it will hold good with regard to princes; for I think a prince should have some such persons about him as make arms their only profession.

Fabrizio. A kingdom that is well governed ought to be still more afraid of such persons than a Commonwealth; because they are the corrupters of princes; and ministers of their tyranny. It is vain to urge any monarchy that now exists, as an instance to the contrary; for there is not one that is under good regulations. A kingdom that is well constituted never gives the sovereign power to its prince in anything but the command of its armies; in which case alone it is absolutely necessary he should have it; because sudden resolutions are often necessary, and such as cannot be carried into execution so speedily as they ought to be, except the supreme command is lodged in the hands of one man: in other matters, nothing ought to be done without his council; and therefore his counsellors should take particular care not to let such men be too near his person, as would be continually advising him to make war, whether it is necessary or not, because they cannot tell how to support themselves in time of peace.

But I will enlarge a little further upon this subject, and not infill merely upon a kingdom that is perfectly well governed and constituted, but content myself (for argument's sake) with such as we see at this time. I say then that even in such Governments those persons are much. to be feared who make war their only business; because the strength of all armies, without doubt, consists in their infantry: so that if a prince has not power enough over his infantry to make them disband and return cheerfully to their former occupations when a war is over, he is in a fair way to be ruined. For no sort of infantry can be so dangerous as that which is composed of people who make war their only calling: because a prince must either keep them continually engaged in war, or in constant pay during the time of peace, or run the *risque* of being stripped of his kingdom: but it is impossible for any prince, either to keep them continually engaged in war, or in constant pay when it is over; and therefore he must run no small *risque* of losing his kingdom.

Whilst the Romans continued wise and good they never suffered any of their citizens to make war their only employment, (as I said before) though they were able to keep them in constant pay, because they were continually at war: but in order to avoid the inconveniencies which might have ensued from the toleration of such a custom, they changed their forces (as they could not alter the times) in such a manner, that at the end of every fifteen years, their legions were filled with new men that were in the flower of their youth: for they took none but such as were betwixt eighteen and thirty-five years of age, in full health and vigour; and never kept them till they grew old and infirm, as the same people afterwards did in more corrupt times. For Augustus, and after him Tiberius, more careful to establish and increase their own power than to promote the public good, began to disarm the Roman people (in order to make them more passive under their tyranny) and kept the same armies continually on foot upon the confines of the Empire: but not thinking those sufficient to keep the Senate and people in due awe, they raised other forces, called the *Pretorian Bands,* which were always quartered either in the city or near it, and served not only as guards to the emperor's person, but to bridle the people.

Afterwards, however, when the emperors suffered the men who composed those bands to lay aside all other occupations, and to make war their sole profession, they soon became insolent and formidable, not only to the Senate, but to the emperors themselves; many of whom they put to death, and then disposed of the Empire as they pleased, taking it from one, and giving it to another: nay it frequently happened that different emperors were elected by different armies at the same time; which soon occasioned the division of that Empire, and at last the utter ruin of it. A prince therefore who would reign in security, ought to make choice of such men alone for his infantry, as will cheerfully serve him in war when it is necessary, and be as glad to come back to their own houses after it is over; which will always be the case with those that have other occupations and employments to live upon: for which purpose, when a peace is concluded, he should order his generals and great officers to return to their respective charges and governments; the gentlemen to the care of their estates; and the private men to their particular callings: that so everyone may be ready to enter into a war to procure a good peace, and no man presume to disturb the peace, in order to stir up a war.

Cosimo. Indeed, Sir, I think there is much truth and reason in what you have said, but as the substance of it is so very different from the judgement I had formed to myself of these matters, I cannot say that I am altogether satisfied in some respects: for I know several lords and gentlemen who are supported by the profession of arms alone in time of peace; as yourself for instance, and some others of your rank and quality., who receive pensions from princes and states: I see likewise many soldiers, still kept in pay for the security of fortresses and other cities; so that it appears to me that there is sufficient employment and occasion for them all in time of peace.

Fabrizio. Surely you cannot be of that opinion: for if there was no other reason to convince you of the contrary, the small number of men that is reserved to garrison those places might be a sufficient answer to your objection. What proportion is there betwixt a few regiments of infantry that are necessary to defend some strong places in time of peace, and those that are to be kept in pay for the prosecution of a war? Are not many more wanted in time of war to reinforce those garrisons, besides the numbers that are to be employed in the field, which are always disbanded as soon as a peace is concluded? As to the common standing Guards that are requisite in any state (which need not be many) Pope Julius II. and your own republic have sufficiently shewn the world how dangerous they thought those people who made war their only occupation, by dismissing them for their insolence, and hiring Swiss Guard in their room, who are not only born and brought up in strict obedience to laws, but picked and chosen by the state in a proper and regular manner: your objection therefore that soldiers of every kind are necessary, and may find sufficient employment in time of peace as well as war, must naturally fall to the ground.

But why horse and *gens d'armes* should be kept in pay in times of peace, perhaps may not appear so obvious: nevertheless, if we consider the matter thoroughly, it may easily be accounted for from the corruption of the times. For it is a bad custom introduced by men who make a trade of war, and would be attended with many dangerous consequences in a state, if any considerable number of them was kept in pay; but as there are seldom enow to make up an army of themselves, they can do no great mischief at present; though they have formerly, as I shewed before in the cases of Francisco Sforza, his father, and Braccio da Montone. It is a bad custom however, and such as I approve not.

Cosimo. Would you have none at all then? Or if you would have any, in what manner would you raise and employ them?

Fabrizio. As a militia; not like the *gens d'armes* of France (who are as insolent and dangerous as our own) but after the manner of the ancients, who always raised their cavalry out of their own subjects; and after a war was over, sent them home again to support themselves upon their respective occupations, as I shall shew more at large before I have done with this subject. So that if troops of horse are kept together, and receive pay, and live entirely upon it, even in times of peace, it is owing to corruption and bad government. And though indeed I myself and some other commanders, whom I know, receive pensions and stipends in time of peace, I must confess I think it a very corrupt custom: for a wise and well governed republic ought never to keep such commanders in constant pay, but rather to employ its own citizens in time of war, and afterwards to dismiss them to follow their former occupations.

So likewise a prince, if he would act wisely, should not allow a pension or stipend to anyone in time of peace, except by way of reward for some signal piece of service, or in order to avail himself of some able man in time of peace as well as war. And since you have pitched upon me as an example of this kind, I will take the charge to myself and make the best apology I can. I say then, that I never made war my sole business and occupation: my profession is to govern my subjects well, to defend and protect them: for which purpose, I study the arts both of peace and war; and if I am rewarded and esteemed by the prince whom I have the honour to serve, it is not so much for the experience I have in military affairs, as because he is pleased to retain me as one of his counsellors in time of peace.

A prince therefore who would govern wisely should admit no other sort of persons into his confidence: for if his counsellors are too fond either of peace or war, they will lead him into errors and inconveniencies. Thus much I thought myself obliged to say in consequence of what I proposed at first: and if it is not satisfactory, I make no doubt but you will be able to find others who can give you better information in the things you seemed so desirous of knowing. You begin however, I dare say, to be aware how difficult a matter it must be to revive the military discipline of the ancients at present, what preparations are necessary for that purpose, and what occasions and opportunities are wanting to accomplish it. But if you are not already tired with what I have said, I could throw a little more light upon this subject, by comparing the particulars of our modern practice and institutions with the discipline of the ancients.

Cosimo. If we were desirous at first to hear you enter into a discussion of these points, we can assure you that what you have already said has redoubled that desire: we thank you therefore most heartily for the satisfaction you have given us, and earnestly desire the favour of you to proceed.

Fabrizio. Since it is your pleasure then, I will deduce this matter from the fountain-head; that so I may be enabled to explain myself with more perspicuity, and you to understand me the better.—Whoever engages in a war must endeavour by all means to put himself in a condition to face his enemy in the field, and to beat him there if possible. For this purpose, it is necessary to form an army; and to form an army, he must not only raise men,: but arm, discipline, and exercise them frequently, both in small and large bodies; he must teach them to encamp and decamp, and make the enemy familiar to them by degrees, sometimes by marching near them, and sometimes by taking post in a situation where they may have a full view of them. These preparations are absolutely necessary in a field war, which is the most effectual and honourable of all others: and a general who knows how to conduct such a war, to form and draw up an army, and to give an enemy battle in a proper and soldier-like manner, cannot err much in other respects: but if he is deficient in this part of his profession (though he be ever so able a man in other points) he will never bring a war to a happy conclusion: besides, if he wins a battle, it cancels all other errors and miscarriages; but if he loses one, it effaces the memory of ail his former merits and services.

To form an army therefore, it is necessary in the first place to make choice of proper men for that purpose, which the ancients termed *delectus*, but we call *lifting* or *levying*, Those then who have prescribed rules in the Art of War, are unanimously of opinion that such men should be raised in temperate climates, that so they may be both brave and quick of apprehension; for it has been generally observed that hot countries produce men that are quick and sharp witted, but not courageous; and on the other hand, that the inhabitants of cold countries are for the most part hardy and brave, but of dull and heavy understandings. This rule indeed might be followed by a prince who had the whole world at command, and could raise his men where he pleased.

But to give a rule which may be observed by any state, I say that every prince or republic should raise their men in their own dominions, whether hot, cold, or temperate: for we see by ancient examples, that good discipline and exercise will make good soldiers in any country, and that the defects of nature may be supplied by art and industry; which in this case are more effectual than nature itself. Besides, the raising of men in any other country cannot properly be called *delectus*, or *making a choice*; because that term signifies to pick and cull the best men in a province, and implies a power to chuse such as are unwilling, as well as, those that are willing to serve; which cannot be done in any country but your own: for in territories that are subject to another state, you must be content with such as are willing to serve you, and not expect to pick and chuse whom you please.[1]

Cosimo. But you may either take or refuse whom you think fit of those that are willing to serve you; and therefore that may be called *delectus*.

Fabrizio. You are right in one respect: but consider the defects to which such a choice is subject, and you will find that it is no choice at all. In the first place, those that are not your own subjects, but yet are willing to enter into your pay, are so far from being the belt men, that they are generally the worst: for if there be any scandalous, idle, incorrigible, irreligious wretches, any runaways from their parents, any blasphemers, common cheats, or fellows that have been initiated into every kind of villainy, those are the people that commonly lift under your banners; and what sort of soldiers they are likely to make I leave everyone to judge for himself. Now when they are more of these that offer their service than you want, you may indeed pick and chuse out of them; but you can never make a good choice, because they are all so bad.

It often happens however, that there are not so many, even of these, as you have occasion for to fill up your regiments: so that you must

---
1. See *The Prince* chapters 22-24.

be obliged to take them all and then surely you cannot so properly be said to make a *delectus, a choice*, as to raise men at any rate. Of such disorderly people our Italian armies and those of most other nations are composed at present, except in Germany; because our princes have it not in their power to make any man serve in their wars except he is willing. Consider with yourselves therefore whether it is possible to revive the discipline of the ancients in armies which are raised in this manner.

Cosimo. What other method would you take then to raise them?

Fabrizio. That which I recommended before: a prince should chuse them out of his own subjects, and exert his authority in such a choice.

Cosimo. Do you think any part of the ancient discipline might be revived in an army thus chosen?

Fabrizio. Without doubt it might, if such an army was commanded by the sovereign of a principality, or by one of the governing citizens of a Commonwealth, who is appointed commander in chief during the time of his office; otherwise it would be a very difficult matter to do it.

Cosimo. Why so?

Fabrizio. I will explain that to you more at large hereafter: let it suffice at present to say, that no good can be done any other way.

Cosimo. Well then, since these levies are to be made in your own dominions; is it better to draw the men out of the country or out of towns?

Fabrizio. All authors who have written upon this subject agree, that it is better to take them out of the country; because such men are inured to hardships and fatigues, to endure all sorts of weather, to handle the mattock and spade, to throw up ditches, to carry heavy burdens, and are, generally speaking, more temperate and incorrupt than others. But as Horse as well as Foot are necessary in an army, I would advise that the Horse should be taken out of towns, and the Foot out of the country,

Cosimo. Of what age would you have them?

Fabrizio. If I was to raise a new army, I would chuse them from seventeen to forty years of age: but, if I was only to recruit an old one, I would have none above seventeen.

Cosimo. I do not well understand the reason of this distinction.

Fabrizio. I will tell you the meaning of it then. If I was to raise an army, or establish a militia, in a state where there was none before, it would be necessary to take the best and most docible men I could find of all ages, (provided they were neither too young nor too old to carry arms) in order to discipline them in such a manner as I shall inform you of in its proper place: but if I was to raise men only to recruit on army that had been long on foot, I would take none above seventeen, because there would be men enow of riper age in such an army.

Cosimo. Then you would put your troops upon the same footing with those in our country?

Fabrizio. Yes; but I would arm, and officer, and exercise, and discipline them, in a manner that I fancy is not known amongst yours.

Cosimo. You would have trained bands, I suppose?

Fabrizio. Why not, Sir?

Cosimo. Because several wise and able men disapprove of them.

Fabrizio. That cannot well be surely. Some men perhaps may be accounted wise and able, though they really are not so.

Cosimo. The bad proof those bands have always made seems to countenance that opinion.

Fabrizio. Are you sure it is not owing to your own fault rather than any defect in them, that they have always made so bad proof? Perhaps I may convince you that it is, before we part.

Cosimo. We shall be much obliged to you for so doing. But in the first place I will tell you upon what accounts these troops are disapproved of, that so you may be the better enabled to refute the objections that are made to them. It is said then, that they are either of little or no service and if a prince or state confide in them they are sure to be ruined; or, if they are good soldiers the person that commands them may seize upon the Government himself by their assistance. To confirm this, the example of the Romans is cited, who lost their liberties by keeping up such forces: the case of the Venetians and the King of France is likewise instanced for the same purpose; the former of whom make use of foreign troops only, to prevent any of their own citizens from seizing upon the Government; and the latter has disarmed all his subjects in order to rule them with more ease.

But the unserviceableness of these troops is further urged for the following reasons: the first is, that they are raw and inexperienced; the second, that they are compelled to serve: for when people are grown up to years of maturity, they seldom learn anything perfectly; and surely no material service can be expected from men who are forced into the army whether they will or not.

Fabrizio. All these objections seem to be made by very short-sighted people, as I shall shew presently. For as to the unserviceableness of these bands. I say that no troops can be more serviceable than such as are chosen out of one's own subjects; nor can those subjects be raised in a better or more proper manner. And since this will not admit of dispute, I shall not throw away any more time in endeavouring to prove it; especially as there is sufficient evidence of it in the histories of all nations. What has been said concerning inexperience and compulsion, I allow to be just and reasonable: for inexperience is the mother of cowardice, and compulsion makes men mutinous and discontented: but both experience and courage are to be acquired by arming, exercising, and disciplining them in a proper manner, as I shall plainly demonstrate to you.

As to the matter of compulsion, I answer, that such men as are to be raised by the command of their prince, should neither be altogether volunteers, nor yet forcibly compelled into the service: for if they were to be altogether volunteers, the mischiefs would ensue which I just now mentioned, it could not properly be called a *delectus*, and few would be willing to serve. Compulsion, on the other hand, would be attended with no less inconveniencies; and therefore a middle course ought to be taken, and without either treating men with downright violence, or depending entirely upon their own voluntary offers, they should be moved by the obedience they think due to their governors, to expose themselves to a little present hardship, rather than incur their displeasure: and by these means (their own will seeming to co-operate with a gentle sort of compulsion) you will easily prevent those evils which might otherwise result from a spirit of licentiousness or discontent.

I will not venture however to affirm, that an army composed of such men is invincible; for even the Roman legions were often routed, and Hannibal himself was at last conquered: so that it is impossible to model any army in such a manner as to prevent it from being ever defeated. The wise and able men therefore of whom you speak, should not be so peremptory in pronouncing such forces altogether unserviceable, because they have sometimes lost a battle; for though they may happen to be defeated once or twice, they may be victorious afterwards, when they have discovered the causes that contributed to their defeat, and provided remedies against them; especially as their disgrace (when the causes of it come to be looked into) may probably be owing rather to bad conduct in the commanders than any defect in the institution itself: your acquaintance therefore instead of condemning one, should endeavour to correct the other; and how that is to be done I will shew you as we proceed.

In the meantime I shall convince you how little foundation there is for the objection which you urge, that such bands, under the command of an aspiring subject or citizen, may deprive a prince or republic of their authority and dominions: for it is certain that no subjects or citizens, when legally armed and kept in due order by their masters, ever did the least mischief to any state: on the contrary, they have always been of the highest service to all governments, and have kept them free and incorrupt longer than they would have been without them. Rome continued free four hundred years, and Sparta eight hundred, though their citizens were armed all that while: but many other states which have been disarmed have lost their liberties in less than forty years.

No state therefore can support itself without an army, and if it has no soldiers of its own, it must be forced to hire foreign troops, which will be much more dangerous; because they are more liable to be corrupted, and become subservient to the ambition of some powerful citizen, who may easily avail himself of their assistance to overturn the established government, when he was nobody to deal with but an unarmed and defenceless multitude. Besides, every state must naturally be more afraid of two enemies than one; and that which takes foreign troops into its pay, will be apprehensive of them, as well as of its own forces: for which indeed you will see there is sufficient reason, if you remember what I said just now concerning Francisco Sforza: whereas a state which employs no troops but such as are composed of its own subjects has only one enemy to fear.

But to omit all other proofs which might be adduced to support this point, I shall only lay it down as a certain truth, that no man ever yet founded a monarchy or a republic but he was well assured the subjects, if armed, would always be ready and willing to defend it: and if the Venetians had acted as wisely in this respect as in others, they might have erected a new monarchy in the world: for the neglect of which, they are the mere inexcusable, as they had arms put into their hands by their first legislators: but not being possessed of much territory by land they employed their strength chiefly at sea, where they carried on their wars with great spirit, and made considerable acquisitions.

At last, however, when they were obliged to engage in a land war for the relief of Vicenza, instead of trusting some citizen of their own with the command of their forces, they took the Marquis of Mantua into their pay. Now if this false step, which clipped the wings of their ambition, and put a stop to their further aggrandizement, was owing to an opinion, that though they knew how to make war at sea, they did not at land, it was a simple and ill-founded diffidence: for a sea-commander who has been used to fight the winds and waves, as well as the enemy, will sooner make a good land-officer where he has nothing to deal with but men, than a land-officer will make a good sea-commander.

The Romans, who were most expert in land-wars, but knew little of naval affairs, being engaged in a quarrel with the Carthaginians, who were very powerful at sea, did not take either Grecian or Spanish forces into their service, though they were the best seamen in the world at that time; but left the command of that expedition to their own land-officers, who made a descent upon the enemy's coast, and subdued the whole country. But if the Venetians acted in the above manner out of apprehension that if they did otherwise, some one of their own citizens might seize upon the Government, it was an unreasonable jealousy: for (not to repeat what has been already said) if none of their sea-commanders ever made themselves masters of any town upon their coasts; much less occasion had they to fear that any of their citizens who commanded their armies should make use of them for such a purpose.

If they had considered this, they would have been convinced that tyranny and usurpation are not owing to the citizens being armed, but to a weak government; and that whilst a state is well conducted, it has nothing to fear from the arms of its subjects: the resolution therefore which they took upon that occasion was a very imprudent one, and brought great disgrace and many misfortunes upon them. As to the error which the King of France is guilty of in disarming his subjects, instead of keeping them well disciplined and ready for war, (an instance which you urge against me) every impartial man must own that it is a great default in judgement, and has much weakened that kingdom.

But I have made too long a digression, and may seem perhaps to have forgot my subject: yet I was in some measure obliged to do it, in answer to your objections, and to shew you that a state ought by no means to depend upon any troops but such as are composed of its own subjects; that those subjects cannot be raised in any manner so well as by way of trained bands: and that there can be no better method devised to form an army, or militia, or to introduce good order and discipline amongst the soldiers.

If you ever read the institutions established by the first kings of Rome, particularly by Servius Tullus, you must remember that the *Classes* which he formed, were a sort of trained bands, or bodies of men fit to bear arms, out of which, an army might presently be raised upon any sudden emergency for the defence of the state.——But to return to your levies, I say again that if I was to recruit an old army, I would take men of about seventeen years of age; but if I was to raise a new one, and to make it fit for service in a short time, I would take them of all ages betwixt seventeen and forty.

Cosimo. Would you have any regard to their respective trades or occupations?

Fabrizio. Some authors who have written upon this subject, will not admit of fowlers, fishermen, cooks, pimps, or any other sort of people who make an occupation of pleasure or sporting; but prefer ploughmen, smiths, farriers, carpenters, butchers, hunters, and such like: but, for my own part, I should not so much consider the nature of their profession as the goodness of the men, and which of them would be the most serviceable. For this reason I should sooner make choice of husbandmen, and such as have been accustomed to labour in the fields, as more useful in an army than any other kind of people: next to these, I would take smiths, carpenters, farriers, and stone-cutters, of whom it is necessary to have many; because they are very often wanted, and it is a good thing to have soldiers that can turn their hands to more services than one.

Cosimo. But how may one distinguish those that are fit for war from those that are not?

Fabrizio. I will first inform you of the method I would take for raising levies to form a new army; because I shall have an opportunity of mentioning several things at the same time, that are necessary in the choice of men to recruit an old one.—I say then, we must judge whether a man is fit for service, either from the experience we have had of his former behaviour, or from probable conjecture: but in such as are altogether raw men, and never served before, (of whom we must suppose all new levies chiefly, if not wholly, to consist) we can have no experience of their fitness: upon which account, we must have recourse to such conjectures as we may be able to form from their age, their occupation, and appearance.

Of the two first we have already spoken; it only remains therefore to say something of the last. Some, like Pyrrhus, would have their soldiers tall and large of stature; others, like Julius Caesar, prefer such as are active and vigorous: of which they form a conjecture from the symmetry of their limbs, and the vivacity of their aspect. Some that have treated of this subject, accordingly recommend those that have quick and lively eyes, muscular necks, wide chests, brawny arms, long fingers, small bellies, round sides, spare legs, and little feet, which are for the most part signs of strength and agility; two qualities that are principally necessary in a soldier.

But above all, we ought to have strict regard to their morals and behaviour: otherwise we shall make choice of such as having neither modesty nor honesty, will be a scandal to an army, and not only become mutinous and ungovernable themselves, but sow the seeds of corruption amongst others; for it is not to be expected that any virtue or commendable quality can be found in such men. Here perhaps it may not appear impertinent (nay indeed it seems absolutely necessary) to put you in mind of the method taken by the Roman consuls, as soon as they entered upon their office, to raise the forces that were wanted for the service of that year; that so you may be more fully convinced of the importance of such a choice.

Upon these occasions then, (as their republic was almost continually engaged in war) being obliged to make choice of some that had served before, and others that were altogether raw men, they had an opportunity in one case of pitching upon such as they knew by experience were fit for their purpose, and were forced in the other to make use of those that seemed to be so from probable conjecture. It should likewise be observed that such levies are made either for present service, or to be disciplined in order to be employed when occasion shall require. But as I have hitherto spoken of those only that are to be raised and disciplined for future service, in countries where there was no army before, and consequently no proper choice can be made from any experience of such men as are fit for soldiers, I shall continue that subject: because it is an easy matter either to raise good recruits or form armies for immediate service, in places where a military force has been once established; especially, if the rulers of the state have sufficient authority to enforce it, as the Romans did of old, and the Swiss do at this day: for though there must of course be many new men, yet there will also be so many veterans, in this sort of levies, that both together will soon make a very good army.

The Roman emperors, however, when they began to keep up garrisons and standing armies upon the confines of the Empire, thought fit to appoint certain masters or instructors to teach and discipline their *tirones* (or new raised men) in warlike arts and exercises, as we may see in the life of the Emperor Maximus: an institution observed at home only whilst Rome continued free; but in such a manner, that the young Romans who had been trained up, and inured to this sort of discipline, made excellent soldiers when a *delectus* was necessary, and they were called out into the service of their country: but afterwards, when this custom of training up the youth at home was left off by the emperors, they were forced to make use of the method I just now mentioned—But to return to the method observed by the Romans in making their levies.

As soon as the consuls (who always conducted their wars) had entered upon their office, they began to raise forces, each consul having two legions allotted him, which consisted of Roman citizens only, and were the main strength and flower of their armies. For this purpose, they first appointed twenty-four military *tribunes*, fix to each legion; whose office resembled that of our lieutenant-colonels, or commanders of a battalion. This done, they called all the people together that were able to bear arms, and placed the *tribunes* of each legion apart: after which, those officers cast lots out of which tribe or class they should begin their choice; and upon which tribe so ever the lot fell, they took four of the best men out of it, one of whom was made choice of by the *tribunes* of the first legion, another by those of the second, another by those of the third, and the last fell to the share of the fourth.

After this, they picked out four more, out of whom, the first was chosen by the *tribunes* of the second legion, the second by those of the third, the third by those of the fourth, and the fourth by those of the first. When this were thus disposed of, four others were drawn out: the first of whom was taken by the third legion, the second by the fourth, the third by the first, and the fourth by the second; thus varying the turns of their choice out of all the tribes, till the four legions were all equal and complete. Now these levies might be employed in immediate service, as I said before: and since they consisted of men, many of whom had been tried, and the rest well exercised and disciplined at home, such a choice might be made partly from experience, and partly from conjecture: but where the men are altogether raw and untried, and must be exercised and disciplined from the beginning to make them fit for future service, the choice must be made by conjecture alone, founded upon their age and appearance.

Cosimo. What you have said appears to be very just: but before you proceed any further, I could wish you would gratify my curiosity in one point, winch you have put me in mind of by saying, that where the levies that are to be made have not been used to military service before, they must be chosen by conjecture: for I have heard great fault found with our militia in many respects, especially with regard to their number; some being of opinion that if they were fewer, they might be better chosen; that it would not be so troublesome and inconvenient to the country, nor to the men themselves; and that they might have larger pay, which would make them more content and ready to obey your commands. I should be glad to know therefore, whether you would have a large or small number of such people, and how you would proceed in the choice of them in either case.

Fabrizio. Without doubt is it much better to have a large number than a small one; for where there is not a great number, it is impossible ever to have a good militia: as to the objections which you say some others have made to it, I shall presently shew you the futility of them.—I say then, in the first place, that the smallness of the number does not make them the better soldiers, especially in a country where there is plenty of men, as in Tuscany; for if you are to chuse them from experience, you will find very few there that have had any trial, as not many have been in the field; and of those few, there are hardly any that have given the least mark of worth, or deserve to be preferred to others; so that whoever wants to raise men in this country can have no assistance from experience, but must depend wholly upon conjecture.

Since this is the case, I should be glad to know what I am to do, and by what rules I must make my choice of a certain number, if twenty well-looking young fellows should be brought before me. Surely everybody must allow, that it would be the best way to arm and exercise them all (since it will be impossible to judge at first fight which of them will make the best proof) and defer your choice till they have all had the same exercise and instruction: for then you will easily perceive which of them are most spirited and active, and likely to be the most serviceable. Upon the whole therefore, the maxim of chusing but few, that they may be so much the better, is simple and ill grounded.

As to a large number being troublesome and inconvenient, both to the country and the men themselves, I answer that no number of such men, whether small or great can be troublesome or inconvenient to anyone; for nobody is hindered by being a militia-man from pursuing his usual occupation, or following his necessary affairs; since they are only obliged to meet together, and to be exercised on holidays, which can be of no prejudice either to the country or themselves; on the contrary, it would be a great recreation to both: for young men instead of being idle at those times, or perhaps spending their leisure in something worse than idleness, would go to these exercises with pleasure, and others would not be a little entertained with such a spectacle.

In answer to the objection, that a small number may be better paid, and consequently will be better satisfied and more obedient to command, let it be considered that no number of militia (how small so ever) can be kept in continual pay in such a manner as to be always satisfied with it. Let us suppose (for example) a militia to consist of five thousand men, whose, pay (if they are to be paid to their satisfaction) will amount to at least ten thousand *ducats per* month. But in the first place, five thousand foot are not sufficient to make up an army; and in the next, a monthly payment of ten thousand *ducats* would be an insupportable burden upon most states, and yet not enough to keep their soldiers in content and obedience: so that though the expense would be extravagant, your army would be so inconsiderable that it would not be able to defend your own dominions, much lets to act offensively upon occasion.

If you increase their pay or their number, it will still be more difficult to pay them: and if you diminish either, they will become dissatisfied and unserviceable. Those who talk of raising a militia therefore, and of paying them when they have nothing thing for them to do, talk of things that are either impossible, or will answer no end: but it is highly necessary, I own, to pay them, and well too, when they are called out to serve their country. If such an establishment however should happen to occasion any little inconvenience to the community in time of peace, (which yet can hardly be) surely that must be much over-balanced by the conveniences and advantages which result from it: for without a regular and well-ordered militia there is no living in security.

I conclude then, that those who are for keeping up but a small militia, that so they may be able to pay them the better, or for any other of the reasons you have alleged, are greatly mistaken: for (which makes still more for my opinion) any number, be it ever so considerable, will be continually diminishing upon your hands through many unavoidable accidents; and therefore a small one would soon dwindle away to nothing. Besides, when your militia is numerous, you may employ a considerable force at once, if you see occasion; which must always have a greater effect than a small one, and be much more for your reputation. I might add, that if you raise but a small number of militia in a large country, and design to have them well exercised, they must of course be at such a distance from each other, that they cannot all be got together upon the days and at the places appointed for that purpose, without great trouble and inconvenience: and if they are not duly exercised they will be good for nothing at all, as I shall shew in its proper place.

Cosimo. You have fully refuted the objections I started upon this head, I must confess: but I have another doubt within myself which I should be glad to have solved. The persons I mentioned before seem to think, that a great number of armed men must naturally occasion much confusion and disorder, and frequently tumults in any country.

Fabrizio. This notion is altogether as ill grounded as those which have already been discussed, as I hope I shall be able to convince you. For if a militia can occasion any disorders, it must either be amongst themselves or others; which may easily be prevented, if such an establishment is not so badly constituted and regulated as to defeat the end of its institution. For if it is properly conducted, it naturally suppresses all disturbances amongst its own constituents, instead of fomenting them; because they are under the command of superiors: and if the inhabitants of the country where you raise a militia are either so little used to war that they are in a manner unarmed, or so united amongst themselves, that they have no factions, it will secure them against the fear of foreign enemies, but cannot in anywise contribute to divide them.

For men who are well disciplined will always be as tender of violating the laws when they have arms in their hands, as when they have not; and will continue so if they are net corrupted by their commanders; which it will be no difficult matter to prevent, as I shall shew you presently. But if the people are warlike and yet given to faction, such an establishment is most likely to reunite them: because, though they may have arms and chiefs of their own; yet their arms are such as will be of no service to their country, and their chiefs only serve to foment divisions and animosities, instead of promoting union and tranquillity: whereas this institution furnishes them with arms that will be serviceable to their country, and chiefs to suppress their differences. For when any man thinks himself injured or offended in a divided country, he immediately applies to the head of his faction, who, in order to keep up his own interest and reputation, is obliged to assist him in taking revenge, instead of discouraging violence.

But a chief appointed by public authority acts in a quite different manner: so that by establishing a good and well ordered militia, divisions are extinguished, peace restored, those people that were unarmed and dispirited, but united, continue in union and become warlike and courageous; others that were brave and had arms in their hands, but given to faction and discord before, become united, and turn those arms and that courage upon the enemies of their country, which they formerly used to exert against each other. But to prevent a militia from injuring others, or overturning the laws and liberties of their country (which yet cannot be effected but by the power and iniquity of the commanders) it is necessary to take care that the commanders do not acquire too great an authority over the private men.

Now authority of this kind is either natural or accidental: to guard against the one, it should be provided that an officer should not have any command over the men that were raised in the district where he was born: but over such only as were drawn out of ether places where he has no natural interest or connections: as to the other, it may in a great measure be prevented by changing the officers, and sending them to command in different parts every year: for a long continuation of command over the same people is apt to create too strict an union betwixt them, which may easily be converted to the prejudice of the Government.

How serviceable this method has been to those that have followed it, and how fatal the neglect of it to others, plainly appears from the histories of the Assyrian and Roman Empires; where we find that the former continued above a thousand years without any sedition or civil war; which was entirely owing to the custom which the Government observed of changing the commanders of their armies every year, and sending them into different provinces. On the contrary, the omission of this custom in the Roman Empire, (from the time of Julius Caesar) was the occasion of all the civil wars betwixt the commanders of different armies, and of all the conspiracies which those commanders afterwards formed against the emperors.

But if any of the first emperors (especially of those that were esteemed the best, as Adrian, Marcus Aurelius, Severus, or some others like them) had been provident enough to have changed their generals at certain times, that Empire would have enjoyed more tranquillity and existed longer: for then those commanders could not have had an opportunity of rebelling, the emperors would have lived in greater security, and the Senate (when the throne became vacant) would have had more authority, and consequently have acted with more judgment in the choice of a successor. But (whether it proceeds from ignorance, or inattention, or indolence in mankind, I know not) it is certain that bad customs are seldom changed, let who will be at the helm, or what example so ever may be brought either to discredit them, or recommend an opposite measure.

Cosimo. I am afraid I have broke in upon the order you proposed to yourself, and led you away from your subject, by asking impertinent questions; for behold from talking of levies we are got to another topic: so that if I had not desired you would excuse my freedom when we began this conversation, I should have thought myself obliged to ask your pardon for it.

Fabrizio. You need not make any apology for that, Sir, since what has been said is nothing more than was necessary to shew the nature of a militia: an institution which (as it is condemned by many) I have taken upon me to defend and explain; and therefore it behoved me to point out the best manner of raising one. But before I descend to other particulars, I should say something concerning the choice of cavalry. These troops were anciently chosen from amongst the richest citizens (with due regard, however, to their age and other qualifications) and there were but three hundred of them in a legion: so that the Romans never had above six hundred horse in a consular army.

Cosimo. Would you have these troops likewise trained up and disciplined at home, in order to employ them upon occasion?

Fabrizio. Most certainly; and it is absolutely necessary to do so, if you would have cavalry of your own, and not be obliged to take up with those that make a trade of hiring themselves out to anybody that wants them.

Cosimo. In what manner would you chuse them?

Fabrizio. As the Romans did. I would take them out of the richest of the people; I would officer them as others are officered at present: I would have them well-armed, well-exercised, and disciplined.

Cosimo. Would it be proper to allow them any pay?

Fabrizio. To be sure: but as much only as would be sufficient to keep their horses: for if you gave them anymore, it would be so burdensome to your subjects that they would murmur at it.

Cosimo. What number would you have; and how would you arm them?

Fabrizio. That is another matter: but I will answer your question after I have told you how the infantry ought to be armed and prepared for the field.

Book 2

What arms and armour were chiefly used by the ancients, Concerning the arms and armour made use of at present, and the invention of the pike. Whether the ancient or modern way of arming is the better. How infantry ought to be armed; and of the necessity of cavalry. Which of the two are most to be defended upon. How the ancients exercised their soldiers: and in what manner they should be exercised at present. How many men a regiment should consist of: and how they should be disciplined end exercised in battalions and companies. Concerning the three principal ways of drawing up a battalion in order of battle. Of rallying soldiers after they have been dif ordered, and making a whole battalion face about at a time. How to draw up a battalion in such order as to face an enemy on any side. How to draw up a battalion with two horns, and another in a hollow square. Of the baggage and carriages belonging to a battalion, of the necessity of many officers; and the usefulness of drums and other military music. A digression concerning military virtue; and to what it is owing that it is now become so rare. What number of horse is necessary in a regiment; and how many carriages ought to be allowed them for their baggage.

Fabrizio. Now we are provided with men, it is time to arm them; for which purpose, let us see what arms where chiefly used by the ancients, and chuse the best. The Romans divided their infantry into heavy and light-armed companies: the light armed were called *Velites*; under which name were included all those that made use of slings, bows, and darts: the greater part of them wore *casques* upon their heads for their defence, and a sort of target or buckler upon their left arm. They fought in no order, and at a distance from the heavy armed foot, who had helmets which reached down to their shoulders, *cuirasses*, and *brigandines*, which covered their bodies and thighs, greaves and gauntlets upon their legs and arms, a shield about four feet long and two broad, plated with an iron rim or border at the top to defend it from the edge of sharp weapons, and another at the bottom to keep it from being damaged by frequent rubbing against the ground.

Their offensive weapons consisted of a sword about a yard long on their left side, a dagger on the right, and a dart in their hand (called *pilum*) which they threw at the enemy at the first charge. Such were the arms with which the Romans conquered the world. Some old writers indeed say, that besides these, they had a spear like what we call an *espontoon* or *half pike:* but I cannot see how so troublesome a weapon could be made use of by those that carried shields; which must hinder them from using both hands at once; and for one it must be too unwieldy. Besides, such weapons could be of no service, except in the front of an army where there is room to manage them; which would be impossible in the other ranks: for those (as I shall shew hereafter) must be drawn up thick and close together, since that is the best way of forming an army, though perhaps it may be attended with some inconveniencies.

All such weapons therefore as exceed the length of four feet are of little or no service in close fight: for if you have one of those spears, and are obliged to take both hands to it (admitting that your shield was no incumbrance to you) you could not annoy an enemy with it that presses hard upon you: but if you make use of one hand only, in order to avail yourself of your shield with the other, you must take hold of it by the middle of the staff; and then there will be so much of it behind you, that those who are upon your back will prevent you from making any use of it. To convince you then that the Romans either never had any such spears; or that, if they had, they were of little or no service, read the account which Livy gives of their most remarkable battles, and you will find that he very seldom makes mention of any spears, but tells us, that as soon as they had thrown their darts, they fell upon the enemy with their swords.

I would have nothing at all to do with these spears then, but trust to the sword and buckler, and such other weapons and armour as the Romans made use of.—The armour of the Greeks was not so heavy as that of the Romans: but for offensive weapons, they depended more upon the spear than the sword; especially the Macedonian Phalanx, which was armed with spears above twenty feet long, called *sarissae* with which they broke in upon the enemy, and yet kept good order in their own ranks: and though some authors say they had shields too; yet I cannot see (for the reasons abovementioned) how they could manage them and the spears at the same time. Besides, in the battle betwixt Paulus Æmilius and Perfeus King of Macedon, I do not remember any mention made of shields, but of the *sarissae* only, which were very troublesome to the Romans: so that I imagine the Macedonian Phalanx was like the Swiss regiments at present, whole strength lies wholly in their pikes, The Roman infantry, besides their armour, likewise had crests and plumes upon their *casques* and helmets, which afforded an agreeable spectacle to their friends, and served to strike a terror into their enemies.

As to the armour of their cavalry, it consisted at first of a round shield and a helmet; the rest of their body was uncovered. Their arms were a sword and a long thin javelin or lance with an iron head, so that being incumbered with a shield and a lance at the same time, they could use neither of them properly; and their bodies being in a great measure uncovered, were not a little exposed to the enemy. But afterwards they were armed like the infantry; excepting that they still carried a small square shield, and a thicker lance, armed at both ends, that so if one should be broken off, they might avail themselves of the other. With these weapons, and this sort of armour for their horse and foot, the Romans subdued the whole world; and it is reasonable to suppose from their success that they were the best appointed armies that ever existed.

Livy himself indeed, when he is comparing their strength with that of an enemy, often tells us, that in their armour, their weapons, their discipline and courage, they were much superior: for which reason I have chosen to speak more particularly of the arms and armour of the conquerors than of the conquered.———It now remains that I say something of those that are in use at present. The infantry cover their body with a *demi-cuirass*, or iron breast-plate which reaches down to their waist; they have a spear eighteen feet long, called a pike, and a broad sword by their side: this is their common way of arming themselves: for very few of them have back plates, greaves, or gauntlets, and none at all any *casques* or helmets; and those few instead of pikes, carry halberds about six feet long with sharp points, and heads something like a battle-axe: they have likewise musketeers amongst them, instead of the slingers and bowmen employed by the ancients.

These arms and this sort of armour were invented, and are still used by the Germans, particularly by the Swiss: (as at time of first publication), for being poor, but desirous at all times to defend their liberties against the ambition of the German princes, (who are rich and can afford to keep cavalry, which the poverty of the Swiss will not allow them to do) they are obliged to engage on foot, and therefore find it necessary to continue their ancient manner of fighting, in order to make head against the fury of the enemy's cavalry. Upon this account they still use the pike, a weapon that enables them not only to keep off the horse, but very often break and defeat them; and without which, men of the greatest experience in military affairs say, that infantry are good for little or nothing.

The Germans accordingly put so much confidence in this sort of infantry, that with fifteen or twenty thousand of them they will attack any number of horse; of which we have had many instances of late; and such is the general opinion of their excellence from the many remarkable services they have done, that since the expedition of Charles VIII. into Italy, all other nations in Europe have adopted the same weapons and manner of fighting; the Spaniards in particular have got very great reputation by it.

Cosimo. Which method of arming would you recommend, the German, or that of the ancient Romans?

Fabrizio. The Romans without doubt, and I will shew you the advantages and disadvantages of them both. The German infantry are able not only to sustain the shock of cavalry, but to break them; they are more expeditious upon a march and in forming themselves; because they are not overloaded with arms. On the other hand, they are much exposed to wounds, both at a distance and when they are close engaged, because they are so slightly armed; they are of no great service in storming a town, or even in a field battle where they meet with a vigorous refinance.

But the Roman infantry knew how to deal with cavalry as well as the German; their armour was such that they were not so liable to be wounded either in close fight or at a distance; they both attacked, and sustained an attack much better, on account of their targets; they did more execution with their swords when they fought an enemy hand to hand, than the Germans can do with their pikes; and though the latter have swords, they are not capable of doing any great execution with them, because they have no targets. The Romans were so well armed and so secure under the shelter of their targets, that they were very serviceable in storming a breach. So that they laboured under no other inconvenience but the weight of their armour; which yet they got the better of by accustoming themselves to carry heavy burdens, and to endure all other sorts of hardship and fatigue, which made that matter easy and familiar to them.

You must consider likewise that infantry are often obliged to engage other infantry and cavalry together: and that if they cannot sustain the shock of cavalry, (or even if they can) and are yet afraid of facing another body of infantry that is better armed and disciplined than themselves, they are of little account. Now if you will compare the German infantry with the Roman, you will find the former very fit to oppose cavalry (as I said before), but that they would certainly have the disadvantage, if they were to engage other infantry that were no better than themselves, if they were armed and appointed like the Romans: so that one is to be preferred to the other, because the German are only fit to cope with horse, but the Roman knew how to deal both with horse and foot.

Cosimo. I should take it as a favour if you would give us some particular instance of this by way of illustration.

Fabrizio. You will find many in history, where the Roman infantry have beat infinite numbers of horse, and none where they have been worsted by other infantry, either through any deficiency in their own arms, or advantage of those in an enemy. For if there had been any deficiency in their own, and they had met with other people that armed their soldiers better than they did, they could not have made such prodigious conquests, without laying aside their own method and arming themselves in the same or a better manner: but as they never did this, we may fairly conclude they never found any other people who excelled them in that respect.

But this cannot be said of the German infantry: for they have always made bad proof when they have been engaged by other infantry as obstinate and well conducted as themselves: which must be owing to the advantage the enemy had over them in their arms. Philip Visconti, Duke of Milan, being invaded by an army of eighteen thousand Swiss, lent Count Carmignuola against them, who was at that time commander in chief of his forces. But Carmignuola having no more than six thousand horse and a small body of foot, and coming to an engagement with them, was presently defeated with great loss. As he was an able soldier however, he saw what advantage such an enemy had over cavalry; and having raised another army, he went to look for the Swiss a second time: but when he came near them, he ordered all his *gens d'armes* to dismount and fight on foot; which they did with such success that they killed fifteen thousand of the enemy, and the rest, seeing no possibility of escaping, threw down their arms and surrendered.

Cosmo. How is this to be accounted for?

Fabrizio. I told you a little while ago: but as you seem either to have forgot, or not to have understood what I said, I will repeat it. When the German infantry, who (as I said before) are but indifferently provided with defensive armour, and make use of the sword and the pike for their offensive weapons, come to engage an enemy that is well-armed at all points (as the *gens d'armes* were, whom Carmignuola caused to dismount) they are easily defeated: for the enemy has nothing to do but to receive their pikes upon their targets, and to rush in upon them sword in hand; after which, the danger is chiefly over: for the German pikes are so long, that they cannot avail themselves of them in close fight, nor will their swords stand them in any great stead, as they are so slightly defended, and are engaged with enemies that are completely armed from head to foot.

So that whoever considers the advantages and disadvantages on each side, will see that those who are so poorly armed have no remedy against an enemy that is completely armed, when he charges home, and has sustained the first push of the pikes. For when two armies are resolved to engage, and advance upon each other every moment, they must of necessity soon come close together: and though some of the men in the first ranks on one side, may either be killed or overthrown by the pikes on the other, there will be enow left to carry the day: hence it came to pass, that Carmignuola made such a slaughter amongst the Swiss, with little or no loss on his own side.

Cosmo. It must be considered that Carmignuola's men were *gens d'armes*, though they were on foot, and covered all over with armour, which enabled them to do what they did: I should think it would be a good way therefore, to arm infantry in the same manner.

Fabrizio. If you would recollect what I said concerning the armour which the Roman infantry made use of, you would be of another opinion; for men who have *casques* upon their heads, their bodies defended by shields and *cuirasses*, their legs and arms covered with greaves and gauntlets, are better able to defend themselves against pikes, and to break in upon them, than *gens d'armes* on foot: of which I will give you a modern example or two. A body of Spanish infantry being transported from Sicily into the Kingdom of Naples, to relieve Gonsalvo da Cardova, who was shut up in Barletta by the French, Monsieur d'Aubigni was sent to oppose their march with some *gens d'armes* and about four thousand Swiss foot.

When they came to engage, the Swiss pressed so hard upon the enemy with their pikes, that they soon opened their ranks: but the Spaniards, under the cover of their bucklers, nimbly rushed in upon them with their swords, and laid about them so furiously, that they made a very great slaughter of the Swiss, and gained a complete victory. Everyone knows what numbers of Swiss infantry were cut to pieces at the Battle of Ravenna in the same manner: for the Spanish foot having closed with the Swiss, made so good a use of their swords, that not one of the enemy would have been left alive, if a body of French cavalry had not fortunately come up to rescue them: after which, the Spaniards, however, drew up close together in good order, and made a handsome retreat with little or no loss.

I conclude therefore, that no infantry can properly be called good, but such as are able not only to make head against cavalry, but against any other sort of infantry whatsoever: and this must be entirely owing to their discipline and manner of arming, as I have often said before.

Cosimo. How then would you have them armed?

Fabrizio. I would take some of the Roman arms and armour, and some of the German; half of my men should be armed with one, and half with the other; for if in every six thousand foot, three thousand were provided with swords and shields like the Romans, two thousand with pikes, and one thousand with muskets, like the Germans, it would be sufficient for my purpose, as I shall shew you presently. For I would place my pikemen either in the front of the battle, or where I thought the enemy's cavalry were most likely to make an impression: and the others I would post in such a manner as to support the pikemen, and push forwards when a way was opened for them: which I think would be a better method of arming and drawing up a body of infantry, than any other that is used at present.

Cosimo. So much for infantry. I should now be glad to know whether you would recommend the ancient or modern way of arming cavalry.

Fabrizio. Considering the war saddles and stirrups which are now in use, and were not known to the ancients, I think men must sit much firmer on horseback at present than they could do formerly. I think likewise, our way of arming is more secure, and that our *gens d' armes* are capable of making a greater impression than any sort of cavalry the ancients ever had. I am not of opinion however, that we ought to depend any more upon cavalry in general than they did in former times: for, (as I said before) we have often seen them shamefully beaten of late by infantry; and indeed they must always come off with the worst when they engage infantry that are armed and appointed in the manner abovementioned.

Tigranes, King of Armenia, brought an army of an hundred and fifty thousand horse into the field (many of whom were armed like our *gens d' armes* at present, and called *cataphratti*) against Lucullus the Roman general, whose army confided only of six thousand horse and fifteen thousand foot: upon which Tigranes said, "they were more like the train of an ambassador than an army." Nevertheless, when they came to engage, the king was routed: and the historian, who gives us an account of that battle, imputes the defeat entirely to the little service that was done by the *cataphratti*, whose faces were covered in such a manner that they could hardly see, much less annoy the enemy, and their limbs so overloaded with heavy armour, that when any of them fell from their horses, they could hardly gee up again, or make any use of their arms.

I will venture to affirm therefore, that such states as depend more upon cavalry than infantry, will always be weak and exposed to ruin; as Italy has been in our times; for we have seen it over-run from one end to the other, and plundered by foreigners, merely because its princes have made little or no account at all of infantry, and trusted solely to cavalry. It is right however to have some cavalry to support and assist infantry; but not to look upon them as the main strength of an army; for they are highly necessary to reconnoitre, to scour the roads, to make incursions, and lay waste an enemy's country, to beat up their quarters, to keep them in continual alarm, and to cut off their convoys; but in field battles, which commonly decide the fate of nations, and for which armies are chiefly designed, they are fitter to pursue an enemy that is routed and flying than anything else: and consequently are much inferior to foot.

Cosimo. Here I could wish to have two difficulties resolved. In the first place, everybody knows that the Parthians never used any other forces but cavalry in their wars, and yet they shared the world with the Romans: in the next, I can neither see how infantry can be able to sustain cavalry; nor to what the strength of the one, and the weakness of the other is owing.

Fabrizio. I either told you before, or designed to tell you, that what I intended to say concerning the Art of War should be limited to Europe; and therefore shall think myself excused from accounting for the conduct of the Asiatic nations. I cannot help observing to you, how–

ever, that the discipline of the Parthians was quite different from that of the Romans: for the former all fought on horseback, in a loose and irregular manner, which is not much to be depended upon: the latter, on the contrary, fought chiefly on foot in close and regular order: and their success was various according to the nature of the countries in which they happened to fight.

For in enclosed places, the Romans generally got the better; and the Parthians had the advantage in large open plains; and indeed the nature of the country they had to defend was very favourable to their manner of fighting; for it was flat and open, a thousand miles from any sea-coast, with so few rivers, that they might sometimes march two or three days together without seeing one, and was also very thin of towns and inhabitants: so that the Roman armies which marched but slowly on account of the heaviness of their armour, and the good order they observed, were much annoyed by an active and light-armed enemy, who always fought on horseback, and were at one place overnight, and perhaps fifty or sixty miles off the next day: in this manner the Parthians availed themselves of their horse with so much success, that they ruined the army conducted by Crassus, and reduced that under the command of Mark Anthony to the utmost distress.

But (as I said before) I shall confine myself to Europe alone in what I have to say of these matters, and quote only the examples of the Greeks and Romans in former times, and the Germans at present—Let us come now to the other point if you please, *viz.* what it is that makes infantry superior to cavalry.—I say then, in the first place, that cavalry cannot march through all roads, as foot can; and they are slower in their motions, when it is necessary to change their order: for if there should be occasion to retreat when they are advancing, or to advance when they are retreating; to wheel off to the right or left; to move when they are halting, or to halt when they are in motion, it is certain they cannot do it so soon as infantry; and if they are thrown into confusion by some sudden shock, they cannot rally so easily when the shock is over.

Besides, it often happens that a brave and spirited fellow is put upon a pitiful horse, and a coward upon one that is unruly and ungovernable; in either of which cases, some disorder must ensue. Why then should it seem wonderful that a firm and compact body of foot should be able to sustain an attack of cavalry; especially as horses are sensible animals, and when they are apprehensive of danger, cannot easily be brought to rush into it? You should likewise compare the force that impels them to advance, with that which makes them retreat, and you will then find, that the latter is much more powerful than the former; for in one case, they feel nothing but the prick of a spur, but in the other, they see a rank of pikes, and other sharp weapons presented to them; so that you may see both from ancient and modern proofs, that good infantry will always be able not only to make head against cavalry, but generally to get the better of them.

But if you object, that the fury with which the horses are driven on to charge an enemy, makes them regard a pike no more than a spur; I answer, that though a horse be upon his career, yet he will bate of his speed when he comes near the pikes; and when he begins to feel the points of them, he will either stand stock still, or wheel off to the right or left. To convince yourself of this, try if you can ride a horse against a wall, and I fancy you will find very few, if any, how spirited so ever they may be, that can be forced to do it. Julius Caesar, before an engagement which he had with the Swiss in Gaul, not only dismounted himself, but caused all his cavalry to dismount, and sent their horses away to a place at some distance from the field of battle, as fitter for flight than to fight upon.

Notwithstanding these natural impediments, however, to which cavalry are subject, a general who commands an army, which consists chiefly of infantry, should always lead them through roads upon his march, where he cannot be attacked by cavalry without great trouble and inconvenience; and such roads may easily be found in most countries. If he marches over hills, they will protect him from the fury of their career, which you seem to think irresistible: if he marches through a flat country, the hedges, and ditches, and woods, will generally secure him; every little bank or thicket, how inconsiderable so ever, every vineyard or plantation, is sufficient to embarrass cavalry, and to prevent their acting with any material effect; and if they come to engage, it is probable they may meet with the same impediments in a field of battle as upon a march; for the least obstruction spoils their career, and damps their ardour.

The Roman armies, however, I must tell you, put such confidence in their armour and manner of fighting, that if it was in their power to choose one place, that was rough and confined, in order to shelter them from the fury of the enemy's cavalry, and to prevent them from extending their lines; or another where such cavalry might act with the greatest advantage, they always made choice of the latter.——But now we have armed our infantry, it is time to exercise them: let us see therefore in what manner the Romans used to exercise their infantry before they were suffered to engage an enemy; for though soldiers may be well-chosen and armed, they will never be good for anything if they are not diligently exercised. Now this exercise ought to be of three kinds. In the first place, they must be taught to endure all sorts of hardship and fatigue, as well as to be dexterous and agile: in the next, to handle their arms well: and lastly, to observe orders, and obey command, and to keep their ranks and stations, whether it be upon a march, or in battle, or in encamping; which are the three principal operations of an army, and if they are well executed, a general will come off with reputation even when he loses a battle.

The ancients therefore had very strict laws and ordinances to enforce the constant practice of these exercises in every particular: their youth were accustomed to run races, to leap, to pitch the bar, and to wrestle; all which are very necessary qualifications in soldiers: for swiftness of foot will enable them to be beforehand with an enemy in seizing an advantageous post, to come upon them on a sudden, and to overtake them when they are flying: if they are nimble and dexterous, they will know how to avoid a blow, and find no difficulty in getting over a fosse or breastwork: and if they are strong, they will be able to carry their arms with more ease; to make a greater impression upon the enemy, or to sustain a shock the better. But above all, they should be inured to carry heavy burdens, which is very necessary: for upon some great and pressing occasions, they may be obliged to carry provisions with them for several days, besides their arms, which they could not do if they were not accustomed to such things: and by these means great dangers are often avoided, and sometimes glorious victories obtained.

To accustom their young men to their armour, and to teach them how to handle their arms with dexterity, the ancients used to clothe them in armour which was twice as heavy as that which they were to wear in battle; and instead of a sword, they put a thick cudgel in their hands which was loaded with lead in the inside, and much heavier than a sword: after this, they fixed posts in the earth about six feet high, and so firm that no blows could move them; upon which the young men used to exercise themselves with their cudgel and buckler, as if they had been real enemies, sometimes making a stroke at the top, as if it had been the head or face of a man, sometimes at the right or left side, sometimes at the lower part, sometimes advancing briskly upon it, and at others retreating a step or two; by which means they became dexterous and expert, not only in defending themselves, but annoying an enemy, and the weight of their false arms made their true ones seem light and easy to be wielded.

The Romans taught their soldiers rather to thrust than to cut with their swords, because thrusts are more dangerous, harder to be warded off, and he that makes them does not expose his own body so much, and is sooner ready to repeat a thrust than a full stroke. Do not think it strange, however, that the ancients were so exact and particular in things, which to you, perhaps, may seem trifling and ridiculous: but consider, that when men come to fight hand to hand, every little advantage is of great importance; and I must beg leave to tell you, that several good authors have entered into a much more minute and circumstantial detail of these matters than I have done: for the ancients thought nothing conduced more to the welfare and security of their country, than to have a great number of men well disciplined, exercised, and ready for war; knowing, that neither riches nor magnificence, but the reputation of their arms alone, could keep their enemies in awe and subjection; and that defects in other things may sometimes be remedied, but that in war, where the fatal consequences of them are immediately felt, they admit of no remedy.

Besides, expertness in these exercises makes men bold and courageous in battle; for instead of being afraid, everyone is eager to distinguish himself in such points as he knows he excels in. The ancients therefore, took great care to make their youth perfect in all military exercises: for they likewise accustomed them to throw darts, that were much heavier than those they carried in war, at the posts I mentioned before, which taught them to be very expert in the use of that weapon, and made their arms strong and macular. They were also taught how to use the crossbow, the longbow, and the sling, and in all these things there were mailers appointed on purpose to instruct them: so that when they were called out to serve in the wars, they were so well prepared that they wanted nothing to make them excellent soldiers, but to be taught how to keep their ranks upon a march or in battle, and to obey orders: which they quickly learnt by being incorporated with others who had served a long time, and were thoroughly experienced in that part of discipline.

Cosimo. What exercises would you recommend to such as are to compose our infantry at present?

Fabrizio. most of those which I have already mentioned, as running, wrestling, leaping, carrying heavy arms, the use of the crossbow, the long-bow, and the musket; which last is a new weapon, you know, but a very useful one. To these exercises I would accustom all the youth in the country, but those in particular who are destined to be soldiers: and for this purpose, I would set aside all holidays and idle times. I would likewise have them taught to swim, which is very necessary; for all rivers have not bridges over them, nor can they expect to find boats always ready to transport them: so that if your soldiers cannot swim, you will lose many advantages and opportunities of doing great things.[1]

The reason why the Romans exercised their youth in the Campus Martius was because the Tiber ran close by it; that so when they were fatigued, they might refresh themselves in the river, and learn to swim.—I should also chuse (like the ancients) to have those properly exercised that are to serve in the cavalry; because it not only teaches them to ride well, but to avail themselves of their strength in a better manner. For which purpose, they had wooden horses, upon which they exercised themselves, vaulting upon them sometimes with armour on, and sometimes with none, without any assistance, and on either side of the horse: so that upon a signal or word of command from their instructors, they were all either mounted or dismounted in a moment.

Now as these exercises both for horse and foot were practiced without any difficulty or inconvenience in former times, they might easily be introduced again amongst the youth of any state if the governors of it so pleased; as in fact they have been in some of the western

---

1. When the ancient Greeks would upbraid anyone with extreme insufficiency, they told them in a proverbial manner, "that he could neither read nor swim." Julius Caesar was also of opinion, that swimming was of great use in war, and he himself found it so; for chusing most commonly to march on foot, as Alexander the Great also did, he always swam over the rivers in his way, when expedition was required. When he was in Egypt, being forced to get into a little boat for his safety, and so many people leaping in with him, that it was in danger of linking, he chose, though he was of an advanced age, to commit himself to the sea, and swam. to his fleet, which lay about two hundred paces off, holding his pocket-book above water in his left hand, and drawing his armour in his teeth. Sueton. in J. Caesar Sect. 64. Another time, during the war he was engaged in with Petreius and Afranius, he commanded his whole army to pass a river by swimming, without any manner of necessity.

———*rapuitque ruens in praelia miles. Quod fugiens timuisset iter, mox uda receptis Membra fovent armis, gelidosque a gurgite, cursu Restituunt artus.* Lucan. L. iv. v. 151. &c.
(*The soldier rushing through a way to fight which he should have been afraid to have taken in flight; then with their armour they cover wet limbs, and by running restore warmth to their numbed joints*)

nations, where they divide the inhabitants into classes, which take their respective names from the different sorts of arms they make use of in battle: and as these consist of pikes, halberds, muskets, and bows, the man that carry those weapons are called pikemen, halberdeers, musketeers, bowmen, or archers. Every inhabitant is likewise obliged to declare in which of these classes he chuse s to be enrolled: and as some of them cannot be fit to bear arms, either on account of their age or some other impediment, they make a *delectus* or choice out of each class, and call those who are thus chosen *jurati*, because they make them take an oath of fidelity and obedience.

These *jurati* then are called together upon holidays, and exercised in the use of such arms as they take their name from; every class having its particular place assigned by the Governors of the State, where it is to rendezvous and be exercised; and every man belonging to it, as well as the *jurati*, is to appear and bring his proportion of money with him to defray the expenses that are occasioned by those meetings. What therefore is actually done by others, I should think might be done by our countrymen: but they are grown so lazy and degenerate that they will not imitate anything that is good; though it was entirely owing to such exercises that the ancients had such excellent infantry, and that the states in the west, abovementioned, have much better at present than we have for the Romans either exercised them at home during the time of their republic, or abroad, under the reign of their emperors, as I have said before; but the Italian states will not exercise them at home, and abroad they cannot, because they are not their own subjects, and therefore will do nothing but what pleases themselves.

Hence it comes to pass, that these military exercises are now wholly neglected, and all manner of discipline is at an end; which is the true reason why many states, especially in this country, are become so weak and contemptible.—But to resume our subject. It is not sufficient to make a good army, that the soldiers are inured to hardships and fatigue, strong, swift, and expert in the use of their arms: they must likewise learn to keep their ranks, to obey the word of command, and signals by drum or trumpet, and to observe good order, whether they halt, advance, retreat, are upon a march, or engaged with an enemy: for without a strict attention to these points, an army will never be good for any thing: as it is certain that a parcel of disorderly and ill-disciplined men, though ever so brave, are not so much to be depended upon as others who are not so courageous by nature, but orderly and well-disciplined; for good order makes men bold, and confusion cowards. But that you may better comprehend what I am going to say, it is necessary to premise, that every nation has had particular corps, or bodies of soldiers in their armies and militias, which though differing in their names, varied but little in the number of men they were composed of; as they generally confided of six, or at most, of eight thousand.

Thus the Romans had their legions, the Greeks their *phalanxes*, the Gauls their *catervae*, and the Swiss at present (who are the only people that have any traces of the ancient military institutions left amongst them) what we should call regiments in our country: but they all divided them into battalions or smaller bodies, as best suited their purposes. Let us then call them by the name that is most familiar to us, and form them according to the best dispositions that have been made, either by the ancients or moderns. Now as the Romans divided their legion, which consisted of betwixt five and six thousand men, into ten *cohorts*, we will also divide our regiment, which is to consist of six thousand foot, into ten battalions of four hundred and fifty men a-piece; of whom four hundred should be heavy armed, and the other fifty light armed.

Of the heavy-armed, let three hundred have swords and targets, and be called targetmen; another hundred should have pikes, and be called ordinary pikemen; the other fifty light-armed men must carry muskets, crossbows, halberds, and targets, whom we will call by the old name of ordinary *velites;* so that in the ten battalions there will be three thousand targetmen, one thousand ordinary pikemen, and five hundred ordinary *velites*; that is to say, four thousand five hundred. But as our regiment is to consist of six thousand men, we must add fifteen hundred more; of whom a thousand must have pikes, and be called pikemen extraordinary; the other five hundred should be light-armed, and called *velites* extraordinary; and thus one half of our infantry would be composed of targetmen, and the other of pikemen, and others armed in a different manner.

Every battalion should have a lieutenant colonel, or particular commander of its own, four captains, and forty corporals, besides a captain and five corporals of the ordinary *velites*. Over the thousand pikemen extraordinary, there should be three commanders or lieutenant colonels, ten captains, and an hundred corporals; in the *velites* extraordinary, two lieutenant colonels, five captains, and fifty corporals.

I would then appoint a colonel or commander of the whole regiment, with his drum and colours; which every one of the commanders abovementioned should likewise have: so that the whole would consist of ten battalions, composed of three thousand targetmen, a thousand ordinary pikemen, as many extraordinary, five hundred ordinary *velites*, five hundred more extraordinary, in all six thousand: amongst whom, there would be six hundred corporals, fifteen lieutenant colonels, fifteen drums and colours, sixty-five captains, and the colonel with his colours and drum.—You see I have been guilty of some repetition: but it is purely to make you understand me the better, and that you may not be puzzled or perplexed when I come to speak of drawing up an army in order of battle.—I say then, that all princes and governors of republics should arm their militia in this manner, and form them into such regiments; of which they ought to raise as many as their dominions will admit; after which, having divided them into battalions according to the directions I have just now given, in order to make them perfect in their discipline, it will be sufficient to exercise them battalion by battalion: and though one battalion has not men enow in it to form a competent army of itself, yet by this means, every man may learn to do his own duty.

For two things must be observed in all armies: first, that the men be taught what they are to do in their respective battalions; and next, how every battalion is to act when it is joined with others to form an army: and those that are ready and expert in the first, will soon learn the second; but such as are not perfect in one, can never be taught the other. Every battalion then must first be taught separately to keep good order in its own ranks upon all occasions, and in all places; and afterwards, how to act in conjunction with the rest, to attend to the drums and other instruments, by which all motions are regulated and directed in time of battle; to understand from the difference of sounds, whether it is to maintain its ground, or to advance, or retreat, or wheel off, or face about. So that when the men know how to keep their ranks in such a manner that no sort of ground nor any manoeuvre can throw them into disorder; when they understand what they have to do by the beat of the drum or found of the trumpet, and where to take their station, they will soon learn how to act in concert with the other battalions of their regiment, when they are assembled to form an army.

But as it is necessary to exercise them all together sometimes, the whole regiment should be assembled once or twice a year in time of peace, to be formed like an army with front, flanks and rear in their proper places, and to be exercised for some days, as if they were preparing to engage an enemy. Now since a commander draws up his forces for battle, either upon sight of an enemy, or in apprehension of one that is not far off, his army should be exercised according to the occasion, and shewn in what order it is not only to march, but to engage, if need should require; with particular instructions how to act, if it should be attacked on this or that side. But when he would prepare his men to attack an enemy that is in sight, he should shew them how and where to begin the attack, whither they are to retreat if they should be repulsed, who are to take their places, what signals, sounds, and words of command they are to observe, and inure them to sham fights in such a manner, that they may be rather desirous than afraid to come to a real one.

For it is not the natural courage of men that makes an army bold, but order and good discipline: because, when the first ranks know whither to retreat, and who are to advance in their place if they should be worried, they will always fight with spirit, having relief so near at hand: nor will the next ranks be daunted at the misfortune of the first, as they are prepared for such an event, and perhaps not sorry for it, because they may think it will give them the glory of a victory which others could not obtain. These exercises are particularly necessary in an army newly raised, and they ought not to be neglected in one that is composed of veterans; for though the Romans were trained up to the use of arms from their youth, yet their generals always exercised them in this manner with great assiduity for some time before they expected to come to an engagement: and Josephus tells us in his history, that even the very suttlers and rabble that used to follow their armies, often did good service in battle by having seen the soldiers frequently exercised, and learned to handle their arms, and keep firm in their ranks.

But armies composed of new men, which have been raised either for present service, or to be formed into a militia in order to be employed upon occasion, will be good for nothing at all, if the battalions are not first exercised separately, and afterwards all together: for as good order and discipline are absolutely necessary, great care ought to be taken to keep them up amongst those that know their duty, and greater still to instruct such as are entirely ignorant of it: to effect which, a wise and able commander will spare no pains.

Cosimo. You seem to have deviated a little from your point, I think: for before you have told us how a single battalion ought to be exercised, you talk of exercising a whole army, and preparing it for battle.

Fabrizio. You say very true indeed; and I confess my zeal for these exercises and institutions, and my concern at their being now so much neglected, have led me a little out of the way, and occasioned me to break in upon the order I had proposed to myself. But I will return to it.—You may remember that I told you it is of the utmost importance in disciplining a battalion to make the men keep their ranks well: for which purpose, it is necessary to exercise them in the manner called snail-fashion[2]; and as I said there should be four hundred heavy-armed foot in a battalion, I will keep to that number.

These four hundred men must be formed into eighty ranks, of five in each rank, which should learn both how to extend themselves, and how to reduce themselves into closer order, whether they are moving slowly or briskly: but in what manner this is to be done, is easier to comprehend by seeing it actually performed than from any description; which is not absolutely necessary here, because everyone who has the least experience in military affairs knows the method of it, and that its chief use is to accustom the men to keep their ranks.

But let us now proceed to draw up a battalion. There are three principal ways then of doing this: the first and best of which is to draw it up close and compact in the form of an oblong square: the second is to form it in a square with two wings [3] in front: and the third is to throw it into a square with an area or vacancy in the middle, which is commonly called a hollow square.

The first may be effected two ways; one, by doubling the ranks, that is, by receiving the second rank into the first, the fourth into the third, the sixth into the fifth, and so on; that so where there were eighty ranks before with five men in every rank, they may be reduced to forty with ten in a rank, and by doubling them a second time, to twenty with twenty in a rank. This will make an oblong square: for though there will be as many men in the files as in the ranks, yet the men in the ranks must stand so close together as to touch each other, but those in the files must be at least four feet distant one from another: so that the square will be longer from the front to the rear, than from the extremity of the right flank to that of the left; that is, the files will be longer than the ranks.

---

2. That is (I suppose) to teach them how to contract or extend themselves upon occasion, as that animal does.
3. The original says "*con la fronte cornuta, i. e.* with a horned front:" the word *corno* in the Italian language, like *cornu* in the Latin, signifying a *horn* as well as the wing of an army.

The fifty ordinary *velites* belonging to the battalion must not be mixed with the other ranks, but polled on each flank, and in the rear, when it is formed.—The other way of drawing up a battalion close and compact in the form of an oblong square is better than this, and therefore I will be more particular in describing it. You remember, I take it for granted, of how many private men and what officers it is to consist, and how they are to be armed: without further repetition then, I say, that the battalion must be formed into twenty ranks, with twenty men in every rank; that is to say, five ranks of pikemen in the front, and fifteen of targetmen in the rear: there must be two captains in the front, and two in the rear: the lieutenant colonel or commander of the battalion with his colours and drum mull take post in the interval betwixt the five ranks of pikemen and the fifteen of targetmen: the corporals are to be placed upon the two flanks, one as the extremity of each rank in such a manner, that every one of them may have his men by his side; those on the right will have them on their left, and those on the left will have them on their right: the fifty ordinary *velites* should be posted upon the flanks and in the rear of the battalion.

Now in order to throw it into this form; you must draw it up in eighty ranks, with five men in every rank, and placing the *velites* by themselves either in the front or the rear, every captain must put himself at the head of his company or hundred men, of twenty ranks of five men in each; of which the five front ranks, or those immediately behind him, must be pikemen, and the rest targetmen. The lieutenant colonel or commander of the battalion with his drum and colours, are to be placed in the interval betwixt the pikes and targets of the second company, and will take up the room of three targetmen: twenty corporals must be placed upon the left flanks of the ranks commanded by the first captain; and twenty more upon the right flanks of the ranks commanded by the last captain: and it must be observed that the corporals of the pikemen must carry pikes themselves, and those of the targetmen must have targets and swords.

Your ranks being thus disposed, if you desire to form them in order of battle to face an enemy, you must cause the captain of the first twenty ranks to halt with his men, the captain of the second twenty, to keep advancing, but inclining a little to the right, close along the flank of the first twenty, till he comes abreast of their captain, and there to halt himself: the third is then to advance with his men in the same manner by the right flank of the other two companies, till he is in a line with the two first captains, and there to halt as they do: after which, the fourth captain and his company are to move forward likewise by the right flank of those that are already joined, and halt when he has advanced as far as the other three: all which being executed, two of those captains must immediately quit the front rank and take post in the rear; and then the battalion will be formed in an oblong square as it was by the other method.

The *velites* must likewise be ported on each flank as they were before: one of these ways is called doubling the ranks in a right line; the other, doubling them by the flanks: the former is the easier of the two; the latter more convenient, and may be better adapted to answer different occasions. For in the former you must conform to the number, because five doubled makes ten, ten twenty, twenty forty; so that if you double your ranks in a right line, you cannot make a front of fifteen, or twenty-five, or thirty, or thirty-five, but must be governed in that by the number in your first rank; and as it is often necessary to form a front of six or eight hundred foot, doubling your ranks in a right line would throw the men into confusion.

I therefore like the latter method best: and though perhaps there may be more difficulty in it, yet that will soon be surmounted by frequent practice and exercise. I say then it is a matter of the utmost importance to have soldiers that know how to take their proper stations in a moment: for which purpose, it is necessary to form them into such battalions, to exercise them all together, to teach them to march either quick or slow in all directions, and to keep such order, that no pass or defile, how rough or difficult so ever, can oblige them to break their ranks. For if soldiers can do this, they are good soldiers, and may be called veterans, though they have never seen the face of an enemy: but if they have been in a thousand battles, and are ignorant in this point, they are no better than raw men.

What has been said, relates only to drawing up a battalion in closer order when it is marching in small ranks: but after that has been done, if it should happen to be thrown into disorder, either by the nature of the country through which it is obliged to march, or by an enemy, or by any other accident, and you want to reduce it to its former order immediately; there lies the main point and chief difficulty: to surmount which, much exercise, and practice, and experience are necessary; and therefore the ancients spared no pains to make their soldiers ready and expert in rallying whenever they were thrown into confusion. For this purpose, two things, are necessary, *viz.* that there should be several peculiar marks of distinction in every battalion; and that the same men should always be placed in the same ranks. For instance, if a man was stationed in the second rank at first, let him continue in it ever after; and not only in the same rank, but in the very same place of it: and that he may not be at a loss how to do that, there must be several peculiar marks to guide and direct him, as I said just now.

In the first place, it is necessary the colours should be such as to be easily distinguished from those of all other battalions, when several are joined together: in the next, that the lieutenant colonels, captains, and other officers should wear different plumes: and lastly (which is of still more importance) that every corporal should be distinguished by some particular mark: in which the ancients were so remarkably careful and exact, that they caused their numbers to be marked upon their *casques* in great figures, as the first, second, third, fourth, and so on: but not thinking that sufficient, every targetman had the number of his rank and his place in that rank engraved upon his target.

When men are thus distinguished from each other, and accustomed to know and keep their respective stations, it is an easy matter to rally them if they are thrown into confusion: for when the standard is once fixed, the captains and corporals will presently know their stations; and resume them (whether on the right or left) at a due distance from it: the private men likewise, being guided by their usual marks and the difference of colours, will presently fall into their proper ranks and places: just as when you are to put together the staves of a barrel, if you have marked them before it was taken to pieces, you may easily do it; but if those staves have not been marked, you will find it exceeding difficult, if not impossible.

These things may soon be learned by frequent practice and exercise, and are not easily forgotten: and thus the new raw men being instructed by the veterans, a whole province by such exercise may be made good and experienced soldiers in time.—It is necessary also to teach your men to move all at a time, when there is occasion, in such a manner as to make either flank or rear become the front, or the front become either the rear or one of the flanks; which may easily be effected by causing every man to face at once towards any particular part, which then will become the front. It is true that when they face to either flank, it will make some alteration and disproportion in the ranks, because the distance which will then be betwixt the front and the rear, will not be so great as that betwixt one extremity of the flanks and the other; which is quite contrary to the form in which a battalion ought to be drawn up: this however may soon be rectified by well-exercised and experienced soldiers, and therefore cannot occasion any great disorder.

But there is another manoeuvre of great importance, in which still more readiness and expertness are requisite; and that is, when a whole battalion is to move all at once like one solid body; for instance, when it is to wheel to the left about in such a manner as to front on that side where the left flank was before: for then those that are on the left at the extremity of the front rank must stand fast, and those that are nearest them on the right must move so slow, that the rest who are farther from them on the right, and those at the other extremity of that rank, may not be obliged to run; otherwise, they will be in great confusion.——Now as it always happens, when a battalion is attacked on its march from one place to another, that the companies which are not posted in the front are forced to fight either in one of the flanks or the rear, and the battalion is under a sudden necessity of making a front where that flank, or perhaps the rear, was before; in order to form those companies in due proportion and order; all the pikes are to be placed in that flank which is to become the front, and the corporals, captains, and lieutenant colonel must take their respective posts as in the method of forming a battalion above described.

To effect this then, in forming the battalion into eighty ranks of five men in every rank, you must put all the pikemen into the twenty first ranks, with five of their corporals in the front rank, and five in the last of that company: and then the other sixty ranks, or three companies, will wholly consist of targetmen; in the first and last rank of which there must be five corporals. The lieutenant colonel, with his standard and drum, are to take post in the centre of the first company of targetmen, and the four captains at the head of their reflective companies. When it is thus formed, if you would have all the pikemen upon the left flank, you must double the companies one by one by their right flanks: but if you would have them on the right flank, you must double them by the left: and thus the battalion will have all its pikemen upon one flank, the corporals in the front and rear, the captains in the front, and the lieutenant colonel in the centre.

This is the order it is to observe whilst it is marching: but upon the approach of an enemy, if you would have its front where one of the flanks was before, you have nothing to do but to order your men to face to that flank where the pikemen are, and then the whole battalion, with all its ranks and officers, are presently changed, and in the order I described before: for every man will be in his proper station, except the captains, and they will loon take their pods. But when a battalion is marching forwards, and apprehensive of being attacked in the rear, the ranks must be so disposed that the pikemen may be posted there: for which purpose, five ranks of them should be placed in the rear of every company, instead of its front where they are usually stationed: in all other respects let the ordinary disposition be observed.[3]

Cosimo. If I remember right, you told us that this manner of exercise is calculated to reduce all the battalions of a regiment into the form of an army; and that in was sufficient for such a purpose. But if it should happen that this battalion of four hundred and fifty men should be obliged to fight by itself, how would you draw it up in that case?

Fabrizio. The lieutenant colonel should consider in the first place, where it will be most necessary to place his pikemen, and to post them there accordingly; which may easily be done without breaking in upon the above mentioned disposition: for though that is the order which should be observed by a battalion when it acts in conjunction with others against an enemy; yet it may serve upon all other occasions. However, in shewing you the two other methods of drawing up a battalion, which I promised you a little while ago, I will answer your question more particularly: but they are seldom used; and if ever, it is when a battalion is to act alone and independent upon all others.—In order then to form a battalion with two wings (or two horns) in the front, you are to dispose your eighty ranks of five men in a rank in this manner. In the first place, you must post a captain at the head of twenty-five ranks, which are to consist of two pikemen on the left, and three targetmen on the right.

Next to the five first ranks, let there be twenty more, with twenty corporals polled in them; all of them betwixt the pikemen and the targetmen, except the five which carry pikes; for they must be placed amongst the pikemen. After these twenty-five ranks thus drawn up, let there be polled another captain at the head of fifteen ranks of targetmen. In the interval betwixt this company and the third, the lieutenant colonel, with his colours and drum, is to post himself at the head of the third company, consisting of fifteen ranks more of targetmen.

The third captain is to take post at the head of the fourth company, which is to consist of twenty-five ranks, every one of which is to have three targetmen on the left, and two pikemen on the right: and after the five first ranks there must be twenty more with corporals in them

---

3. The *valites* then, we are to suppose, must be stationed as before.

polled betwixt the targetmen and the pikemen; in the rear of this company the fourth captain is to take his station. If then you would form these ranks thus drawn up into a battalion with two wings, you must order the first captain to halt with his twenty-five ranks, and the second to make a motion to the right, and then to advance with his fifteen ranks of targetmen to double the right flank of the twenty-five ranks that have halted, till he comes abreast of the rank that is the fifteenth from their rear, and there to halt himself.

After this, the lieutenant colonel, with his fifteen ranks of targetmen, is to do the same on the right flank of the two first companies. Last of all the third captain, with his twenty-five ranks, and the fourth captain in the rear of them, is to move to the right, and then advance along the light flank of the other three companies, but not to halt till his rearmost rank is in a line with their rearmost rank: ell which being done, the captain of the first fifteen ranks of targetmen must quit his station, and repair to the left of the rearmost rank, and the fourth captain to the right of it. In this manner you will have a battalion of twenty-five ranks, some consisting of five, and others of twenty men: with two wings (one at each angle of the front) each of which will consist of ten ranks of five men a-piece, and a space betwixt the wings large enough to receive ten men abreast.

The colonel takes post in this open, a captain at the front of each horn, and another at each angle in the rear of the battalion; two files of pikemen and twenty corporals are placed on each flank. The wings may serve to secure the carriages and baggage, as well as the artillery, if there be any: the *velites* may be ranged along the flanks, on the outside of the pikemen.—Now in order to reduce this horned battalion into a hollow square, you need only to take eight of the rearmost of those fifteen ranks that have twenty men a-piece in them, and place them immediately in the front of the two wings, which will then become the flanks of the hollow square. In the area left in the middle, the lieutenant colonel is to take place with his colours and drum: and it may likewise receive the carriages and baggage, but not the artillery, which is to be planted either in the front or on the flanks.—These are the methods that may be taken to form a single battalion when it is to pass alone through dangerous and suspected places; but the solid battalion, without wings or area in the middle of it, is certainly the best: nevertheless, either one or other of those forms may be necessary sometimes to secure the carriages, baggage, &c.

The Swiss have likewise several forms of drawing up their battalions: one of them is in the shape of a cross; in the spaces betwixt the arms of which, they place their musketeers to shelter them from the full shock of an enemy; but as such battalions are only fit to engage separately, and it is my intention to shew in what manner several battalions united must fight, I shall not give myself the trouble of describing the order they observe.

Cosimo. I think I sufficiently comprehend the method that is to be followed in exercising the men of whom your battalion consists; but if I mistake not, you said you would add a thousand pikemen extraordinary, and five hundred *velites* extraordinary, to the ten battalions of which your regiment is to be composed. Would you not cause them also to be exercised?

Fabrizio. Certainly, and very well too: for I would exercise the extraordinary pikemen, by companies at least, if not altogether, in the discipline of the battalion: for I should employ them more than the ordinary pikemen, especially upon particular occasions, as in convoys, escorts, plundering, and the like. As to the *velites*, it may suffice to exercise them separately at home in their particular method of fighting, without bringing them into the field: for as they are to fight in a loose and detached way, there is no occasion to call them together when the rest of the battalion is assembled to be disciplined in their own manner.

You must therefore (as I said before, and beg leave to say again) take great care to exercise your battalions in such a manner, that the men be taught to keep their ranks, to know their proper stations, to rally or alter their disposition in a moment, when they are either got into troublesome defiles, or are apprehensive of being attacked, or disordered by an enemy: for when they are perfect in these things, they will easily comprehend their duty when joined with, others to form an army. So that if any prince or republic would be at the trouble of establishing this discipline and these exercises, they would always have good soldiers enow in their dominions to make them superior to their neighbours, and put them in a condition to give law to others, instead of receiving it from them.

But such is the degeneracy of the times we live in, and these things are so far from being in any esteem at present, that they are totally neglected and laughed at: which is the reason that our armies are now good for nothing; and that if there be yet any officers or private men amongst us who have the least share of experience, courage, or abilities of any kind, they have no opportunity of shewing them.

Cosimo. How many carriages would you assign to a battalion?

Fabrizio. In the first place, no captain or corporal should be suffered to ride upon a march; and if the colonel desired to ride, it should be upon a mule, and not upon a horse. I would allow him two baggage horses, one to every captain, and two betwixt three corporals; because I would lodge three of them together when they are in camp, as I shall shew in its proper place. So that every battalion should have six and thirty horses to carry its tents, kettles, hatchets, mattocks, spades, with other such implements and utensils as are necessary in an encampment, and anything else that may be useful or convenient, if there is room for it.

Cosimo. Though I believe all the officers in your battalion may be necessary, yet I should be afraid that so many would create confusion.

Fabrizio. That might be the case if they were not all under the command of one person; but as they are, they rather serve to preserve and promote good order; and indeed it would be impossible to keep it up without them: for a wall that is weak and tottering in every part, may be better supported by many props and buttresses, though they are but feeble ones, than by a few, be they ever so substantial; because their strength cannot be of much service at any considerable distance. For this reason, there ought to be a corporal over every ten soldiers in all armies, who should be a man of more spirit and courage, at least of greater authority, than the rest, in order to animate them both by his words and example, and exhort them continually to keep firm in their ranks, and behave themselves like men.

How necessary these things are, may plainly appear from the example even of our own armies, all which have their corporals, drums, and colours, though none of them do their duty. As to corporals, if they would answer the end for which they were first appointed, every one of them should have his particular men under him, should lodge with them, should charge with them, and always be in the same rank: for then they might keep them so regular and compact in their several stations, that it would be almost impossible for any enemy to break or disorder them; and if that should ever happen, they might presently be rallied: but in these times they are employed in other purposes of a different nature, and do nothing as they ought to do, though their pay is considerable.

It is the same with regard to colours, which are still continued, rather to make a fine shew, than for any other use that is made of them. Whereas the ancients availed themselves of them as guides and directions in case of disorder: for as soon as the colours were fixed, every man knew his post, and immediately returned to it. They likewise knew how and when to move, and when to halt, by the motion of halting of the colours: and therefore it is necessary there should be many different corps in an army, and that every corps should have its particular ensign, and marks of distinction: for then it will know what it has to do, and act with spirit. The soldiers then are to observe the motion of their ensigns, and the ensigns the beat of the drum; for that, when rightly managed, is a direction to the whole army, which is to act and move in a certain measure and pace, according to its different founds, that so it may know how to keep due time and order.

For this purpose, the ancients had their pipes and fifes, and other sorts of military music, perfectly adapted to different occasions: and as a man that is dancing, and keeps time with the music, cannot make a false step; so an army that properly observes the beat of its drums cannot easily be disordered. The ancients, therefore, used to vary the sounds and notes of their military music according to the occasion, and as they wanted either to excite, or abate, or confirm the ardour of their soldiers: and as their tunes and marches were different, they gave them different names: the Doric was calculated to inspire men with resolution and firmness; the Phrygian excited martial ardour, or rather fury: for Alexander the Great (as it is said) being at dinner one day, and hearing a Phrygian march sounded, was so transported with it, that he leaped up from the table and drew his sword, as if he had been going to charge an enemy.

It would be very useful then, either to revive these measures, or invent new ones for such purposes; but if that cannot be done, those at least should not be neglected or laid aside, which teach soldiers to obey command: and these may be varied and adapted in such a manner, that by frequent use and exercise, they may learn to distinguish them, and know their signification: but at present our drums are chiefly employed to make a noise and parade.

Cosimo. I should be very glad to be informed (if you have ever considered the matter) how it comes to pass that we are so degenerated, and that not only these exercises, but all manner of military discipline, are now fallen into such neglect and disuse amongst us.

Fabrizio. I will give you my opinion of the matter very freely, Sir. You know then, there have been many renowned warriors in Europe, but few in Africa, and fewer still in Asia: the reason of which is, that the two last mentioned quarters of the world have had but one or two monarchies, and very few republics; and that Europe, on the contrary, has had several kingdoms, but more republics.

Now men become great and excellent, and shew their abilities accordingly as they are employed and encouraged by their sovereigns, whether they happen to be kings, princes, or republics: so that where there are many states, there will be many great men; but where there are few of the one, there will not be many of the other. In Asia, there were Ninus, Cyrus, Artaxerxes, Mithridates, and some few others like them. In Africa (without having recourse to the early times of the ancient Egyptians) we read of Massinissa, Jugurtha, and some Carthaginian commanders of eminent note; the number of whom, however, is very small in companion of that which Europe has produced: for in this quarter of the world, there have been numbers of great men that we know of, and many more without doubt, whose memories are now extinguished by the malevolence of time: because every state being obliged to cherish and encourage men of merit and abilities, either out of necessity or for other reasons, where there are many different states, there must of course be many great men.

Asia, on the contrary, has not produced many extraordinary men: because that quarter of the globe being subject in a great measure to one monarchy, of so large an extent that most parts of it languish in continual inactivity, cannot form any considerable number of men for great and glorious enterprises. The same may be said of Africa; though indeed there have been more able commanders in that country than in Asia; which was owing to the republic of Carthage: for there will always be a greater number of such men in republics than in monarchies; because merit is generally honoured in the former, but feared in the latter: from whence it comes to pass, that able men are cherished and encouraged in one, but discountenanced and suppressed in the other.

If we consider Europe in the next place, we shall find that it was always full of principalities, kingdoms, and republics, which lived in perpetual jealousy of each other, and being obliged to keep up good discipline in their armies, were under a necessity of honouring and encouraging military merit. For in Greece, besides the Macedonian Monarchy, there were several republics, every one of which produced many great and eminent men. In Italy, there were the Romans, the Samnites, the Tuscans, and the Cisalpine Gauls: France, Germany, and Spain abounded with republics and principalities: and if we do not read of so many great men in any of them as amongst the Romans, that is owing to the partiality of historians, who generally follow the stream of fortune, and content themselves with praising the conqueror. It is But reasonable however to suppose, there were a great many illustrious men amongst the Samnites and Tuscans, as they supported themselves against the Romans an hundred and fifty years.

The same may be supposed of France and Spain: but the merit which most authors are so shy of allowing to particular men, they are forward enough to celebrate in whole nations, when they tell us, with what bravery and resolution they exerted themselves in defence of their liberties. Since it is manifest then, that where there are many states there will always be many able men, it is certain, that when the number of those states is diminished, the number of such men will likewise decrease by degrees, as the effect must cease when the cause is taken away. Thus, when the Roman Empire had swallowed up all the kingdoms and republics in Europe and Africa, and most of those in Asia, merit and abilities met with no countenance anywhere but at Rome: so that great men began to grow scarcer and scarcer in Europe, as well as in Asia, till at last, there were hardly any to be found; for as all manner of spirit and worth was extinguished, except amongst the Romans, so when they became corrupt, the whole world in a manner was corrupted, and the Scythians poured by swarms into an Empire, which, having extinguished the virtue of most other nations, was not able to preserve its own.

And though that Empire was afterwards dismembered by those barbarians, yet the several parts into which it was cantoned never recovered their pristine vigour; for, in the first place, it is a very difficult matter, and requires a long course of time, to revive good order and discipline when it is once abolished: and in the next, the Christian Religion has wrought such a change in the manners and customs of mankind, that they are now no longer under a necessity of defending themselves with such a degree of obstinacy and despair as they did in former times. For then, all such as were vanquished in battle, where either put to death, or carried into perpetual slavery in the enemy's country, where they spent the remainder of their lives in labour and misery.

If a town was taken, it was either demolished, or the inhabitants were stripped of their goods, dispersed all over the world, and reduced to the last degree of poverty and wretchedness: so that the dread of these evils obliged them to keep up good discipline in their armies, and to honour all those that excelled in the Art of War. But at present, these terrible apprehensions are in a great measure dissipated and extinguished: for after an army is defeated, those that fall into the hands of the conqueror are seldom or never put to death; and the terms of their ransom are made so easy, that they do not long continue prisoners.

If a town has changed sides an hundred times, it is not demolished, nor are the inhabitants either dispersed or stripped of their possessions: the word they have to fear is being laid under contribution: so that men now no longer care to submit to the rigour and continual hardships of military discipline, to ward off evils which they are but little afraid of. Besides, the provinces of Europe are subject to few heads at present, in comparison of what they were formerly: all France is under the dominion of one king; all Spain under that of another; and there are not many principalities or republics in Italy; so that the petty states find protection under the wings of the strong, and those that are more powerful are not afraid of utter ruin, even if they should be conquered, for the reasons already given.

Cosimo. But we have seen many towns sacked, and some kingdoms entirely ruined within these last five and twenty years: examples, which ought to serve as warnings to others to provide for their security by reviving the ancient military discipline and institutions.

Fabrizio. You say very true: but consider what towns those were which suffered in that manner, and you will find they were not states, but inferior members of states: if Tortona was sacked, Milan was not; Capua suffered, but Naples escaped; Brescia and Ravenna felt the lash of the conqueror, but Venice and Rome came off with impunity: so that these examples are not sufficient to make a state change its purpose; but rather determine it to persevere in its resolution, when it sees it can at any time redeem itself from destruction by a ransom; for it will not expose itself and its subjects to the continual fatigues of military discipline and exercises, when they seem not only unnecessary, but attended with much trouble and inconvenience.

As for the dependent members which ought to be most affected with these examples, it is not in their power to save themselves; and those states which have already been ruined, see their error when it is too late to correct it, whilst others, which have not yet shared the same fate, take no pains to prevent it; chusing to live a lazy indolent life, free from trouble and inconvenience, and to rely upon fortune rather than their own virtue: for seeing there is so small a proportion of virtue now left amongst mankind, that it has but little influence in the affairs of the world, and that all things seem to be governed by fortune, they think it better to follow her train, than contend with her for superiority.

To evince the truth of what I have said, if further proof is wanting, let us consider the state of Germany at present, which being full of principalities and republics, abounds with great and able commanders; and indeed, whatsoever is worthy imitation in the military discipline of these times, is owing to those states, which being jealous of their neighbours, and abhorring the thoughts of slavery (a condition which seems not much dreaded in some other countries) take all proper means to defend their liberties, and therefore continue free and respectable.—This, I think, may suffice to shew the causes of our degeneracy, and the present neglect of military discipline amongst us; but I cannot tell whether you are of the same opinion: perhaps what I have said has either not given you the satisfaction you wanted, or not been thoroughly understood, and consequently may have left some doubts upon your mind.

Cosimo. None at all, Sir, I assure you: on the contrary, I perfectly comprehend what you have said, and am very well satisfied with it; but beg the favour of you to resume our subject, and to let us know in what manner you would dispose your cavalry in these battalions, what number of them you would have, and how they should be armed and officered.

Fabrizio. You might think, perhaps, I had forgot that, but I have not; though I have but little to say of cavalry, for two reasons. In the first place, because the main strength of an army consists in its Infantry; and in the next, cavalry, even in these times, are much better disciplined than infantry; and if they are not superior, they are equal however to the cavalry of the ancients. I have already shewn how they ought to be exercised; and as to their arms, I would arm both the *gens d'armes* and the light horse as they are armed at present: but the light horse should mostly consist of crossbow men, with some musketeers amongst them, which, though of little service in other respects, are yet very necessary to frighten the country people, and drive them from passes, which perhaps they may have undertaken to defend: for they are more afraid of one musketeer, than of twenty men that are armed in any other manner.

With regard to their number (as I proposed at first to take a Roman legion for my model) I should think three hundred good horse in a regiment would be sufficient; of which an hundred and fifty should be *gens d'armes*, and the rest light horse; with a captain, a cornet, fifteen corporals, and a drum to each troop: every ten *gens d'armes* should have five baggage horses, and every ten light horsemen, two, which (like those belonging to the infantry) should carry their tents, kettles, horse-furniture, and other implements and utensils. Do not think this out of compass, for every one of our *gens d'armes* have four horses allowed them for that purpose; but that is an abuse; for in Germany they have no other horse than that which they are mounted upon, and only one carriage to every twenty for their baggage.

The Roman heavy-armed horse had no more; but the *triarii* indeed were always quartered near their cavalry, and obliged to assist them in dressing and taking care of their horses: an example which might easily be followed in these times, as I shall shew more particularly, when I come to speak of encampments: for surely what was formerly done by the Romans, and is still practised by the Germans, may be effected at present, and therefore those that omit or neglect these things are much to be blamed. These squadrons being raised and enrolled in the same manner with the rest of the Regiment, should sometimes be reviewed with the other battalions, when they are assembled, and exercised in skirmishes and sham-fights with them, to make them well acquainted with each other, and perfect in those exercises. So much for this head. Let us now proceed to draw up an army in such an order of battle, as is most likely to ensure us a victory, when we come to engage an enemy; for this is the end for which all armies are raised, and that so much care and pains are to be taken in disciplining them.

Book 3

The order of battle observed by the Romans. Of the Roman Legion, the Macedonian Phalanx, and the Swiss Regiments. That it is the best way to use fart of the Roman arms and armour; and part of the Grecian. Of what number of men the Roman armies generally consisted. A method of drawing up a regiment or army recommended. A description of a battle. Reasons for the several manoeuvres in it. Concerning the general exercises of an army.

Cosimo. Since we are going to vary the subject, I beg leave to resign my office of interrogator in this conversation; for, as I hate presumption in others, I would not willingly seem guilty of it myself. I therefore lay down the dictatorship, and give up my authority to any other person in company, that will please to accept of it.

Zanobi. It would have been very grateful to us all, if you would have continued in that office; but since you decline it, be pleased at least to say, which of us you depute to succeed you in it.

Cosimo. I desire to leave that to Signor Fabrizio.

Fabrizio. I freely accept it: and think we should follow the example of the Venetians, who always appoint the youngest to speak first in their councils and assemblies; especially as the art of speaking well is properly the exercise of youth, and therefore we may suppose young men the best qualified to talk of the several duties and exercises of war, as well as the fitted to put them in execution.

Cosimo. The lot then falls upon you, Luigi: and as I myself am much pleased with my successor, I make no doubt but he will be equally agreeable to you all. Let us lose no more time however, but return to our subject.

Fabrizio. I know very well, that in order to shew how an army ought to be drawn up in order of battle, it would be necessary to describe the method in which the Greeks and Romans formed their troops for that purpose: but as this is done at large by ancient historians, I refer you to them, and omitting several other particulars, shall speak only of such as are absolutely necessary to be adopted by those that would improve our present system of military discipline: for which purpose, I will shew you at the same time, how an army ought to be formed in order of battle at present, how it is to be exercised in sham fights, and in what manner to behave in real engagements.

The greatest error then that a general can be guilty of in drawing up an army for battle, is to give it but one front: because in so doing, he commits himself and his fortune entirely to the event of the first conflict: and this is the effect of having lost the method, observed by the ancients, of receiving one line into another: for without that, those in the front can neither be supported nor relieved in the time of action; both which, were effectually performed by the Romans. Now to point out the method by which these things were effected, I must tell you that they divided their legion into the *hastati*, the *principes*, and *triarii*; the first were placed in the front or first line of the army in thick and close array; the *principes* in the second line, but in looser order; and the *triarii* in the third, with still larger intervals betwixt the men in their ranks, into which they could admit both the *principes* and *hastati* upon occasion.

Besides these, they had their slingers, bowmen, and other light-armed soldiers, who were not incorporated with these ranks, but posted on the right and left betwixt the cavalry and infantry in the front. These light-armed forces used to begin the engagement, and if they made any impression upon the enemy (which seldom happened) they pursued their advantage: but if they were driven back, they retreated either along the flanks of the army, or through certain intervals of it left open for that purpose, to cover the suttlers and servants, and other unarmed people that followed the camp.

After this, the *hastati* advanced against the enemy, and if they were repulsed, they retreated leisurely into the spaces left for them amongst the *principes*, and again advanced with them to renew the battle: but if this line also was overpowered, it fell back into the *triarii*, and all three, being thus joined together, made their third attack with greater vigour and strength than ever; and if that miscarried, the day was loft, because they had no other resource or means of relief left.

The cavalry were stationed on each side of the infantry, in the form of two wings, and sometimes engaged the enemy's cavalry, and sometimes supported their own infantry, as occasion required. This method of renewing the attack three several times, with a continual increase of strength and vigour, can hardly be withstood, except either your fortune be very bad indeed, or the resolution of the enemy much greater than that of your own forces.—The Greeks were strangers to this method of renewing the front of their *phalanxes*; and though they were very well officered, and consisted of many ranks, yet they made but one body, or rather one front.

To relieve each other, one rank did not retire into another (as the Romans did) but one single man advanced into another's place when it was vacant; which was effected in this manner. When their *phalanx* was drawn up in files (which we will suppose to consist of fifty men apiece) with its front towards the enemy, all the six first ranks might engage at once: for their lances (which they called *sarissae*) were so long, that those of the sixth rank reached over the shoulders of the men in the first. In the time of action therefore, if any man in the first rank was either killed or disabled, the man that was next behind him in the second rank presently stepped into his place; the person immediately behind him in the third rank filled the vacancy in the second, and so on; the ranks in the rear continually filling up the deficiencies of those in the front: so that all the ranks were constantly kept full and entire, except the rearmost, which was exhausted at last, because there was no other to reinforce it.

These *phalanxes* therefore might be wasted away and annihilated by degrees, but seldom could be broken; as the close order and grossness of their body made them in a manner impenetrable.—The Romans at first formed their legions in this manner, in imitation of the Grecian Phalanx: but growing out of conceit with it at last, they divided them into more corps, as *cohorts* and *manipuli*, or companies, being convinced that such bodies have most life and vigour in them, as have the most officers to animate and inform them, and are divided in such a manner that each division can act separately and support itself.

The Swiss Regiments at present, are likewise formed upon the model of the ancient *phalanxes*, and follow their method both in closeness of order and relieving their ranks: and when they come to engage, they are placed on the flanks of each other, but not in a parallel line. They have no method of receiving the first into the second, if it should be repulsed; but in order to relieve each other, they place one regiment in the front, another a little behind it on the right; so that if the first is hard pressed, the second may advance to its assistance: a third is placed behind both these, and on the right too, at the distance of a musket-shot; that so, if the other two should be driven back, it may advance to relieve them, and all of them have sufficient room either to retreat or advance without falling foul upon one another; because great bodies cannot be received into each other like little ones; and therefore the little distinct corps, of which the Roman Legions were composed, are the most proper both to receive and relieve each other: and that the method observed by the Swiss is not so good as that which was taken by the ancient Romans, appears very plainly from the success of the Roman Legions, which always got the better of the Grecian Phalanxes whenever they happened to engage them; because both their arms and armour, and their way of receiving one rank into another, were much better than the arms and discipline, and close order, of the *phalanx*.

Now, in order to form an army upon the model of both, I would make the Grecian Phalanx my pattern in some respects, and the Roman Legion in others: and therefore, as I told you before, I would have two thousand pikemen in my regiment, armed after the manner of the Macedonian Phalanx, and three thousand men with swords and targets like the Roman Legion. I have divided my regiment into ten battalions, as the Romans did their legion into ten *cohorts*: like them too, I have appointed *velites* to begin the battle: and as I have retained the arms of both nations, I would likewise in some measure imitate the order and discipline of each: for which reason I have taken care that the five first ranks of every battalion should consist of pikemen, and the rest of targetmen; that so it might be enabled not only to sustain the shock of the enemy's cavalry in the front, but to make an impression upon their infantry, and to open it in such a manner to the right and left that the targetmen may come in to complete the victory.

Now if you consider this method, and the nature of these arms, you will find how well they are calculated for that purpose: because the pikes are of admirable service against horse, and amongst infantry they do no small execution before they come to fight hand to hand: for after that, they are of no use at all: upon which account, the Swiss place one rank of halberdiers behind every three ranks of pikemen, to give them room to make use of their pikes; bur that room is not sufficient. Placing our pikemen then in the front, and the targetmen behind them, they serve both to sustain the enemy's horse, and open and disorder their foot: but after the battle is joined, and they become useless, the targetmen advance with their swords, which are weapons that may be managed in the closest fight.

Luigi. We are impatient to hear how you would draw up an army, thus armed and appointed, in order of battle.

Fabrizio. I was just going to do it. You must know then, that a consular army amongst the Romans did not exceed two legions; that is to say, about eleven thousand foot, and six hundred horse; but they were composed wholly of their own citizens. Besides these, they were furnished with as many more of both sorts by their friends and allies, which they divided into two bodies, called the right and left wing, and stationed them on each flank of their main battle; but they never suffered the number of these auxiliaries to surpass that of their legions; though there was generally a larger proportion of cavalry amongst them than in their own forces. With such an army, consisting of about twenty-two thousand foot, and two thousand good horse, a consul went upon most expeditions: but when the enemy was very formidable, they lent out two consuls with two such armies united.

You must know likewise, that in the three principal operations of an army, *viz.* upon a march, in an encampment, and in battle, they constantly posted their legions in the centre, rightly judging that the forces in which they reposed the greatest confidence should always be compact and united; as I shall shew you when I come to speak more particularly and distinctly of these three operations. But these auxiliary infantry, by their union and daily conversion with the legionary infantry, soon became as serviceable as they were: for they were exercised and disciplined in the same manner, and formed in the same order before an engagement: so that when we know how the Romans drew up one legion for that purpose, we know in what manner they drew up a whole army: and as I said they formed their legion in three lines, in such a manner that one line might receive another, I have consequently told you how they drew up their whole army in the day of battle.

To form an army then in order of battle after the manner of the Romans, as they had two legions, I will take two regiments; by the arrangement of which, you may see how a whole army is to be drawn up: for if you would add any more, there is nothing further to be done but either to multiply or enlarge the ranks. It will be needless, I suppose, to put you in mind of how many foot a regiment consists, that there are ten battalions in it, what sort of arms and armour they have, how many companies there are, and what officers in each, what number of *velites* and pikemen both ordinary and extraordinary, how many targetmen, &c. for when I spoke of these things a little while ago, I desired you to take particular notice of them, and to remember them as absolutely necessary to give you a clear idea of the whole arrangement: and therefore, without any repetition of that kind, I shall proceed to draw up my army.

For this purpose, I would place the ten battalions of one regiment on the left, and the ten of the other on the right. Those on the left are to be formed in this manner.—Post five battalions on the flank of each other in the front, with an interval of eight feet betwixt every one of them; and let the space which they occupy be two hundred and eighty two feet in breadth, and eighty in depth. In the rear of these five I would place three others, at the distance of eighty feet, one of which should be in a right line with the battalion that is on the left flank of those in the front; the second with that on the right flank; and the third with that in the centre: so that these three will take up as much ground both in breadth and depth as the other five: but though the space betwixt every one of those five is but eight feet, I would have the space betwixt these three to be sixty-six.

In the rear of these I would post the two remaining battalions at the distance of eighty feet, one of them in a right line with that on the left of the three last mentioned, and the other with that on the right; with an interval betwixt one and the other of ninety-two feet. The ground therefore which all these battalions, thus formed, take up, will be two hundred and eighty-two feet in breadth, and four hundred in depth. The pikemen extraordinary I would range along the left flank of these battalions at the distance of forty feet, and I would make an hundred and forty ranks of them of seven men in every rank: so that they would cover the whole left flank of the Battalions draw up in the manner I have described, and there would be forty ranks remaining to guard the baggage, suttlers, and other unarmed people who follow the camp in the rear of the army, after porting the captains and corporals in their proper places.

Of the three lieutenant colonels belonging to them, I would place one at the front, another in the centre, and another in the rear. But to return to the front of the army; next to the pikemen extraordinary, I would place the five hundred *velites* extraordinary, and allow them to take up a space of eighty feet. Next to them on the left, I would place my *gens d'armes*, and allow them a space of four hundred and fifty feet: and next to them, my light horse, whom I would allow the same space. The ordinary *velites* I would leave with their respective battalions in their proper places, (that is, in the intervals betwixt one battalion and another) to be attendants as it were upon them; unless I should think fit to put them under the cover of the pikemen extraordinary; which I would do sometimes, and sometimes I would not, according as it was most for my advantage.

The colonel of the regiment, with his colours and drum, I would place either in the centre of that space which is left betwixt the first and second lines of the battalions, or in the front of them, or in the interval betwixt the last of the first five and the pikemen extraordinary, as I saw most convenient; with sixty, or at least thirty picked men about him, who should not only carry his orders properly and distinctly to the different parts of the army, but be able to repel the enemy if he should be attacked.—In this manner I would form the regiment on the left, which would be just one half of the army, and will occupy a space of five hundred and seventy-two feet in breadth, and four hundred in depth, exclusive of the space taken up by the forty ranks of pikemen extraordinary that are to guard the baggage, &c. in the rear, which will be two hundred feet.

The other regiment I would draw up in the same manner on the right of this, with an interval betwixt them of sixty feet: and at the head of this interval I would place some pieces of artillery, behind which, the general of the army should take post with his standard and drum, and two hundred picked men at least, most of them on foot; of whom there should be ten or more fit to carry any orders; and he himself should be mounted and armed in such a manner that he might command either on horseback or on foot, as occasion required.

As for artillery, ten fifty pounders would be sufficient for the reduction of a town; and I would make use of them rather to defend my camp than in a field engagement; for my field pieces should be ten or fifteen pounders, and these I would place. along the front of the whole army, except the ground was such that I could place them conveniently and safely in the flanks where the enemy could not come at them. This method of drawing up an army may answer the end both of the Grecian Phalanx and the Roman Legion: for you have the pikemen in the front, and all the rest of the infantry are so formed in their proper ranks, that either in charging an enemy, or sustaining the charge, they may (like the *phalanx*) recruit their front ranks out of those in the rear.

On the other hand, if they are so hard pushed that they are obliged to give way, they may retreat into the intervals of the second line, and advance again in conjunction with it to face the enemy: and if they are repulsed the second time, they may retire into the spaces betwixt the battalions in the third line, and renew the battle with still greater vigour: so that, according to this method, you may reinforce your ranks either in the Grecian or the Roman manner.

As to the strength of such an army, no body can be more compact: for each wing is perfectly well fortified in every part, both with officers and private men properly armed, and appointed in such a manner, that if there is any apparent weakness in it, it must be in the rear where the carriages and suttlers, &c. are stationed; and even those are covered by the pikemen extraordinary. Being so well fortified therefore on all sides, an enemy cannot attack it anywhere but it will be ready to receive him: for the rear is in no danger; because if the enemy be so strong that he is able to attack you on every side at once, it must be madness in you to take the field against him.

But supposing he should be superior to you in number by one third, and his army as well armed and drawn up as your own; if he weakens it in order to attack you in several parts at the same time, and you happen to break in upon him in any one, the day is your own. As to cavalry, you have nothing to apprehend from them; for the pikemen which environ you on all sides will sufficiently secure you against their fury, even though your own should be repulsed. Your officers are so conveniently posted, that they may do their duty with ease; and the spaces betwixt one battalion and another, and betwixt every rank, not only serve to receive each other upon occasion, but give the officers sufficient room to go backwards and forwards with orders from the general.

Now as I told you before, that the Romans had about twenty-four thousand men in their armies, I would have our army consist of the same number: and as their auxiliaries learnt their discipline and order from their legions, I would have our auxiliaries likewise formed upon the model of our regiments. These things may easily be effected by a little practice: for in adding two other regiments to the army, or the same number of men that it consists of (let it be what it will) you have nothing to do but to double your ranks by placing twenty battalions on the left, instead of ten, and as many more on the right; or to extend or contract them, according to the nature of the ground, and the posture of the enemy.

Luigi. I perfectly understand you, Sir. Methinks I see your army drawn up for battle. I am impatient to have it begin. For Heaven's Sake do not turn Fabius Maximus upon us: if I do, I am afraid I shall be tempted to abuse you as the Romans did that great man.

Fabrizio. I am ready. The signal is given. Do not you hear our artillery? It has fired and done but little execution amongst the enemy. The *velites* extraordinary and light horse have set up a great shout and begun the attack with the utmost fury. The enemy's artillery has made one discharge; and being ill-pointed, their balls have gone over the heads of our infantry without doing them any hurt: but to prevent it firing a second time, our *velites* and light horse endeavour to make themselves matters of it: a body of the enemy post themselves before it; so that the artillery on both sides is become useless. See with what courage and dexterity our men charge them: the expertness they have acquired by long exercise and discipline, inspires them with confidence: the battalions move forward in regular pace and good order, with the *gens d'armes* on their flanks to attack the enemy: our artillery draws off through the space that was left vacant by the *velites* to make room for it.

See how the general encourages his men, and assures them of victory. Observe our *velites* and light horse returning, and extending themselves along the flanks of our army, to see if they can meet with any of the enemy's light-armed forces there.—The two armies are now engaged: see with what firmness and silence our men receive the charge: do not you hear the general giving his orders to the *gens d'armes* to maintain their ground, and not to advance upon the enemy, nor desert the infantry upon any account whatsoever? You see a party of our light horse have now detached themselves to charge a body of the enemy's musketeers that were coming to take us in flank; and how the enemy's cavalry are advancing to support them: but the musketeers, to avoid being entangled betwixt them, are retiring to their own army. See with what resolution and dexterity our ordinary pikemen handle their weapons: but the infantry on each side are now come so close together that our pikemen can no longer make any use of their pikes; and therefore, according to their usual discipline, they retreat by degrees till they are received by the targetmen.

You see how a large body of the enemy's *gens d'armes* have in the mean time disordered our *gens d'armes* on the left, who retire (as they had learnt before) into the pikemen extraordinary, and being supported by them, not only make head against the enemy again, but repulse them with great slaughter. Now the ordinary pikemen of the first battalions have retreated amongst the targetmen; they leave them to maintain the battle, and behold what havoc they make amongst the enemy; with what confidence and security they press upon them; see how close they are engaged with them, they hardly have room to manage their swords.

The enemy are embarrassed and falling into confusion: their pikes are too long to do any further execution, and their swords are of no service against men that are so well secured by their armour. What a carnage! what a number of wounded men! They begin to run away. See, they are flying on the right and on the left. The battle is over; we have gained a glorious victory.—It might have been more complete however, if we had exerted our whole strength. But you see we were under no necessity of employing either our second or third line, as the first was sufficient to do the business: so that I have nothing mere to add upon this occasion; except it be to answer any objection or doubt you may have to propose.

Luigi. You have carried everything before you with such amazing rapidity, that I cannot well tell whether I ought to start any objection or not. With submission however to your superior judgement, I will make bold to ask you a question or two. Be so good therefore to tell me, in the first place, why you would suffer your artillery to fire no more than once: and why you ordered it to be drawn off so soon, without making any sort of use of it afterwards.

In the next place, you managed that of the enemy just as you pleased, and had it pointed so ill, that it could do no execution: which indeed I suppose may be the case sometimes; but if it should happen (as I believe it often does) that the shot should take place, what remedy would you prescribe? And since I have mentioned artillery, I will here propose all that I have to say upon that subject, that so we may have no occasion to return. to it hereafter. I have heard many people laugh at the arms and armour, and military discipline, of the ancients, and say they would be of little or no service at all now, since the invention of artillery, which would break all their ranks, and beat their armour to pieces: so that it would be folly to draw up a body of forces in such order as cannot be maintained, and undergo the fatigue of carrying armour, which can be no means secure them.

Fabrizio. Your objections are of several kinds; and therefore you must have patience if you expect a particular answer to them all. It is true our artillery made but one discharge, and I was in some doubt whether I should suffer even that; because it is of more importance to keep one's self from being hurt, than to annoy the enemy. Now in order to secure yourself from artillery, you must either keep out of the reach of its shot, or place yourself behind a wall, or a bank, or some fence of that kind; there is no other cover that I know of, and that must be very strong. But when an army is drawn up in order to engage, it cannot skulk behind a wall or a bank, nor yet keep at such a distance as not to be annoyed by the enemy's artillery. Since there is no method then to shelter one's self from it, the general must have recourse to such means as will expose him and his men to the least danger; for which purpose, the best, and indeed the only way, is to make themselves masters of it, if possible, and as soon as they can.

To do this, it is necessary that a body of your men should march up, and rush suddenly upon it; but not in close order: because the suddenness of the attack will prevent it from firing more than once; and when your men are thinly drawn up, it cannot do much execution amongst them. Now a compact body of regular forces is not at all proper for this service: for if it moves fast, it must naturally fall into disorder of itself; and if it extend and weakens its ranks, it will presently be broken by the enemy: upon which considerations, I drew up my army in a manner that was most proper for such an attempt; for having placed a thousand *velites* in the wings of it, I ordered them to advance, together with the light horse, as soon as our artillery had fired, to seize upon that of the enemy.

This is the reason why I would not suffer our own to make a second discharge, lest the enemy should have time to do the same, as they easily might have done, and perhaps before our artillery was loaded again, if I had not taken these means to prevent it. So that the only way to make the enemy's artillery of no service, is to attack it as soon as possible: for if they desert it, it falls into your hands of course; but if they defend it, they must place a body of forces before it, and then they will not dare to fire it again, because their own men must be the chief sufferers by it.—These reasons, I think, might be sufficient of themselves, without quoting any examples to support them: but as antiquity furnishes us with many, I will give you one or two.

When Ventidius had resolved to come to an engagement with the Parthians (whose strength consisted chiefly in their bows and arrows) he differed them to advance almost to the very entrenchments of his camp before he drew out his army: and this he did, that he might fall suddenly upon them, and before they could make use of their arrows. Caesar tells us, that in a battle with the Gauls, they made so sudden and furious an attack upon him, that his men had not time to throw their darts at the enemy, as the Romans always used to do. Now from these instances, we see, that in order to secure an army in the field from the effects of any weapons or engines that annoy them at a distance, there is no other way, but to march up to them as fast as possible, and get possession of them, if you can, or at least to prevent their effects.

Besides all these, I had still another reason which determined me to fire my artillery no more than once: perhaps it may seem trifling to you; but with me it has much weight. There is nothing that occasions greater confusion and embarrassment amongst a body of men, than to have their fight dazzled or obstructed: a circumstance which has been the ruin of many gallant armies that have been blinded either by the sun or clouds of dust: and what can contribute more to that than the smoke of artillery? It would be more prudent therefore to let the enemy blind themselves, than to go blindfold yourself to seek them: for which reason, I would either not make any use of artillery at all, or if I did (to avoid censure now great guns are in such credit) I would plant it in the flanks of my army; that so when it was fired, the smoke might not blind the men in my front, where I would have the flower of my army.

The effects of that may be seen from the conduct of Epaminondas, who going to engage the enemy, caused all his light horse to trot backwards and forwards a great pace in the front of their army, which raised such a dust that it threw them into disorder, and gave him an easy victory over them.—As for my seeming to have pointed the enemy's artillery as I pleased, and made the shot fly over the heads of our infantry; I answer, that it much oftener happens so than otherwise: for infantry stands so low, and it is so nice a matter to manage heavy pieces of cannon well, that if you either elevate or lower them ever so little too much, in one case the balls will fly quite over their heads, and in the other, they strike into the earth, and never come near them: the least inequality of ground likewise is a great preservation to them; for any little bank or brake betwixt them and the artillery, serves either to intercept the shot, or divert their direction.

And as to cavalry, especially *gens d'armes* (because they are drawn up in a closer order, and stand so much higher than light horse, that they are more exposed to danger) they may continue in the rear of the army till the artillery has fired. It is certain that small pieces of cannon and musket-shot, do more execution than heavy artillery; against which, the best remedy is to make a resolute attack upon it as soon as possible: and if you lose some of your men in it, (which must always be the case) surely a partial loss is not so bad as a total defeat. The

Swiss are worthy of imitation in this respect: for they never decline an engagement out of fear of artillery; but always punish those with death who offer to stir out of their ranks, or shew the least sign of being frighted at it.

I caused my artillery therefore to be drawn off as soon as it had been discharged, in order to make room for the battalions to advance; and made no further mention of it, as a thing of no consequence after the two armies had joined battle.—You say likewise, that many people laugh at the arms and armour, and military discipline of the ancients, as good for nothing since the invention of artillery: from whence one would be apt to imagine the moderns had made effectual provision against it. If so, I should be glad to hear what that provision is; for I confess I know of none, nor do I think it possible to make any, but what I have already mentioned. Why do our infantry at present wear corslets? and why are our *gens d'armes* covered with armour from head to foot? If they despise this manner of arming among the ancients, as of no service against artillery, why do they continue to use it themselves?

I could likewise wish to be informed, why the Swiss, (like the ancients) form their regiments of six or eight thousand foot, drawn up in close order; and for what reason all other nations have began to imitate them; since that method exposes their armies to no less danger, (with regard to artillery) than many other institutions that were in vogue amongst the ancients, but are neglected and laid aside at present? These are questions, which I fancy the people whom you mention cannot easily answer: but if you would propose them to soldiers of judgement and experience, they would tell you, that they arm themselves in that manner, not because they think such armour will effectually secure them against cannon balls, but because it will defend them against crossbows, pikes, swords, and many other offensive weapons, which an enemy may make use of.

They will tell you further, that the close order observed by the Swiss, is necessary to make an impression upon the enemy's infantry, to sustain their cavalry, and to prevent themselves from being easily broken: so that we see soldiers have many other things to dread besides artillery, against which this order, and this sort of arms and armour, serve to secure them. Hence it follows, that the better an army is armed, and the closer and stronger it is drawn up, the less it has to fear: and therefore the persons whose opinion you alleged not long ago, must either have had very little experience, or not have considered the matter in the light they ought to have done.

For since we find that only the pikes and close order of the ancients, (still in use amongst the Swiss, as at time of first publication) have done such wonderful service, and contribute to much to the strength of our armies at present; why may we not conclude, that the rest of the military institutions observed by the ancients (but now entirely laid aside and neglected) might be equally serviceable? Besides, as the fury of artillery does not make us afraid of drawing up our battalions in close order, like the Swiss; certainly there can be no other disposition contrived that can make us more apprehensive of its effects.

Further, if we are not terrified at the enemy's artillery in laying siege to a town, when it may annoy us with the greatest security, and we can neither come at it, nor prevent its effects, because it is covered by walls; but must endeavour to dismount it with our own cannon, which perhaps may require much time, and expose us to a continual fire all the while; why should we so much fear it in the field, where we may presently either make ourselves masters of it, or put a stop to its firing? The invention of artillery therefore, is no reason, in my opinion, why we should not imitate the ancients in their military discipline and institutions, as well as their courage: and if this matter had not been thoroughly discussed in a piece lately published, (*Political Discussions*, book II) I would have dwelt longer upon it at present: but for brevity's fake I refer you to that discourse.

Luigi. I have read it, and am of opinion upon the whole, that you have sufficiently shewn, that the best remedy against artillery, is to seize upon it as soon as you can; that is, in a field battle. But suppose the enemy should place it in the flanks of their army; where it would still gall you, and yet be so well secured, that you could not make yourself master of it. For in drawing up your army, you may remember that you left an interval of eight feet betwixt every battalion, and of forty betwixt the battalions and the pikemen extraordinary: now if the enemy should form their army in the same order, and place their artillery deep in those intervals, I should think it would annoy you very much, without any *risque* of being taken, because you could not come at it there.

Fabrizio. Your objection carries much weight with it; and therefore I will endeavour either to take it off, or to find same remedy in that case. I told you before, that the battalions, when engaged with an enemy, are in constant motion, and of consequence must draw closer and closer to each other; so that if you leave but small intervals betwixt them for the artillery, they will soon be filled up in such a manner, that it cannot be of any service: but if you make them large, in order to avoid that inconvenience, you must naturally run into a much greater; because you then leave room enough for the enemy to rush into them, and not only seize upon your artillery, but throw your whole army into confusion.

But to make short of the matter, I beg leave to tell you once for all, that it is impossible to place your cannon betwixt your battalions, especially such as are fixed upon carriages: for as they are drawn one way, and point another, they must all be turned into a different direction before they can be fired; and to do that, will require so large a space, that fifty pieces would disorder any army: so that they must of necessity be placed somewhere out of the battalions; and then they may be come at in the manner I have already prescribed. Let us suppose however, that they could be placed within the battalions, and that we could hit upon some medium, which on one hand would prevent the battalions from frustrating the effects of the artillery when they drew closer together; and on the other, not leave the intervals betwixt them so large, that the enemy might push into them: I say, that even then a method might be found to elude its force, by opening counter-intervals in the enemy's army, to let your shot pass through without doing any execution.

For to secure your artillery effectually, perhaps you would place it at the very bottom of the intervals betwixt your battalions; in which case, (to avoid killing your own men) it must be pointed in such a manner, as to throw its shot directly and continually through the interval it is planted in; and therefore, by opening such another interval right over-against it in the enemy's army, they will pass through it without doing them any damage at all: for it is a general rule, always to give way to such things as cannot be opposed; as the ancients used to do when they were attacked by elephants and armed chariots.

You see I gained a victory with an army formed and appointed in the manner I recommended; and I must beg leave to repeat (if what I have already said be not sufficient) that such an army must of necessity defeat any other, at the very first onset, that is armed and drawn up like ours at present, which, for the most part can make but one front, is entirely unprovided with targets, and not only armed in such a manner, that they cannot defend themselves against an enemy that closes with them, but so formed, that if they post their battalions flank to flank, they make their lines too thin and feeble; and if they place them in the rear of each other, not having any method of receiving one another, they soon fall into confusion, and are easily broken. And though indeed they are divided into three bodies, called the vanguard, the main-battle, and the rearguard; yet this division is of no use, except upon a march, or to distinguish them in an encampment: for in engagement they are combined, and therefore all liable to be defeated at once by the first shock.

Luigi. I further observed in your late battle, that your cavalry were repulsed, and forced to take cover under the pikemen extraordinary, by whose assistance, they not only made head against, the enemy a second time, but repulsed them in their turn. Now I am persuaded that pikemen may support cavalry in a thick and close drawn-up body like the Swiss regiments: but in your army there are but five ranks of pikemen in the front, and seven on the flanks; so that I cannot see how they can keep off a body of horse,

Fabrizio. Though I told you before, that six ranks of pikemen might charge at a time in the Macedonian Phalanx, yet I must now add, that if a Swiss regiment consisted of a thousand ranks, no more than four or five of them at most could charge at one: for their pikes being eighteen feet long, three feet we may imagine must be taken up betwixt one hand and the other: so that the first rank would have but fifteen feet to make use of: in the second, besides the three feet betwixt the men's hands, as much more must be taken up by the distance betwixt one rank and another, and then there would be but twelve feet of the pike that could be of any service: the third, for the same reasons, would have but nine feet; the fourth but six; and the fifth but three: the other ranks behind could make no use at all of their pikes, but serve to recruit and support the first five ranks, as we have shewn before.

If then five of their ranks could keep off the enemy's cavalry, why cannot our five do the same, as they likewise have other ranks in their rear to support them, though they have not pikes like the others? And if the ranks of pikemen extraordinary, which are placed upon the flanks of our army, may seem to you too thin, they may be reduced into a square, and posted on the flanks of the two battalions in the rear; from which place they may succour either the front or rear, and assist the horse upon occasion.

Luigi. Would you always then make use of this form and order of battle, whenever you are to engage an enemy?

Fabrizio. No. I would always suit my order of battle to the nature of my ground, the quality and number of the enemy, as I shall shew you before we part. But I recommended this order not only as the best, (as it certainly is) but as a rule to direct and assist you in forming others: for every art has its general rules and principles upon which it is founded. One thing however, I would have you remember, and that is, never to draw up an army upon any occasion in such a manner, that the front cannot be relieved by the rear: for whoever is guilty of that error, prevents the greatest part of his army from doing him any service at all, and will never gain a victory over an enemy that has the least degree either of courage or conduct.

Luigi. I confess I have still another ejection to the order in which you disposed your army. You made your front consist of five battalions, posted on the flank of each other: your second line of three: and your third of two. Now I should think it would be better to invert that order: for surely it must be more difficult to break that army which is stronger and stronger the farther you penetrate into it, than another that is weaker and weaker.

Fabrizio If you will please to recollect that the third line in the Roman Legions was composed of six hundred *triarii* only, and that they were placed in the rear, you would drop your objection: for you see that, according to that model, I have placed but two battalions in the rear, which yet consists of nine hundred men: so that if I have been guilty of any error in following the example of the Romans in that respect, it is by making my rear stronger than they did. Now though the authority alone of such an example might serve for a sufficient answer to your objection, yet I will give you my reasons for what I have done.—The front ranks of an army ought always to be thick and compact, because they are so sustain the first shock of the enemy, and have no friends to receive into them: for which reason, they should be close and full of men; otherwise they will be loose and feeble.

But as the second line is to receive the first into it upon occasion before it is to engage, there should be large intervals left in it for that purpose; and therefore it must not consist of so many men, as the first: for if the number of them was either larger, or but barely equal, you must either leave no intervals in it, (which would occasion confusion) or if you do, it will be longer than the first, which would be out of proportion, and make a strange appearance. As to what you say of the enemy finding our army weaker and weaker the farther they penetrate into it, it is a manifest error: for they cannot come to engage the second line, till it has received the first: into it: so that they will find the second line much stronger than the first was, when they are both united, and the third line still stronger than either of the other two, because they will then have the strength of the whole army to cope with at once: and as the third line is to receive more men than the second, it is necessary it should have larger intervals in it, and consequently consist of fewer men of its own.

Luigi. I am thoroughly satisfied in this point. But if the five battalions in the front retire into the three that are in the second line; and afterwards those eight into the two that are in the rear, it does not seem possible that the eight battalions in the second line, much less the ten in the third, can be contained in the same space of ground that the first five were.

Fabrizio. To this I answer in the first place, that the space of ground is not the same in that case: for there were intervals betwixt the first five, which are filled up when they retire into the second line, and the second into the third: there was likewise an interval betwixt the two regiments, and betwixt them and the pikemen extraordinary, which all together afford them room enough. Besides, the battalions take up different spaces of ground whilst they keep their ranks, and when they are disordered: for in the latter case, the men either get closer together, or extend themselves. They extend themselves when they are so hard pressed, that they are going to run away; and they keep closer together when they are determined to make an obstinate resistance.

I might add, that when the five ranks of pikemen in the front have done their business, they retire through the intervals betwixt the battalions, into the rear, to make way for the targetmen to advance upon the enemy; where they will be ready for any service, in which the General shall think fit to employ them: for in the front they could be of no further use after the two armies were close engaged: and thus the space allotted will be sufficient to contain the whole army. But if it should not, the flanks being composed of men, and not stone walls, can easily open and extend themselves in such a manner as to make room enough.

Luigi. When the five first battalions retire into the three in the second line, would you have the pikemen extraordinary, whom you place in the flanks of your army, stand fast in their ranks, and form two horns as it were to the army? or would you have them likewise retire with the battalions? In the latter case, I cannot imagine whither they are to retire, as they have no battalions in their rear with proper intervals to receive them.

Fabrizio. If the enemy does not attack them at the same time that the battalions are forced to retire, those pikemen may continue firm in their station, and take the enemy in the flanks, as they are pressing upon the battalions in their retreat: but if they are attacked at the same time (as most likely they will be) they also must retire; which they may do very well, though they have no battalions in their rear to receive them, by doubling their ranks in a right line to the centre, and receiving one rank into another, in the manner I shewed you a while ago. But to double them in order to retreat, you must observe a different method from that which I then spoke of: for in that case, I told you the first rank must receive the second, the third the fourth, and so on: but in this you must begin in the rear instead of the front, that so the ranks may retreat, and not advance in doubling each other. But to answer the whole of what may be objected to the manner in which I conducted the late battle, I must beg leave to tell you again, that I drew it up and caused it to engage, in the first place, to shew you how an army ought to be formed in order of battle; and in the next, how it should be exercised.

The order, I make no doubt, you now perfectly comprehend; and as to the exercise, I say that the regiments ought to be joined together, and exercised in this manner as often as possible; that so the officers may learn to post their battalions in their proper places: for as every private man should know his own rank, and place in that rank, so every lieutenant colonel should know where to station his battalion in the army, and all of them learn to obey their general. They should likewise know how to join one battalion with another, and to take their respective posts in an instant: for which purpose, the colours of every battalion should have their number marked upon them in such a manner as to be visible to everyone, not only to distinguish the battalions from one another, but that the lieutenant colonel of every battalion, and his men, may the more easily know where to find each other.

The regiments ought likewise to be numbered, and their numbers marked upon the colonel's colours, in order to know which regiment is posted on the right, and which on the left; what battalions are placed in the first, second, or third line, &c. There should likewise be regular steps and gradations to preferment in our army: for instance, the lowest officer should be a corporal, the next above him, a captain of fifty ordinary *velites*, the next, a captain of a company in the battalions, the next, the lieutenant colonel of the tenth battalion, the next, the lieutenant colonel of the ninth, the next, the lieutenant colonel of the eighth, and so on in succession, till you come to the lieutenant colonel of the first battalion, who should be next in command to the colonel of the regiment; to which post nobody should be advanced, till he had passed through all the subordinate degrees just now mentioned.

But as there are also three lieutenant colonels of the pikemen extraordinary, and two of the extraordinary *velites*, I would have them rank with the lieutenant colonel of the tenth battalion: for I see no absurdity in having six officers of equal rank in the same regiment, as it may serve to create an emulation amongst them, and excite every one of them to behave himself in such a manner, as to be thought worthy of being preferred to the command of the ninth battalion. Every one of these officers then knowing where his corps is to be posted, the whole army will presently be in proper order, as soon as the general's standard is erected. This is the first exercise an army should be accustomed to; that is, to range itself immediately in order of battle upon occasion: for which purpose, it should be drawn up and separated again, not only every day, but several times in the day.

Luigi. What other marks of distinction would you have upon the colours besides their particular number?

Fabrizio. The general's standard should have the arms of his prince upon it: the others may have the same, with some variation of the field or colours, as the prince shall think fit: for that is a matter of no great moment, provided they are sufficient to distinguish one corps from another. But let us now pass on to another sort of exercise, in which an army ought to be very ready and expert; and that is, the learning to move in due pace and distance, and to keep its ranks when it is in motion. The third kind of exercise is to teach the men to act as they should do, when they are actually engaged with an enemy; to discharge the artillery, to draw it off; to cause the *velites* extraordinary to begin the attack, and then to retire; to make the first line fall back into the second, as if it was hard pressed, and then the second into the third; and afterwards to resume their first stations; and to use them so frequently to these and other such things, that every man may know every part of his duty, which will soon become easy and familiar to him by practice.

The next exercise is to instruct your men in the nature of signals, and how to act by beat of drum, sound of trumpet, or particular motion of the colours: for such orders as are given by word of mouth, they will easily understand. And as different notes and sounds are of great importance, and have various effects, I will tell you what forts of military music were used by the ancients. The Lacedaemonians, as Thucydides informs us, made use of flutes in their armies, as the most proper instrument to make them move regularly and resolutely, but not with precipitation. The Carthaginians, for the same reason, used harps in their first attack: Halyattes, King of Lydia, made use of both: but Alexander the Great, and the Romans, used horns and trumpets, which they thought the fitted instruments to rouse the courage of their men, and inspire them with martial ardour.

But as we have imitated both the Greeks and Romans in arming our men, we will also borrow our military music from each of those nations The general then should have its trumpets about him, as the properest instruments to animate his army, and such as may be heard farther than any other. The lieutenant colonels and other officers of the battalions should have small drums and flutes, not to be played upon as they commonly are, but in the same manner that they are founded at great banquets and other festivities.

With these trumpets the general may presently make his army understand when he would have it either halt, or advance, or retreat; when he would have the artillery discharged, and the *velites* extraordinary move forwards; and by various notes and sounds acquaint them with all the different manoeuvres he thinks necessary to be made: which signals should afterwards be repeated by the drums: and in this the whole army should frequently be exercised, because it is of the utmost consequence. As to the cavalry, they may have trumpets too, but of a smaller size and different sound. This is all that occurs to my memory at present, as necessary for the forming and exercising an army.

Luigi. I have but one question more to propose, and hope it will not tire your patience if I ask why the *velites* extraordinary and light horse in the late battle began the attack with a great shout? whereas there was a dead silence when the rest of the army began to engage. I confess I am at a loss to account for this, and therefore beg the favour of you to explain it to us.

Fabrizio. Various are the opinions of ancient authors concerning this matter; that is, whether those that begin the battle should rush on with furious shouts and outcries, or march up to the attack with silence and composure. The latter way is certainly the most proper to preserve good order, and for hearing words of command more distinctly; the former, to animate your own men, and dismay the enemy:

and as I think some regard ought to be had to all these circumstances, I made one part of my army begin with a great shout; the other with profound silence.

But I do not think a continual shout can be of any service, but quite the contrary; because it will prevent the general's orders from being heard, which must be attended with terrible consequences; nor it is reasonable to suppose the Romans used any such shouts after the first onset; as we read in many parts of their history, that when their armies were beginning to give way, it was often prevented by the exhortations and reproaches of their commanders; and that their order of battle was sometimes changed even in the heat of action; which things could not have been done, if the voice of the officers had been drowned in the shouts of the soldiers.

Book 4

Of several precautions and artifices that are to be made use of both in drawing up an army for battle, and in the action, and after it is over. Two other ways of forming an army. That a general ought never to hazard an engagement, except he either has an advantage over the enemy, or is compelled to it. Some rules to be observed by a general. How to avoid a battle when the enemy is determined to engage at all events. In what manner soldiers are to be animated to fight: and how their ardour is to be abated when it runs to high. That a general ought to be an orator as well as a soldier, and to harangue his men some times, in order to should them to his particular purposes: That religion animates soldiers, and keeps them in their duty. That it is proper to inspire them with a contempt of the enemy; and sometimes to lay them under a necessity of fighting bravely.

Luigi. Since we have gained one glorious victory under my auspices, I do not care to tempt so fickle and inconstant a Deity as Fortune any further: upon which account I desire to give up my post to Zanobi Buondelmonti (the youngest man in company who has not yet filled it) according to the order agreed upon; and dare say he will accept that honour, (or rather trouble) both out of complaisance to me, and because he has naturally more courage and spirit than falls to my share, and will not be afraid of *risquing* another battle, in which he has a chance to be beaten as well as to conquer.

Zanobi. Sir, I shall willingly accept whatever you think fit to confer upon me; though I confess I had much rather have continued an auditor: for the questions you proposed, and the objections you started, whilst you was in the post you now desire to resign, were much more pertinent and necessary than any that occurred to me. But not to throw away any more time in ceremonies, which perhaps may be disagreeable to Signor Fabrizio, let us intreat him to proceed, if we have not already trespassed too much upon his patience.

Fabrizio. That I will do with great pleasure, especially as this change of persons will give me an opportunity of seeing the difference of your respective judgements and dispositions. But I should be glad to know whether you have any more questions to ask relating to the matter we were last engaged in.

Zanobi. I could which to be informed of three things before we quit it; in the first place, whether there be any other way of forming an army in order of battle that you can think of at present? in the next, what precautions are necessary before a general leads his army on to engage the enemy; and if any accident or disorder should happen during the battle, in what manner it is to be remedied?

Fabrizio. I will endeavour to give you what satisfaction I can in these points. But I shall not answer your questions separately and distinctly: because what I shall lay in answer to one question may sometimes possibly serve likewise as an answer to another.—I told you before, that I gave you a general order of battle, which you might easily change into any other, as the number and quality of the enemy, and the nature of your ground, shall require: for you must always act according to those circumstances. But let me desire you to remember that you cannot be guilty of a greater or more fatal error than in making a large extensive front, except your army be very numerous: for if it is not, you ought by all means to form it in such a manner that it may be deeper than it is wide.

For when your army is not so large as that of the enemy, you must have recourse to other expedients, such as drawing it up so that it may be flanked by some river or morass, or securing it in that part by ditches and entrenchments to prevent it being surrounded, as Julius Caesar used to do in his wars with the Gauls. But you must make it a general rule in such cases to contract or extend your front according to the number of your own men and those of the enemy; and when you are superior to them in that respect, you should endeavour to draw them into plains and open places, especially if your army is well disciplined, that so you may extend your front and surround them: for in rough and narrow places your superiority of number will not be of any great advantage to you, because you cannot give your ranks their due extent: upon which account, the Romans always made choice of clear open ground, and avoided such a field of battle as was rough and confined.

On the contrary, if you have but a small army and ill-disciplined, you must seek out for an advantageous situation to shelter your men, and where their inexperience cannot be of much prejudice to you: it will be better still if it be upon an eminence, from whence you may fall down upon the enemy with greater weight. You should take care however not to draw up your army either upon the declivity of a hill, or any place near the skirts of it, where an enemy may get above you: for in that case you will be much annoyed by their artillery, and your men so embarrassed that you cannot annoy the enemy again with your own cannon.

Great regard is likewise to be had to the wind and sun in forming an army for battle: for if you have them in your face, one will dazzle your light with its rays, the other will blind you with dust. Besides, when the wind is against you, it will diminish the force of your blows: and as to the sun, you must not only take care that it is not in your face when the battle begins, but that it may not afterwards be troublesome to you. For which purpose, you should contrive to have it full upon your back at first, if possible; that so it may be a great while before it comes upon your face: as Hannibal did at Cannae, and Marius when he defeated the Cimbrians. If you are inferior to the enemy in horse, post your army amongst vineyards and hedges, and other such impediments, when you have an opportunity; as the Spaniards did not long ago, when they beat the French at Cirignuola in the Kingdom of Naples.

It has likewise often happened that the same armies which have been beaten by others, have beat them again in their turn, only by changing their order and their ground: the Carthaginians, for instance, having been several times defeated by Marcus Regulus, in rough and narrow defiles, were at last victorious by the conduct of Xantippus the Lacedaemonian, who advised them to come down into the plains, where they availed themselves of their elephants and cavalry in such a manner, that they fairly beat the Romans.

I have observed from the conduct of many great generals amongst the ancients, that when they knew where the enemy placed the main strength of their army, instead of employing the flower of their own forces, they appointed the worst they had to oppose them in that quarter, and the best of their troops to oppose the worst of the enemy: but afterwards, when the battle was begun, they ordered their choicest troops not to press upon the enemy, but only to sustain the charge, and the weakest to retire by degrees into the rear of the army: for by these means the best part of the enemy's army is insensibly surrounded, and whilst they think themselves sure of a victory, they are presently thrown into confusion and routed.

Thus, when Cornelius Scipio was sent into Spain against Asdrubal the Carthaginian, being aware that Asdrubal thought he would place the legions (which were his best troops) in the centre of his army, and that Asdrubal would therefore do the same; when they came to an engagement, he changed his usual order of battle, placing the legions in the two wings, and the worst of his forces in the centre of his army. But just before the battle began, he ordered the centre to move forwards very slowly, and the two wings to advance briskly: so that the wings only of both armies were engaged, whilst the centre of each was at such a distance from one another, that they could not come together in due time; and the strongest part of Scipio's army being engaged with the weakest of Asdrubal's, the latter was entirely defeated.

This method might be practised in those times, but it cannot at present, now artillery is in use: for the distance which must be left betwixt the centre of each army would give the artillery time to fire again and again, which would do as much mischief as if they were close engaged. It is time therefore lay it aside, and to have recourse to the method I prescribed a little while ago; that is, to let the whole army engage, and the weakest part of it give way.—If your army is larger than that of the enemy, and you want to surround them without discovering your design, let your own be drawn up with a front equal to theirs, and afterwards, when the battle is begun, let your main body retire by little and little, and the wings extend themselves: by which the enemy will find themselves surrounded and entangled before they were aware of it.

When a general would secure his army in such a manner that he may be almost: certain of not being routed if he comes to an engagement, he should post it in some place from whence he may easily and presently retreat into a safe and defensible situation, as behind a morass, or amongst mountains, or into some strong fortress, whither the enemy cannot pursue him, though he may pursue them upon occasion: as Hannibal used to do in the ebb of his fortune, when he began to be afraid of Marcus Marcellus. Some generals, in order to disturb and disconcert the enemy, have ordered their light-armed troops to begin the battle, and then to retire into their proper station again; and after both armies were, warmly engaged, to sally out from the flanks again and make a second attack, which has sometimes succeeded so well, that the enemy has been thrown into disorder and routed by it.

If you are inferior to the enemy in horse (besides the methods already recommended) you should place a body of pikemen in their rear; and in the heat of action, let the horse open to the right and left to make way for the pikemen to advance upon the enemy, which will certainly give you the advantage over them: some have accustomed part of their light-armed infantry to mingle with their horse, and to fight in conjunction with them, which has been of very great service to them.

But of all those that have excelled in drawing up armies in order of battle, without doubt Hannibal and Scipio shewed the most consummate skill and abilities in the African wars: for as Hannibal's army consisted not only of Carthaginians, but auxiliaries of various nations, he placed eighty elephants in his front; next to them his auxiliaries; behind them, his Carthaginians; and last of all, his Italians, in whom he put but little confidence. His design in this disposition was, that his auxiliaries having the enemy in their front, and the Carthaginians in their rear, should not have an opportunity of running away if they were so inclined; but being under a necessity of fighting, he hoped they might either break or disconcert the Romans in such a manner, that when he advanced with a fresh body of his best troops, he might entirely defeat them.

Scipio, on the other hand, drew up his three lines of *hastati, principes*, and *triarii* (after the usual manner of the Romans) in such order that they might easily support or receive each other. In the front of his army, he left several intervals over against Hannibal's elephants: but to make it appear close and united, he filled them up with *velites*, whom he ordered to give way as soon as the elephants advanced upon them, and retire through the ordinary spaces into the legions, in order to leave a free passage for the elephants: by which means he evaded the fury of those beasts, and coming to a close engagement with the enemy, entirely defeated them.

Zanobi. Now you mention that battle, I remember to have read in some account of it, that Scipio did not suffer the *hastati* to retire into the line of the *principes*, but caused them to file off to the right and left, and take post in the flanks of his army, to make room for the *principes* to advance. Now I should be glad to know for what reason he deviated from the usual order and discipline of the Romans upon this occasion.

Fabrizio. I will tell you. Hannibal had placed the strength of his army in the second line: Scipio therefore, in order to oppose him with equal force, joined his *principes* and *triarii* together, so that the intervals amongst the *principes* being taken up by the *triarii*, there was no room left to receive the *hastati*: upon which account, he caused them to open to the right and left, and wheel off to the flanks. But remember that this method of opening the first line to make room for the second to advance, cannot be made use of but when you have the advantage over the enemy; for then it may easily be put in practice, as it was by Scipio: but if you have the word of the battle, and are repulsed, you cannot do it without exposing yourself to the danger of a total defeat: and therefore it is necessary to have intervals in the second and third lines, to receive your men upon such occasions.—But to return to our subject.

The ancient Asiatics, amongst other inventions to annoy the enemy, had chariots with scythes fixed to their axletrees, which served not only to open the enemy's ranks, but to mow them down as they drove through them. Now there were three ways of guarding against these dangerous machines: for the enemy either drew up in such close order, that they could make no impression upon them; or received them in the intervals betwixt the battalions, as Scipio did the elephants; or made some strong fence against them, as Sylla did in the battle he fought with Archelaus, who had a great number of these armed chariots: for he fixed several rows of sharp-pointed stakes or *palisadoes* in the ground before his first line, which stopped the career of the chariots, and prevented the execution they must otherwise have done.

The new method which Sylla used in drawing up his army at that time, is likewise worthy of notice: for he placed his *velites* and light horse in the rear, and all his heavy-armed men in the front, leaving several intervals in it, through which those in the rear might advance when occasion required; by which means he gained a complete victory.—In order to throw the enemy into confusion after the battle is begun, it is necessary to have recourse to some invention that may strike a terror into them: which may be done either by spreading a report that you have succours corning up, or making a false shew of such supplies at a distance; which has often occasioned such a consternation in an army, that it has been presently defeated.

This stratagem was put in a practice by the Roman consuls, Minucius Ruffus and Accilius Glabrio: Caius Sulpicius likewise mounted a great number of suttlers and servants that followed his camp, upon mules, and other beasts that were of no service in battle; and having drawn them up and accoutred them like a body of horse, he ordered them to make their appearance upon a neighbouring hill, as soon as he was engaged with the Gauls; which had such an effect, that he soon routed them. The same was done by Marius, in a battle which he fought with the Germans—If then these false alarms have such consequences in the heat of an action, what may not be expected from a real one; especially if the enemy is suddenly and unexpectedly attacked either in the flank or in the rear, when they are engaged in the front? But this is no easy matter to effect, except you are favoured in it by the nature of the country: for if it be plain and open, you cannot conceal such a body of your forces as is necessary upon such occasions[1]; but if it abound with woods or mountains, you may lie in ambush and fall suddenly upon an enemy, when he least expects it, and be allured of success.

It is sometimes likewise of great service in time of battle, to raise a report that the enemy's general is killed, or that one part of their army is giving way: and it has been no unusual thing to throw cavalry into disorder by strange noises, and uncommon appearances: thus Craesus brought a great number of camels against the enemy's horse: and Pyrrhus made use of elephants against that of the Romans, which occasioned great confusion and disturbance amongst them. The grand *Signor*, not long ago, routed the Sophi of Persia and the Sultan of Syria, merely by the use of muskets; the explosion of which struck such a terror into their cavalry, that they ran away.

The Spaniards, in their battles with Hamilcar, used to place carriages full of flax, and drawn by oxen, in the front of their armies; and setting fire to the flax as soon as the battle begun, the oxen were so frighted at it, that they rushed in amongst the enemy, and opened their ranks.—Where the nature of the country is such, that you cannot well draw the enemy into an ambush, you may however dig ditches and pit-falls in the plains, and cover them lightly over with brushwood and clods, leaving intervals of solid ground, through which you may retire yourself in the heat of the battle; and if the enemy pursues you, he is undone.

If you are aware of any accident that happens during the action, which you think may dispirit your men, it is the best way either to conceal it, if you can, or to give it such a turn as may serve to produce a quite different effect, as Tullus Hostilius did, and after him Lucius Sylla, who seeing a body of his forces go over to the enemy he was en-

---

1. And yet Hannibal found means to draw the Romans into a sort of an ambush in the middle of a plain, at the famous Battle of Cannae. See the account of that battle by Sir W. Raleigh, in his *History of the World*, book V. chap. 3.

gaged with, and that it had greatly discouraged his own men, immediately spread a report through his army, that it was done for a secret purpose, and by his own order: so that, instead of being daunted, they fought with more courage, and beat the enemy. The same commander having sent a party of soldiers upon some attack, in which they were all killed, and being afraid it might discourage the rest of his army, said in public, that he had sent them upon that errand on purpose to be cut off, because he knew they were a parcel of rascals and traitors.

Sertorius, in a battle with the Spaniards, killed one of his own men who brought him word that one of his generals was slain; imagining that if he published it, it would strike a damp into his army.—It is a very difficult matter to stop an army that is beginning to run away, and to make it charge again: but here we must make a distinction betwixt one that is actually running, and another that is only inclining; for in the first case, it is almost impossible; in the second, there may be some remedy found. Some of the Roman generals have done it by reproaching their soldiers, and upbraiding them with cowardice, as we may instance in the conduct of Sylla, who seeing part of his legions begin to fly before the army of Mithridates, rode up to the head of them with a drawn sword in his hand, and cried out, "If anybody should enquire after your general, tell them you left him fighting in the plains of Boeotia."

Attilius the Roman consul detached a body of his best troops to stop the flight of some others that were running away, and told them that if they did not turn back, they should be attacked by their own friends, as well as by the enemy. Philip of Macedon finding some of his troops were afraid of the Scythians, posted a body of cavalry, in which he most confided, in the rear of his army, with orders to kill any man that offered to quit his rank: upon which, the rest chusing rather to hazard their lives in battle, than to be killed without mercy, if they fled, exerted their courage, and fought so manfully that they beat the Scythians[2].

---

2. Memorable was the behaviour of two Lacedaemonian matrons to their sons, when they had fled from battle, as it is recorded in two Greek epigrams, of which the following are literal translations.
Fugiebat Lacon olim pugnam; obviam vero facta mater Dixit, in pects ense sublato, Vivus quidem tuae matri usque dedecus injungis, Et Strenuae Spartae patrias leges solvis. Si vero occideris meis manibus, mater quidem audiam Infelix, sed in meâ patriâ conservatâ, Mater filium desertorem pugnae post mortem Sociorum Occidit, partus-dolorum recordationem aspernata: Legitimum etenim Sanguinem discernit Lacedaemon Virtute praeliantium, non genere infantium.

Several of the Roman generals have taken a pair of colours out of the hands of an ensign, in the heat of battle, and thrown it into the midst of the enemy, with a promise of a reward to those that should retake it: but this was done not so much to prevent their running away, as to create an emulation amongst their soldiers, and encourage them to fight with great ardour. Having now spoken of such things as are necessary to be done, not only before a battle, but in the time of action, it may not be amiss perhaps to say something of what ought to be done after it is over; especially as I shall be very brief in this point, which yet should not be omitted, because it is a part of our System. I say then, that when you have gained a victory, you ought by all means to pursue it, and to imitate Julius Caesar rather than Hannibal in that respect; the latter of whom lost the Empire of the World, by trifling away his time at Capua, after he had routed the Romans at the battle of Cannae.

Caesar, on the other hand, never rested after a victory, but always pursued and harassed the enemy after they were broken and flying, with greater vigour and fury than he attacked them at first.—But when a general happens to lose a battle, he is to consider in the first place, how to make the best of his loss; particularly if he has any considerable force left. Perhaps he may reap some advantage, either from the neglect, or tardiness, or inadvertency of the enemy: for after a victory, soldiers often grow too remiss and secure, and give the army they have beaten an opportunity of beating them in their turn; as L. Marcius did the Carthaginians, who having slain the two Scipios in battle, and defeated their armies, made little account of the forces that were left under the command of Marcius, till they were attacked and routed by him.

Hence we see, that nothing is so easy to effect, as what the enemy imagines you will never attempt; and that men are frequently in the greatest danger, when they think themselves most secure. But if a general can reap no sort of advantage from his first loss, he should by all means endeavour at least to make it as light and supportable as he can, and to prevent any further damage: for which purpose, he ought to use every method either to divide or retard the enemy, if they pursue him. In the first case, some, when they were aware they could stand their ground no longer, have ordered their inferior commanders to separate and retreat with their forces by different ways to some appointed rendezvous; which has made the enemy afraid of dividing his forces, and suffer all or moil of them to escape: in the second, many have suffered the best of their baggage and effects to fall into the enemy's hands upon the road, that so whilst they were busy in plundering and ransacking that, they might have time to save themselves.

The artifice made use of by Titus Dimius, to conceal the loss he had sustained in battle, is not unworthy of notice: for after he had fought from morning till night, and had a great number of his men killed, he caused most of them to be buried in the night: so that the next day, when the enemy saw so many of their own men, and so few of the Romans killed, they looked upon themselves as worsted, and immediately began to retreat—And now I think I have in a great measure answered your questions; though not so distinctly and particularly perhaps, as you expected. It is true, I have something yet to add concerning the method of forming armies in order of battle: as some generals have drawn up their forces in the shape of a wedge, with its edge in the front; imagining that form to be the best adapted to penetrate and open the ranks of an enemy.

To provide against this, the other side commonly drew up their army in the form of a pair of open shears, to receive the wedge in the vacuity, and so to surround and attack it on every side. Upon this occasion, let me recommend a general rule to you: which is, that in order to frustrate any of your enemy's designs, it is the best way to do that of yourself, which he endeavours to force you to: for then you may proceed in a cool and orderly manner, and turn that to your advantage, which he intended as the means of your ruin: but if you are compelled to it, you will surely be undone.

To confirm the truth of this, it is needless to repeat what I have said before: for when the enemy advances in a wedge, with a design to open, and as it were to cleave your army asunder, if you open it yourself in the form abovementioned, it is certain you must cut him to pieces, and he cannot much hurt you. Hannibal placed elephants in the front of his army, to break in upon that of Scipio: but Scipio having opened a way for them himself, gained a complete victory by it. Asdrubal likewise posted the flower of his army in the centre of his front, for the same purpose: but Scipio ordering his front to open and file off, disappointed his intention, and defeated him: so that when such designs are known, they are generally frustrated, and prove the ruin of the contrivers,

I think I have likewise something left to say, relating to the precautions which a general should make use of before he leads on his army to battle: for, in the first place, I am of opinion, that he should never come to engagement, except he either has an advantage over the enemy, or is compelled to it. Now the advantage may arise from the nature of the ground, the order, superiority, or bravery of his army: and he may be compelled to engage, by a conviction, that if he does not, he must inevitably be ruined: which may happen, either when he has no money to pay his troops, and they begin to mutiny and talk of disbanding; or when he has no provisions left, and must otherwise be starved; or when he knows the enemy daily expects to be reinforced: for without doubt, in such circumstances, he ought always to engage; because it is better to try your fortune whilst there is any chance of victory (though ever so small) than to sit still and be sure to be undone.

It is therefore as great a fault in a general not to hazard an engagement upon such occasions, as it he had a fair opportunity of gaining a victory, and neglected it, either out of ignorance or cowardice. Some advantages may result from the negligence and misconduct of the enemy; and others from your own vigilance and good conduct: many armies have been routed in passing rivers, by an enemy, who has waited till one half of them has been transported, and then fallen upon them; as Caesar did upon the Swiss, when he cut off a fourth part of their army, which was separated from the rest by a river they had palled. Sometimes an enemy is so jaded and fatigued by too rash and hasty a pursuit, that if your men have had a little time to rest and refresh themselves, you have nothing to do but to face about and gain a victory.

If an enemy offers you battle early in the morning, you ought not to draw out your army to fight him immediately; but rather to let his men wait under arms for some hours, till their ardour is abated, and then to come out of your entrenchments and engage him, as Scipio and Metellus did in Spain; the former, when he had Asdrubal upon his hands, and the latter, Sertorius. If the enemy has diminished his strength, either by dividing his army (as the Scipios did in Spain) or upon any other occasion, you ought by no means to omit that opportunity of fighting him. Most prudent generals have chosen rather to receive the enemy, than to attack them: because the fury of the first shock is easily sustained by men that stand firm and resolute, and ready prepared in their ranks: and when that is over, their fury commonly subsides into languor and despair.

By proceeding in this manner, Fabius routed both the Samnites and the Gauls: but Decius, his colleague, taking the other course, was defeated and slain. Some generals, who have thought the enemy superior to them, have chosen to defer a battle till the evening that so if they should be worsted, they might save themselves under shelter of the night: others who have known that the enemy would not fight at particular times, out of reverence to the laws of their religion, have taken that opportunity to attack and defeat them: of which advantage Julius Caesar availed himself against Ariovistus in Gaul, and Vespasian against the Jews in Syria. But above all things, a general should take care to have men of approved fidelity, wisdom, and long experience in military affairs, near his person, as a fore of council; from whom he may learn, not only the state of his own army, but that of the enemy's; as which of them is superior to the other in number; which of them is the better armed and disciplined; which of them is the stronger in cavalry; which of his own troops are fitted to undergo hard service and fatigue; and whether his infantry or cavalry are likely to be of most service.

Let them well consider the nature of the country where they are; whether it be more advantageous to the enemy or themselves; which of the two can be most conveniently furnished with provisions and other supplies; whether it be better to come to an engagement directly, or to defer it; and what advantage or disadvantage may accrue from time: for it sometimes happens, that when soldiers see a war protracted, and a battle put off from time to time, they lose their ardour, and become so weary of hardships, that they grow mutinous and desert their colours. It is likewise of great importance to know the qualities and disposition of the enemy's general, and of those that are about him; for instance, whether he is bold and enterprising, or cautious and timid.

He should next consider how far he can confide in his auxiliaries; and be particularly careful not to bring his army to an engagement, if he perceives his men are in the least dispirited or diffident of victory: for it is a bad omen indeed, when they think an enemy invincible. In such circumstances, you must either endeavour to avoid a battle, by following the example of Fabius Maximus (who always took the advantage of situations where Hannibal durst not attack him) or, if you think the enemy will attack you, how advantageous so ever your situation may be, you must entirely quit the field, and canton your forces in different towns and fortresses, to tire him out with sieges and blockades.

Zanobi. Is there no other way of avoiding an engagement?

Fabrizio. I think I told some of you in a conversation we once had before upon this very point, that an army in the field cannot possibly avoid an engagement, if the enemy is determined to fight it at all events; except it suddenly decamps, and removes to the distance of fifty and sixty miles, and always keeps retreating as they advance. Fabius Maximus never refused to fight Hannibal: but did not chuse to do it without an advantage; and Hannibal, considering the manner in which he always took care to fortify himself, was too wise to force him to it: but if Fabius had been attacked, he must either have fought him at all events, or run away.

Philip of Macedon, the father of Perseus, being at war with the Romans, encamped upon the top of a very high hill, to avoid coming to an engagement with them: but they attacked and routed him there. Cingetorex,[3] General of the Gauls, retreated to a considerable distance, that he might not be obliged to fight the Roman army, commanded by Julius Caesar, who had suddenly passed a river that was betwixt them, contrary to his expectation. The Venetians in the late wars, might have avoided a battle with the French, if they had marched away from them (as Cingetorex did from Caesar) instead of waiting till they passed the Adda: but they neither took the opportunity of attacking them whilst they were passing that river, nor could they afterwards retreat; for the French were then so close at their heels, that as soon as the Venetians began to decamp, the French fell upon them and defeated them. In short, there is no other way of avoiding a battle, if the enemy is fully determined to bring you to one: and therefore it is to no purpose to allege the example of Fabius Maximus; for in that case, Hannibal avoided an engagement as much as Fabius.

It often happens, that soldiers are eager to engage, when (considering the superiority of the enemy, the nature of the ground, or some other circumstances) you are convinced you cannot do it without disadvantage, and therefore would willingly decline a battle: it may likewise happen, that either necessity may oblige, or opportunity invite you, to engage when you find your soldiers dispirited and adverse to it; in one of which cases, it is necessary to repress their ardour, and in the other to excite it. In the first, when persuasion and exhortations have no effect, it is the best way to let some part of them be roughly handled by the enemy; that so, both those who have suffered, and those who have not, may learn to be more tractable and conformable

---

3. The author is guilty of a little mistake here; it was not Cingetorex, but Vercingetorex. See *Caef. Com. de Bello Gallico.* lib. VII. cap. xxxv.

to your will another time: for what was the effect of chance in the army of Fabius Maximus, may be done on purpose by any other commander, upon a like occasion. It happened, that not only the general of his cavalry, but all the rest of his army, were very impatient to fight Hannibal; though Fabius himself was utterly against it: which dissension grew to such a height, that at last they divided the army betwixt them.

Fabius, with his troops, kept close in his entrenchments; the other went out and engaged the enemy, but would have been entirely defeated, if Fabius had not at last marched out to his succour: from which example, both the general of his cavalry, and all the rest of the army, were convinced, that it would have been wiser to have submitted to the opinion of Fabius.—As to the means of animating your men, and inflaming them with a desire to engage, it would be a good way, in the first place, to exasperate them against the enemy, to tell them they are despised, to insinuate that you have corrupted some of their officers, and hold a private correspondence with them, to encamp in a situation where you may daily see what they are doing, and now and then take an opportunity of skirmishing with them: for things that are often seen, at last become familiar, and are but little regarded.

If these measures fail, you should treat them with disdain, and harangue them in a weighty and pathetic manner, upbraiding them with cowardice, and endeavouring to make them ashamed of themselves, by telling them, that if the rest have not courage enough to follow you, you will take such or such a regiment, which you know you can depend upon, and fight the enemy with that alone.[4] But to make your men the bolder and more courageous and resolute, you ought above all things, to take care that they may neither send any of their money or plunder away to their own houses, or deposit it in any other place of safety, till the war is over: that so they may be assured, that if they run away, they may save their lives perhaps, but must certainly lose their treasure; the love of which most commonly operates as strongly upon men as that of their life.

Zanobi. You say that soldiers should be animated to fight by haranguing them: would you harangue the whole army then, or the officers only?

Fabrizio. It is an easy matter to induce a few people either to do a thing or to let it alone; for if arguments are not sufficient, you make life of force and authority: but the great difficulty is to make a whole

---

4. As Caesar and Alexander did.

army change their resolution, when the execution of it must either be of prejudice to the public, or thwart your own private schemes and designs; because in that case, you can avail yourself of nothing but words, which must be heard and considered by the whole army, if you would have the whole army affected by them.

For this reason, it is necessary that a general should be an orator as well as a soldier: for if he does not know how to address himself to the whole army, he will sometimes find it no easy task to should it to his purposes. But there is not the least attention shewn to this point at present. Read the *Life of Alexander the Great*, and you will see how often he was obliged to harangue his troops; which otherwise he should never have conducted (rich and loaded with spoil) through the deserts of India and Arabia, where they underwent every fore of hardship and fatigue. Many things may prove the ruin of an army, if the general does not frequently harangue his men: for by that, he may dispel their fears, enflame their courage, confirm their resolution, point out the snares that are laid for them, promise them rewards, inform them of danger, and the way to escape it, rebuke, entreat, threaten, praise, reproach, or encourage, and avail himself of all other arts that can either excite or allay the passions and appetites of mankind.

If any prince or republic, therefore, would make their armies respectable, they should accustom their generals to harangue the men, and the men to listen to their generals.——Religion likewise, and the oath which soldiers took when they were enlisted, very much contributed to make them do their duty in former times: for upon any default, they were threatened not only with human punishments, but the vengeance of the Gods. They had also several other religious ceremonies, which had a very good effect in all their enterprises; and would have still in any place where religion is held in due reverence. Sertorius well knew this, and used to have conferences with a hind, which he said was lent by the Gods to allure him of victory.

Sylla pretended to converse with an image he had taken out of the temple of Apollo; and several have given out that some God or other has appeared to them in dreams and visions, and commanded them to fight the enemy. In the days of our Ancestors, when Charles VII. of France was at war with the English, he pretended to be advised in everything by a virgin sent from Heaven, commonly called *the Virgin of France*[5]; which gained him many a victory.——It is proper also to teach your men to hold the enemy in contempt, as Agesilaus the Spar-

---

5. Or the Maid of Orleans.

tan did: who having taken some of the Persians, caused them to be dripped naked and shewn to his soldiers, that so when they had seen the delicacy of their bodies, they might despise them.

Some commanders have laid their men under a necessity of fighting, by depriving them of all means of saving themselves, except by victory, which is certainly the best method of making them fight desperately: and this resolution is heightened, either by the confidence they have in themselves, their arms and armour, their discipline, good order, and the victories they have lately gained, or by the esteem they have for their general, which arises rather from the opinion they have of his valour and conduct, than from any particular favour they have received of him; or by the love of their country, which is natural to all men. There are various other methods of laying them under the necessity of fighting, but that is the strongest and most powerful, which leaves men no other alternative but either to conquer or die.

Book 5

In what order the Romans used to march through an enemy's country; and how an army ought to be drawn up for that purpose. How to reduce an army into order of battle immediately: and to form it in such a manner that it may be able to defend itself on any side, in case of a sudden attack. Concerning orders that are to be given by word of mouth, beat of drum, or found of trumpet. Of pioneers, and the provisions that are necessary for an army. In what manner the ancients divided the spoil taken from the enemy amongst their soldiers. How to discover ambuscades upon a march. That a general ought to be well acquainted with the country through which he is to pass; and to keep his design secret. What means are to be taken for that purpose. Some other precautions that are necessary upon a march. How to avoid an engagement, if the enemy presses hard upon you, as you are going to pass a river; and in what manner rivers may be passed with safety. How some generals have escaped when they have been shut up in a pass, or surrounded by the enemy.

Fabrizio. I have shewn you how an army ought to be formed that is going to engage, how an enemy may be defeated, and many other circumstances on this subject which may happen through various accidents and occurrences. It is now time therefore, I think, to inform you in what manner I would have an army drawn up, which has not an enemy actually in fight, but expects to be attacked on a sudden; particularly when it is marching either through an enemy's country, or one that is suspected of favouring the enemy.

You must know then, in the first place, that the Roman generals usually sent some troops of horse before their armies to reconnoitre the country, and scour the roads: after them came the right wing, with the carnages and baggage belonging to it in its rear: then followed one of the legions with its carriages; and next to that, the other in the same manner: last of all, came the left wing with its baggage, and the rest of the horse in the rear of all. This was the order which they commonly observed upon a march; and if they were attacked either in the front or rear, they immediately caused all the carriages to be drawn off to the right or left, as best suited their convenience, and the nature of the ground would admit; after which, the whole army, being freed from that incumbrance, faced about to the enemy.

If they were attacked on the right flank, they drew off the carriages to the left, and *vice versa*, converting; the flank that was attacked into a front. This being a very good method, in my opinion, I think it is worthy of imitation; and therefore, upon the like occasions, I would always send my light horse before the army to reconnoitre the country, and scour the roads: the four regiments of which it consists should march next, one after another; every one of them having its own baggage in its rear. And as there are two sorts of baggage, *viz.* that which belongs to individuals, and that which is for the use of the army in general, I would divide the latter into four parts, and assign one fourth of it to the care of every regiment: the artillery, suttlers, and others who attended the camp, should also be distributed amongst them in, the same manner; that so every regiment might have an equal share of these impediments.

But as it sometimes happens, that you march through a country, which instead of being suspected, is professedly your enemy, and where you hourly expect to be attacked, you will then be obliged to change the form and order of your march for greater security; and to draw up your men in such a manner that neither the peasants nor the enemy's army may find you unprepared to receive them on any side, if they should make a sudden attack upon you. In such cases, the Roman generals used to form their armies into an oblong square, so that they might defend themselves on every side, and be ready to fight as well as to march: and I confess I like that disposition so well, that I would follow their example in drawing up the two regiments I have taken for the model of an army, in the same manner upon the like occasions: that is, in an oblong square with a hollow in the middle of it, or four hundred and twenty-four feet on every side.

My flanks then would be that distance from one another; in each of which, I would place five battalions in the rear of each other, with an interval of six feet betwixt every one of them: so that these battalions, would take up the space of four hundred and twenty-four feet in depth, including the intervals betwixt them; every battalion being supposed to take up eighty feet. In the front and rear of the hollow square, I would place the other ten battalions; that is, five of them in the front of it, and five in the rear; in such a manner that four of them abreast of each other should be next to the front of the right flank, and four drawn up in the same manner next to the rear of the left, with an interval of eight feet betwixt every one of them: another I would post next to the front of the left flank, in a line with the four first, and another next to the rear of the right, in a line also with the four others there.

Now as the distance from one flank to another is four hundred and twenty-four feet, and the battalions posted in front of the square (including the intervals betwixt them) will take up no more than two hundred and seventy-four fact, there will remain a vacant space of one hundred and fifty feet betwixt the four battalions on the right, and the single one on the left. There will also be the same room left betwixt the battalions in the rear without any difference; except that the space in the front will be near the left flank, and that in the rear near the right.

In the former of these, I would place my ordinary *velites*, and my extraordinary in the latter, which would not amount to quite a thousand in each space.—But to order it so that the hollow square in the middle of the army should be completely four hundred and twenty four feet on every side, care must be taken that neither the five battalions that are posted in the front, nor the other five in the rear may take up any part of the space that is included betwixt the flanks: for which purpose, the last men on the right and left of the first rank of the battalions in the rear should be close (not in a right line, but rather obliquely) with the innermost man in the last rank of each flank: and the last man on the right and left of the last rank of the battalions in the front, should be close (in the same manner) with the innermost man in the first rank of each flank; and then there will be a space left at every angle or the army large enough to receive a body of three hundred and thirty-three pikemen extraordinary: but as there would still be two more corps of pikemen extraordinary left, each consisting of three hundred and thirty-four men, I would draw them up in a square form in the middle of the area within the army; at the head of which, the general himself, with his proper officers and attendants, should take post.

Now though these battalions thus drawn up march all in one direction, but may be obliged to fight on any side, you must take, care to qualify them properly for that purpose: and therefore the five first battalions being secured on all sides but in their front, must be formed with their pikemen in their foremost ranks. The five last battalions are likewise covered on every side, except their rear; and therefore they must be formed with their pikemen it their rearmost ranks. For the same reason each flank should also have its pikemen in the outermost ranks. The corporals and other officers should take their proper posts at the same time; that so when the enemy comes to engage, every corps, and every member of that corps, may be in its due place, according to the order and method I described before, when I was speaking of ranging an army in order of battle.

The artillery I would distribute along each flank; the light horse should be sent before to reconnoitre the country and scour the roads: and the *gens d'armes* I would post in the rear of each flank, at the distance of eighty feet from the battalions. For it should be a general rule in drawing op an army, always to post your horse either on the flanks or in the rear: because, it you post them in the front, you must either do it at such a distance from the army, that if they should be repulsed by the enemy, they may have time and room enough to wheel off without falling foul upon your infantry, or you must leave proper intervals in the front to receive them in such a manner as not to disorder the rest of your forces.

This is a matter that deserves to be well remembered; for many who have neglected these precautions have been thrown into disorder, and routed by their own men. The carriages, suttlers, and other unarmed people who follow the camp, should be placed in the hollow square, and so ranged that any person upon occasion may have a free passage through them, either from the front to the rear, or from one flank to another. The depth of the whole army, when the battalions are thus disposed, will be five hundred and eighty-four feet from front to rear, exclusive of the horse and artillery: and as it is composed of two regiments, it must be considered how each of them is to be posted.

Now since the regiments are distinguished by their respective marks and numbers, and each of them consists of ten battalions and a colonel, the five first battalions of the first regiment should be posted in the front of the army, and the other five in the left flank; in the angle of which, on the inside, the colonel of it should take his station: after which, the five first battalions of the second regiment should be placed in the right flank, and the other five in the rear, with their colonel in the angle which they make there. When the army is thus formed, you are to put it in motion, and to observe this order during your whole march; which will effectually secure you against any tumultuary attack from the people of the country.

All other provisions for that purpose are unnecessary, except you shall think fit now and then to send a troop or two of light horse, or a party of *velites* to drive them away: for such sort of disorderly people are so afraid of regular forces, that they will never come within reach of their pikes, much less of their swords; but may set up a great shout perhaps, and make a feint of attacking you, like a parcel of curs barking at a mastiff which they dare not venture to come near.

Thus Hannibal all the while he was traversing Gaul to invade Italy, made little or no account of the country people.—For the sake of convenience and expedition upon a march, you should send pioneers before the army to make a clear passage for it: and these pioneers should be covered by the light horse that are sent forwards to reconnoitre the country. In this order an army will march ten miles in a day with great ease, and have time enough to encamp and refresh itself before it is dark: for the usual march of an army is about twenty miles a day.—If you should happen to be attacked by a regular army, it cannot be so suddenly but you will have sufficient time to put yourself in a proper posture of defence: because such an army must move in an orderly manner, and therefore you will be able to draw up your forces, either in the form I have been describing, or in some other of the like nature.

For if you are attacked in the front, you have nothing to do but to draw your artillery from the flanks, and your horse out of the rear, and to post them in the places and at the distances I just now recommended. The thousand *velites* in the front may advance; and having divided themselves into two bodies of five hundred in each, let them take place betwixt the horse and each wing of the army. The void which they leave may be filled with the two corps of pikemen extraordinary,, which were posted in the middle of the hollow square. The *velites* extraordinary, which were in the rear, may divide into two bodies, and range themselves along each flank of the battalions to strengthen them; and all the carriages, suttlers, &c. may draw off through the open space, which will then be left into the rear of the battalions.

The hollow square being thus left empty, let the five battalions, which were in the rear, march up through the vacancy betwixt each flank towards, the front; three of them advancing till they come within eighty feet of those in the front, and the other two halting at the same distance in their rear, with proper intervals betwixt them all. All this may be done in a very little time; and then your order of battle will much resemble the first and principal of those which I recommended some time ago: and if it be closer in the front, it is likewise grosser in the flanks, which will make it so much the stronger.

But as the five battalions in the rear had posted their pikemen in their last ranks for the reasons abovementioned, it will be necessary upon this occasion to place them in their foremost ranks, in order to support the front of the army: for which purpose, they must either wheel to the right or left about (battalion by battalion) all at once, and like one solid body, or the pikemen must pass through the ranks of the targetmen, and place themselves in the front of them, which is a much more expeditious way than the other, and subject: to less disorder. The same must be done upon any attack, in all parts of the army where the pikemen are in the rear of the targets, as I shall shew you. If the enemy presents himself in the rear, you have nothing more to do than to make your whole army face about to that part, and then your rear immediately becomes the front, and your front the rear: after which, you must observe all the directions in forming that front, which I gave you before.

If the enemy is likely to fall upon your right flank, the whole army must turn its face that way, and make the front there, as I have already said; taking care to place your cavalry, *velites*, and artillery according to that disposition; in which alterations there is but little difference, excepting in the distance betwixt each flank, and that which there is betwixt the front and the rear. It is true, that in converting the right flank into the front, the *velites* which are to fill the space betwixt the horse and the wings of the army, should be those that are nearest the left flank; and the two corps of pikemen in the area should advance to fill their places: but before they do that, the carriages, &c. should quit the area, and retire through the open left by the *velites* behind the left flank, which will then become the rear of the army. The other *velites*, which were posted in the rear, should keep their place, that so no opening may be left, because that which was the rear before, will now become the right flank: all the other necessary manoeuvres in this case must be conducted in the manner already prescribed.

What has been said of making a front of the right flank may be applied to the left; as the like manoeuvres and disposition are to be made upon that occasion. if the enemy be so numerous, and drawn up in such a manner that he may attack you on two sides at once, you must strengthen them from those quarters which are not attacked, by doubling their ranks, and dividing all the artillery, *velites*, and cavalry betwixt them. But if he attacks you on three or four sides at the same time, either he or you mull be very imprudent; for surely no wise general would ever expose himself to be attacked on so many sides at once by a powerful and well-ordered army; and on the other hand, the enemy cannot do it with success, except his army is so numerous that he can spare almost as many men as your whole army consists of to attack you on every side.

If then you are so indiscreet as to venture yourself in an enemy's country, or any other place where you may be attacked by an army three times as strong, and as well-disciplined as your own, you have nobody to blame but yourself, if any misfortune happens to you: but if the misfortune is not owing to your own imprudence, but to some strange and unexpected accident, you may save your reputation, though you are totally ruined by it, which was the case of Scipio in Spain, and Asdrubal in Italy. But if the enemy is not much stronger than you are, and attacks you on two or three sides at once, in hopes of throwing you into disorder, that is his error and your advantage: because in that case, he must weaken himself. so much, that you may easily sustain the charge in one place, and attack him vigorously yourself in another; by which he must of consequence be defeated.

This method of drawing up an army therefore, against an enemy who is not actually in fight, but may yet attack you on a sudden, is very necessary; and it is of great importance to accustom your soldiers not only to be formed and to march in this order, but to prepare themselves for battle, as if they were going to be attacked in the front, and then to fall into their former order again, and move forwards: after which, they should be shewn how the rear or either of the flanks may be converted into the front, and then reduced into their first arrangement: all which must be often practised, if you would have your army ready and expert in these exercises.

This is a point which all princes and commanders should carefully attend to: for military discipline consists chiefly in knowing how to command and execute these things; and that only can be called a good and well-disciplined army, which is perfect in the practice of them: and if such a one was now in being, I think it would not be possible to find another that could beat it. If it be said that the forming an army in these squares is attended with a good deal of trouble and difficulty, I allow it; but as it is very necessary, the difficulty must be got over by frequent exercise; and when that is one done, all other parts of military discipline will seem light and easy.

Zanobi. I agree with you that these things are highly necessary, and think you have explained them so well, that nothing material has either been omitted, or can be added. There are two other points however, in which I should be glad to be satisfied: in the first place, when you would convert either the rear or one of the flanks into the front of your army, and the men are to face about to that part, are they to do it by word of command, or by beat of drum, or some other signal? In the next, whether those whom you sent before your army to clear the roads and make a free passage for it, should be soldiers belonging to your battalions, or other sort of people appointed on purpose for that service?

Fabrizio. Your first question is very pertinent: for many armies have been thrown into great confusion, when the general's orders have either not been heard, or mistaken: such orders therefore should be very clear and intelligible, especially upon important occasions: and if they are signified either by beat of drum or sound of trumpet, it should be done in so distinct a manner, that one note or found cannot be mistaken for another: but if they are delivered by word of mouth, you should take great care not only to avoid general terms, and to make use of particular ones, but even in those, not to hazard any that may admit of a double interpretation. Some armies have been ruined by their officers crying out, "Give way, give way," instead of "Retreat;" which should be a sufficient warning never to make use of that expression again. If you want to convert either the rear or one of the flanks into the front, and would have your men turn their face that way, do not say Turn ye, but Face about to the right, the left, or the rear, as the occasion requires. In like manner all other words of command should be plain and simple, as, charge home, stand fast, advance, retreat, &c. and if orders can be delivered clearly and distinctly by word of mouth, let them be given that way; if not, make use of a drum or a trumpet.

As to pioneers, I would depute some of my own soldiers for that service; not merely because the ancients used to do so, but that I might have the fewer unarmed people, and consequently the fewer incumbrances in my army: for which reason, I would take as many as I wanted out of every battalion, who should leave their arms and accoutrements to be taken care of by the men in the next ranks to them, and be furnished with axes, mattocks, spades, and other necessary implements of that kind: so that when the enemy approached they might presently return to their respective ranks in the army, and take up their arms again.

Zanobi. But who must carry their pioneering implements?

Fabrizio. The carriages appointed for that purpose.

Zanobi. I doubt you would not be able to make your soldiers do that sort of work.

Fabrizio. Very easily, as I will convince you before we part: but let us wave that matter at prefect, if you please, because I will tell you in the first place, how I would supply them with provisions: for as we have pretty well fatigued them I suppose with so much exercise, it is now high time to give them a little refreshment.—All princes and commanders should take particular care that their armies may be as light and little encumbered as possible; that so they may be at all times fit and ready for any enterprise or expedition. Now the difficulties occasioned either by the want or too great plenty of provisions, may be reckoned amongst the most considerable that are incident to an army.

The ancients did not give themselves much trouble about furnishing their troops with wine: for when they came into countries where there was none to be had, they drank water with a little vinegar in it to give it a taste: so that instead of wine, they always carried vinegar along with them. They did not bake their bread in ovens; as is usual in towns: for every soldier had a certain allowance of meal or flour, and lard, which being kneaded together, made a very good and nourishing bread. They used likewise to carry a sufficient quantity of oats and barley for their horses and other cattle; for they had herds of oxen, and flocks of sheep and goats, which were driven after the army, and therefore did not occasion any great embarrassment. To these precautions it was owing that their armies would sometimes march for many days together, through desert countries and rugged defiles, without distress or difficulty.

On the contrary, our modern armies, which can neither live without wine, nor eat any bread but was is baked and made as it is in towns (of which they cannot carry a quantity sufficient for any long time) must often either be reduced to great distress, or obliged to provide themselves with those necessaries in a manner that must be very troublesome and expensive. I would therefore re-establish this method in my army, and not suffer any sort of bread to be eaten by the soldiers but what they made themselves: as to wine, I should not prohibit the use of it, if any was brought into the camp; but I would not take the least pains to procure it for them: in all other things likewise relating to provisions, I would follow the example of the ancients, by which many difficulties and inconveniencies might be avoided, and many great advantages gained in an expedition.

Zanobi. We have beat the enemy in a field battle, and afterwards marched our army into his territories, it is but reasonable now that we should make our advantage of it by plundering his country, laying the towns under contribution, and taking prisoners. But first I should be glad to know how the ancients proceeded upon such occasions.

Fabrizio. I take it for granted (as we had some conversation upon this matter once before) that you will allow that wars, as they are conducted at present, impoverish not only those that are beaten, but those also that are conquerors; for if one side loses its territories, the other is at an immense expense in gaining them: which was not the case in former times, when the conqueror was always enriched by the victory. The reason of this is, that the plunder is not now brought to account, as it used to be formerly, but left wholly to the discretion of the soldiers, which occasions two very great disorders, one of which I have already mentioned; the other is; that it makes the soldiers so greedy of spoil, that they lay aside all regard to order and military discipline: from which it has often happened, that the conqueror has had the victory snatched out of his hands.

The Romans, however, who were very attentive to this point, provided against both these inconveniencies, by ordering that all the plunder should belong to the public, who should afterwards dispose of it as they thought fit. For this purpose, they had public officers attending their armies, whom they called *questors* or treasurers, in whose hands all the booty taken in war was deposited; out of which, the consul paid the soldiers, defrayed the expenses of the sick and wounded, and all other necessary charges of the army. The *consul* indeed had a power of distributing some part of the plunder amongst the soldiers, and he often did; but this was not attended with any ill consequence: for when the enemy was conquered, all the spoil that had been taken from them was placed in the middle of the army, and a certain proportion of it given to the soldiers, according to their rank and merit.

This custom made them more intent upon victory than plunder: for after the legionary soldiers had defeated the enemy, they never pursued them, nor even so much as stirred out of their ranks, the cavalry, and other light-armed forces, being employed for that purpose: for if the plunder was to have been the property of the first men that laid hold of it, it would neither have been reasonable or possible to have kept the legions firm and quiet in their ranks; and therefore such a measure must have been of very bad consequence. Hence it came to pass that the public was enriched by a victory, as every consul, when he entered Rome in triumph at his return from the wars, always brought with him the greatest part of the treasure which he had amassed by contributions and plundering the enemy, into the common stock.—The ancients acted very wisely in another point relating to this matter: for they ordered the third part of every man's pay to be lodged in the hands of the standard-bearer of his corps, who was not to be accountable for it till the end of the war.

This seems to have been done for two reasons: in the first place to save their money, which they otherwise might have squandered away in idle and unnecessary expenses, as most young men are apt to do when they have too much in their pockets: and in the next, to make them more resolute and obstinate in defending their colours, as they must know that if the standard was taken, they should lose all their arrears.——A due observation of these institutions, I think, would very much contribute to revive the ancient military discipline amongst us.

Zanobi. When an army is upon a march, it must certainly be exposed to many dangerous accidents, to obviate and avert which, the utmost sagacity and abilities of the general, as well as the most determined bravery of the soldiers, are necessary to be exerted. You would much oblige us, Sir, if you would point out those occasions.

Fabrizio. I shall very willingly comply with your request, since these things are absolutely necessary to be known by one that is desirous of being perfectly instructed in the Art of War. A general then ought above all things to beware of ambushes whilst his army is upon a march; into which he may either happen to fall, or be cunningly drawn by the enemy before he is aware. To prevent the first, he should send out strong parties to reconnoitre the country; and be particularly circumspect if it abounds with woods and mountains, because those are the fitted places for ambuscades, which sometimes prove the destruction of a whole army, when the general is not aware of them; but can do him no harm when he is.

Flights of birds, and clouds of dust, have frequently discovered an enemy: for whenever the enemy approaches they must of course raise a great dust, which should serve you therefore as a sufficient warning to prepare for an attack. It has often happened likewise, that when generals have observed a great number of pigeons or other birds, that usually fly together in flocks, suddenly take wing, and hover about in the air a great while without lighting again, they have suspected there was an ambuscade thereabout; in which case, by sending out parties to discover it, they have sometimes escaped the enemy, and sometimes defeated them.

To avoid being drawn into an ambuscade by the enemy, you must be very cautious of trusting to flattering appearances: for instance, if the enemy should leave a considerable booty in your way, you should suspect there is a hook in the bait; or if a strong party of the enemy should fly before a few of your men, or a few of their men should attack a strong party of your army; or if the enemy runs away on a sudden, without any apparent cause, it is to reasonable to imagine there is some artifice in it, and that they know very well what they are about: so that the weaker and more remiss they seem to be, the more it behoves you to be upon your guard, if you would avoid falling into their snares.

For this purpose, you are to act a double part; and though you ought not to be without your private apprehensions, yet you should seem outwardly to undervalue and despise them: the one will make you more vigilant, and less apt to be surprised; and the other, inspire your soldiers with courage and assurance of victory. You should always remember likewise, that an army is exposed to more and greater dangers in marching through an enemy's country, than in a field battle: upon which account, it concerns a general to be doubly circumspect at such times, The first thing he ought to do is, to get an exact map of the whole country through which he is to march; that so they may have a perfect knowledge of all the towns, their distance from each other, the roads, mountains, rivers, weeds, morasses, and the particular situation and nature of them.

For this purpose, it is necessary to procure several persons by different means, and from different parts, who are well acquainted with those places, whom he should examine separately, and compare their accounts, that so he may be able to form a true judgement of them: besides which, he should send out parties of horse under experienced commanders, not only to discover the enemy, but to observe the quality of the country, and to see whether it agrees with his map, and the information he has received. He must likewise keep a strict eye over his guides, whom he should encourage to serve him faithfully, with promises of great rewards, if they did their duty, and threaten them with the severest punishment, if they deceived him.

But above all things, he ought to keep his designs very secret; which is a matter of the utmost importance in all military enterprises: and to prevent his army from being thrown into disorder by any sudden attack, he should order his men to be constantly prepared for it: for if a thing of that kind is foreseen and expected, it is neither so terrible nor prejudicial when it happens, as it otherwise might have been. Many, in order to prevent confusion upon a march, have placed their carriages and unarmed people near the standard, and ordered them to follow it as close as possible; that so if there should be occasion either to halt or retreat, they might do it with greater ease and readiness; which, I think, is a custom not unworthy of imitation.

A general should also be very careful neither to differ one part of his forces to detach itself from the other whilst they are upon a march, nor to let any of the corps move faster or slower than the rest: for then his army would become weak and unconnected, and consequently exposed to greater danger. It is necessary, therefore, to post officers along the flanks, to keep an uniform pace amongst them, by restraining those that march too fast, and quickening others that move too slow; which cannot be done more properly than by beat of drum, or found of some musical instrument. The roads should also be laid open, and cleared in such a manner, that one battalion at least may march through them at a time, in order of battle.

The quality and customs of the enemy are to be considered in the next place, and whether they usually make their attack in the morning, or at noon, or in the evening, and whether they are more powerful in horse or foot: according to which circumstances, you are to regulate your own proceedings and preparations. But let us suppose some particular case. It happens sometimes that a general is obliged to decamp before the enemy, because he is not able to cope with them, and endeavours to avoid an engagement: but as soon as the enemy are aware of it, they likewise decamp, and press so hard upon his rear, that they must probably come up with him, and force him to an engagement before he can pass a river that lies in his way.

Now, some who have been in this dangerous situation have thrown up a deep ditch in the rear of their army, and filled it with fagots, and other combustible matter, which they have set fire to, and thereby gained time to pass the river in safety, before the enemy could get over the ditch.

Zanobi. I can hardly think such an expedient as this could be of much service, because I remember to have read, that Hanno the Carthaginian being surrounded by the enemy, set fire to a parcel of fagots on that side where he designed to make his push; which had such an effect, that the enemy thinking him sufficiently secured from escaping in that quarter, drew off their guards to another; but as soon as he was aware of that, he ordered his men to throw their targets before their faces, to defend them from the flames and smoke, and to push through the fire; by which means, he got clear with his whole army.

Fabrizio. Very true; but recollect what I said, and compare it with what Hanno did: I told you that the others caused a deep ditch to be thrown up, and filled with combustibles, which they set on fire: so that the enemy had not only the fire but the ditch to pass before they could come at them. Now Hanno had no ditch, and therefore as he designed to pass through the fire, he took care it should not be a very fierce one: otherwise, that alone would have stopped him, without any ditch. Do not you remember that when Nabis was besieged in Sparta by the Romans, he set fire to that part of the town in which he was himself, to prevent the enemy, who had already got possession of some streets, from advancing any farther? by which, he not only stopped them where they were, but drove them entirely out of the town again. But to return.

Quintus Luctatius, the Roman, having the Cimbrians close at his rear, and coming to a river which he wanted to pass, seemed determined to halt there and fight them; for which purpose, he fixed his standard, threw up entrenchments, erected tents, and sent out parties of horse to forage: in short, he acted in such a manner, that the Cimbrians being fully persuaded he designed to encamp there, entrenched themselves, and lent out several parties into the country as he had done; which Luctatius being aware of, immediately struck his tents, and passed the river without any molestation. Some have diverted the course of a river, when they had no other means of passing it, and drawn off one part of the stream other way, till the other has become fordable.

When the current is very rapid, the strongest and heaviest horse should be placed higher up the stream than the foot, to break the force of it, and facilitate their passage, and the light horse rather lower than the foot, to pick up any of them that may happen to be carried away by it: but rivers that are not fordable must be pasted by the help of bridges, pontoons, and other such conveniences; and therefore it is necessary to carry proper materials and implements for the construction of them along with an army.

It happens sometimes that you find the enemy posted on the other side to oppose your passage: in which case, I would recommend an expedient made use of by Julius Caesar in Gaul, who coming to a river, and finding Vercingetorex posted with an army on the opposite bank, marched down one side of it for several days, whilst Vercingetorex marched down the other. At last, Caesar having encamped in a woody part of the country, where he could conceal part of his men, drew three *cohorts* out of every legion, and left them there, with orders to throw a bridge over the river, and to fortify it as soon as he could when he was gone: after which, he pursued his march.

Vercingetorex, in the meantime, observing the number of his legions was the same, and not suspecting that any part of them were left behind, attended his motions as he had done before, on the other side; but when Caesar thought the bridge was finished, he made a sudden counter-march, and finding everything executed according to his orders, immediately passed the river without any opposition.

Zanobi. What rule or mark is there by which one may discover a ford with any certainty?

Fabrizio. A river is always the shallowest and most fordable where you see a sort of a ridge or streak across it, betwixt the tail of a pool and the head of a stream; because there is more gravel and sand left there than in any other place: the truth of which observation has been confirmed by long experience, and therefore it may be depended upon.

Zanobi. But suppose the bottom should either be so rough and broken, or so lost and full of holes, that cavalry cannot pass with safety; what remedy is there in that case?

Fabrizio. I would make hurdles and sink them; over which they might pass with ease.—But to proceed. If a general and his army happen to be inclosed in a pass betwixt two mountains, out of which there are but two ways of extricating himself, one in his front, the other in his rear, and they are both occupied by the enemy, there is still a method left to get clear of them, which has been practiced by others with success in such circumstances; and that is, to throw up a very deep and large ditch in his rear, with an intent, as it may seem, to secure himself effectually on that side, and to take all other methods to make the enemy believe he designs to exert his whole strength in the front, in order to force his way out on that side, if possible, without apprehending any danger in his rear.

The enemy, therefore, in the like cases, having been deceived by theft appearances, have naturally turned their whole force from the rear where they thought they had him safe, to block him up more securely in the front: upon which, he has taken an opportunity of suddenly throwing a drawbridge over the ditch, and escaped that way out of the hands of the enemy. Lucius Minucius, the Roman consul, and his army, being shut up by the enemy in the mountains of Liguria, and seeing to other means to get clear of them, sent a body of **Numidians** which he had with him, very badly armed, and mounted upon poor lean horses, towards the pass that was blocked up by the enemy, who immediately doubled their guards, and took all necessary measures to defend it with vigour upon their first appearance: but perceiving, as they came nearer, what a pitiful figure they made, they drew off part of their guards.

The Numidians being aware of this, presently set spurs to their horses, and made so furious an attack upon those that were left, that they broke through them, and afterwards made such havoc and devastation in the adjacent country, that the enemy were forced to quit their posts, and leave the pass open for Minucius and his whole army to come out of the mountains where they had been shut up. Some generals, when they have been attacked by a much superior force, have drawn up their men very close together, and suffered themselves to be surrounded by the enemy; in order to make their way by one resolute push through that part of their army which they saw was the thinned and weakest; and this method has sometimes succeeded very well. Mark Anthony, in his retreat out of Parthia, observing the enemy attacked him early every morning when he was decamping, and harassed his rear all day long, resolved afterwards not to decamp till noon: upon which, the Parthians concluding he would not move at all that day, returned to their own camp, and left him to continue his march all the rest of the day, without any disturbance.

The same commander, to guard against the arrows of the Parthians, ordered all his men to kneel down when the enemy drew near, and the second rank to cover the heads of the first with their targets, the third of the second, the fourth of the third, and so on: by which means the whole army was under a roof as it were, and safe from their arrows.— —This is all that occurs to my memory at present concerning the accidents that may happen to an army upon a march: if you have no other questions to ask relating to this matter, I will pass on to another part of our subject.

Book 6

What sort of situations the Romans and Greeks made choice of for their encampments. The form of an encampment. Concerning the centinels and guards that are posted about a camp: and the necessity of observing who goes out and comes into it. Of military justice, and the method taken by the ancients in punishing offenders. That the ancients allowed neither women nor gaming in their armies. Their method of decamping. That they used to encamp in healthful situations, and where they could neither be surrounded by an enemy, nor cut off from provision. Directions concerning provisions. How to encamp more or less than four regiments or legions; and what number of men is sufficient to fight an enemy. What means some generals have used to get clear of any enemy. How to make a prince become suspicious of his counsellors and confidants, and to divide his forces. How to suppress mutiny and discord in an army. In what manner the ancients interpreted had omens and other sinister events. That an enemy should not be reduced to despair: and of several artifices that may be used to decoy and over-reach them. In what manner a suspected town or country is to be secured; and how to gain the affections of a people. That a war should not be carried on in winter.

Zanobi. Since we are going to vary our subject, I beg leave to lay down my office, and hope Battista della Palla will take it up: in so doing, we shall in some measure imitate the example of experienced commanders, who in time of battle (as Signor Fabrizio has informed us) generally place the best of their men in the front and rear of their armies; that the former may begin the attack with vigour, and the latter support it with resolution: Cosimo Rucellai therefore was wisely pitched upon to least the van (if I may use the expression) in this conversation, and Battista della Palla to bring up the rear: Luigi Alamanni, and I, took upon us to conduct the second line: and as we all readily submitted to the charge assigned us, I dare say Battista will do the same.

Battista. I have hitherto suffered myself to be governed entirely by the company, and shall do so for the future. Let us intreat you then, Signor Fabrizio, to proceed in your discourse, and to excuse this interruption.

Fabrizio. If it is any interruption, it is an agreeable one I assure you; for this change of officers, as I told you before, rather refreshes my recollection than otherwise.—But to resume our subject. It is now time to encamp and repose our army in security: for all creatures, you know, naturally require due intervals of rest from their labour, and nobody can properly be said to rest, that does not enjoy security at the same time. You might except perhaps that I should have first encamped my army, and then shewn the order of a march, and last of all, how it should be formed to engage an enemy. But I have done quite the contrary; and indeed I was obliged to it; for as I was to shew what an army upon a march had to do, when it was forced on a hidden to prepare for action, it was necessary to tell you first in what order of battle it should be drawn up.—Now to lodge your men in security, your camp ought to be strong and well governed: the former of which points depends either upon art, or the nature of its situation; the latter, upon care and good discipline in the commander.

The Greeks used to look out for a situation that was strong by nature; and never would encamp in any place that was not fortified either by a mountain or a river, or wood, or some other defence of that kind: the Romans, on the contrary, not depending so much upon nature as art and good discipline in their encampments, constantly made choice of situations where they could range their forces in their usual order, and exert their whole strength upon occasion. Hence it came to pass that the form of their encampments was always the same; because they never swerved from their established discipline, but pitched upon a situation which they could make conformable to it: whereas the Greeks were often obliged to vary the form and manner of their encampments, because they made their discipline give way to the situation of the place, which could not always be the same, or similar.

When the situation therefore was but indifferent, the Romans used to supply that defect by art and industry: and since I have hitherto proposed the conduct of that people as a model in most cases, I would likewise recommend their method in the encampment of their armies: not that I would follow it exactly in every particular, but in such only as may best suit the circumstances of the present times. I have told you more than once already, that they had two legions of their own citizens in their consular armies, amounting to about eleven thousand foot and six hundred horse; besides which, they had eleven thousand more foot composed of the auxiliaries furnished by their friends and confederates: but they never had a greater number of auxiliaries than of their own citizens in those armies; except in their horse, in which they were not so scrupulous.

I told you likewise, that they always posted their legions in the centre, and their auxiliaries in each wing, whenever they came to an engagement; which custom they also observed in their encampments, as you must have read, I dare say, in ancient history; and therefore I shall not trouble you now with a circumstantial detail of the method they followed upon such occasions, but content myself with informing you in what manner I would chuse to encamp an army at present; from whence you will easily perceive what I have borrowed from the Romans.—You know that as they had two legions in a consular army, I have likewise composed mine of two regiments, each consisting of six thousand foot and three hundred horse: you remember into how many battalions I divided them, in what manner they are armed, and by what names the different forces of which they consist are distinguished: you know, lastly, that in drawing them up either for battle or a march, I have made mention of no other troops, but only shewn that when their number is to be doubled, there is nothing more to be done than to double the ranks.

But now I am to shew you the method of encamping, I shall not confine myself to two regiments only, but inform you how a whole army should be disposed of, consisting (like those of the Romans) of two regiments of our own forces, and the same number of auxiliaries: and this I do to give you a clear idea of a complete encampment; for in the exercises and operations which I have hitherto described and recommended, there was no occasion to bring a whole army into the field at once. In order then to encamp an army of twenty-four thousand foot and two thousand horse, divided into four regiments, two of our own subjects and two of auxiliaries, I would observe this method. After I had pitched upon a convenient situation, I would erect my standard in the middle of a square, two hundred feet deep on every side; one of which sides should face the east, another the west, another the north, and another the south: and in this square the general should fix his quarters.

In the next place, (as it was generally the practice of the Romans, and seems worthy of imitation) I would separate my soldiers from the people who do not carry arms, and such as ought to be ready and fit for action from those that are loaded and encumbered in another manner: for which purpose, I would quarter either all or the greater part of my soldiers on the east side of the camp, and the others on the west; making the east side the front, the west the rear, and the north and south the flanks of my camp. To distinguish the quarters of my soldiery I would draw two parallel lines thirteen hundred and sixty feet in length, and at the distance of sixty from each other, from the general's standard towards the east; at the extremity of which, I would have the eastern gate of my camp.

By these means, a passage would formed directly from that gate to the general's quarters of twelve hundred and sixty feet in length, (for the distance from the standard to the extremity of his quarters on every side is an hundred feet) and this interval should be called the main passage. In the next place, let another passage be drawn from the south to the north gate across the main passage, and close by the east: side of the general's quarters, which should be two thousand five hundred feet in length (as it is to reach from one flank of the camp to the other) and sixty in breadth: and let this be called the crossway.

Having thus marked out the general's quarters, and drawn these two passages, I would proceed to provide quarters for the two regiments of my own subjects: one of which I would lodge on the right hand, and the other on the left of the main passage. For this purpose, I would place thirty-two lodgements on the left, and as many more on the right of that passage, leaving a space betwixt the sixteenth and seventeenth lodgement of sixty feet in breadth for a traverse-way to pass through the midst of the quarters of these two regiments, as you may see it marked out in the plan of an encampment which I luckily happen to have in my pocket.

In the front of these two lodgements, on each side of the main passage where they border upon the crossway, I would quarter the commanders of my *gens d'armes*, and their private men in the fifteen lodgements next adjoining to them: for as I have allowed an hundred and fifty *gens d'armes* to each regiment, there would be ten private men in every one of these compartments. The tents of the commanders should be eighty feet broad and twenty deep; and those of their private men thirty in depth and sixty in breadth. But I must here desire you to remember once for all, that whenever I make use of the word breadth, I mean the space that is extended from north to south; and when I speak of depth, I would be understood to design that which ranges from east to west.—In the next fifteen compartments which are to be on each side of the main passage, and on the east of the traverse-way (and to take up the same space with that occupied by the *gens d'armes*) I would quarter my light horse; which being an hundred and fifty in each regiment, would likewise amount to ten in every tent: and in the remaining sixteenth I would lodge their commanders, assigning them the same room with that taken up by the commanders of the *gens d'armes*.

The cavalry then of both regiments being thus provided with quarters of each side of the main passage, will direct us how to dispose of our infantry, as I shall shew you in the next place.

You have observed how I have quartered the three hundred horse belonging to each regiment, and their officers, in thirty-two lodgements on each side of the main passage, beginning from the crossway; and that I have left a void space, sixty feet in breadth, betwixt the sixteenth and seventeenth lodgement for a traverse-way. I order then to quarter the twenty battalions, of which the two regiments consist, I would appoint lodgements for two battalions behind the cavalry on both sides of the main passage; each of which should be thirty feet in length and sixty in breadth, like the others, and so close to those of the horse that they should join together.

In every first lodgement, beginning from the crossway, I would quarter the lieutenant colonel of the battalion, who would then be in a line with the commander of the *gens d'armes*: and this lodgement only should be forty feet in breadth, and twenty in depth. In the next fifteen lodgements reaching to the traverse-way, I would quarter a battalion of foot on each side or the main passage; the number of which amounting to four hundred and fifty, there would be thirty in every lodgement. The other fifteen lodgements I would place contiguous to the light horse on each side of the main passage, and on the east of the traverse-way, allowing them the same dimensions with those, on the west: and in each range of these I would quarter one battalion, assigning the sixteenth, which should be twenty feet in length, and forty in breadth, for the lieutenant colonel of the two battalions, who would then be close abreast with the commanders of the light horse.

The two first ranges of lodgements being thus occupied, would consist partly of cavalry, and partly of infantry: but as the cavalry should always be clean and ready for action, and the horsemen have no servants allowed to assist them in dressing and taking care of their horses, the foot of the two battalions that are quartered next to them should be obliged to wait upon them for that purpose: in consideration of which, they should be excused from all other duty in the camp, according to the practice of the Romans.

Leaving a void space then of sixty feet wide, on the back of the lodgements on each side of the main passage, one of which may be called the first way on the right, the other, the first way on the left, I would mark out another range of thirty-two double lodgements parallel to the others, and with their back parts close together; allowing the same dimensions with an interval likewise betwixt the sixteenth and seventeenth for the traverse-way: and in each of these I would quarter four battalions, with their commanders in the first and last of them. In the next place, I would leave another space of sixty feet wide on the back of these two lodgements, for a way which should be called the second way on the right, on one side the main passage, and the second way on the left, on the other: close to which, I would have another range of double lodgements on each side of the main passage, in every respect like the other two; in which I would quarter the four remaining battalions, and their lieutenant colonels: so that all the cavalry and infantry of our own two regiments would be disposed of in six ranges, or lines of double lodgements, with the main passage betwixt them.

As to the two auxiliary battalions (supposing them to consist of the same number and sort of forces) I would place them on each side of our own, in the like order and number of double lodgements: the two first lines of which should be partly horse, and partly foot, and at the distance of sixty feet from the two third lines of our own on each side the main passage, to make room for a way betwixt them, which should be called on one side, the third way on the right; and on the other, the third way on the left. After this, I would mark out two other lines of lodgements, parallel to the first on each side of the main passage, and divided like those of our own battalions, with spaces of sixty feet betwixt them for other ways, which should be numbered and denominated from their situation and distance from the main passage: and then all this part of the army would be quartered in twelve ranges or lines of double lodgements, with thirteen ways or passages betwixt the several divisions of it, including the main passage, traverse, and crossways.

Besides this, I would have a void space left of two hundred feet in width, betwixt the lodgements and the fosse which should encompass them: so that computing the whole distance from the centre of the general's quarters to the eastern gate, you will find that it amounts to thirteen hundred and sixty feet. There are still remaining two vacant intervals, one from the general's quarters to the south, and the other from thence to the north gate of the camp; each of which (reckoning from the centre) is twelve hundred and fifty feet in length. Deducting then from each of these spaces an hundred feet, which are taken up by the general's quarters on each side, and ninety feet on each side for an area or *piazza*, and sixty for a way to divide the two above mentioned spaces in the middle, and two hundred more for the interval betwixt the lodgements and the fosse, there will be a space left of eight hundred feet in breadth, and two hundred in depth, for a line of lodgements on each side; the depth being the same with that of the general's quarters.

These spaces being properly divided, will make forty lodgements on both sides of the general's quarters, each of which will be an hundred feet long, and forty broad: and in these I would quarter the colonels of the several regiments, the paymasters, the quartermaster-general, and in short, all those that had any particular charge or business in the army; leaving some of them vacant for the reception of strangers or volunteers, and attendants upon the general. On the backside of the general's quarters I would make a passage from north to south sixty-two feet wide, and call it the headway, which should run along the west side of the eighty lodgements just mentioned: and then those lodgements, and the general's quarters, would be included betwixt that passage and the crossway.

From the headway I would draw another passage directly from the general's quarters to the western gate of the camp, which should be sixty feet wide, and of the same length with the main passage; and this should be called the market-way. These two passages being drawn, I would make a marketplace, or square, at the beginning of the market-way, over against the general's quarters, and joining to the headway, which should be two hundred and forty feet on every side. On the right and left of the marketplace, I would have a row of quarters, each of which should contain eight double lodgements, which should be thirty feet in depth, and sixty in breadth; that is, sixteen on each hand of the marketplace.

In these I would lodge the supernumerary horse belonging to the auxiliary regiments: and if there should not be room enough, for all of them there, I would quarter those that were excluded in some of the eighty lodgements next to the general's quarters, but chiefly in those that lie nearest the fosse.

It now remains that we should quarter our pikemen and *velites* extraordinary; for you know there are a thousand of the former, and five hundred of the latter in every regiment: so that our own two regiments having two thousand pikemen, and one thousand *velites* extraordinary, and those of the auxiliaries as many more, we have still six thousand foot to dispose of; all of whom I would quarter on the three sides of the fosse, in the western part of the camp. For this purpose, I would have a row of five double lodgements, an hundred and fifty feet long, and an hundred and twenty wide, on the west side, of the north end of the headway, leaving a vacant space of two hundred feet betwixt them and the fosse: which row consisting of ten single lodgements, and every lodgement being thirty feet deep, and sixty wide, would contain three hundred foot; that is, thirty in every one of them.

Next to these (but with an interval of sixty-two feet betwixt them) I would place another row of five double lodgements of the same dimensions; and after that, another; and so on till there were five rows of five double lodgements of the same size, and with the same intervals betwixt them, all in a right line one with another, at the distance of two hundred feet from the fosse on the west of the headway, and on the north side of the camp: so that there would be fifty lodgements in all, which would contain fifteen hundred men. Turning then from the left towards the western gate, I would mark out five other rows of double lodgements in the space betwixt the last of the other five and that gate, of the same contents and proportion, but with intervals of only thirty feet betwixt one row and the other; in which I would likewise quarter fifteen hundred men: and in this manner, all the pikemen and *velites* extraordinary belonging to our own two regiments would be disposed of in ten rows of double lodgements, that is, an hundred single ones, (reckoning ten in a row) along the range of the fosse from the north to the west gate.

In the like manner I would provide for the pikemen and *velites* extraordinary belonging to the auxiliary regiments; quartering them all in ten rows of double lodgements of the same dimensions, and with the same intervals betwixt them, along the range of the fosse, from the west to the south gate; allowing their colonels and other officers to take up such quarters there as should be most convenient for them.

My artillery I would plant all along the banks on the inside of the fosse: and in the vacant space, which would be still left on the west side of the headway, I would lodge all the unarmed people, and impediments belonging to the camp. Now you must know by the word impediments, the ancients meant all the baggage, and people, and stores that are necessary in an army, except the soldiers; as carpenters, joiners, smiths, stone-cutters, masons, engineers, cannoneers (though indeed these last may properly be reckoned soldiers) herdsmen, oxen and sheep for the sustenance of the army. Cooks, butchers; in short, all manner of artificers and implements, together with proper vehicles and beasts of burden to carry the ammunition, provisions, and other requisites. However, I would not assign separate and distinct lodgements for all these things; but content myself with ordering that some passages should be left entirely clear and unoccupied by them.

Of the four void spaces which would be left betwixt these passages, I would appropriate one to the herdsmen and their cattle; another to the artificers of every kind; another to make room for the carriages that contain the provisions; and the last to receive those that are loaded with arms and ammunition. The passages which I would have left quite open, should be the market-way, the headway, and another called the middle-way, to be drawn across the camp from north to south, which should cut the market-way at right angles, and answer the same purposes on the western side of the camp, as the traverse-way does in the eastern. Besides this, I would have still another passage drawn behind the lodgements of the pikemen and *velites* extraordinary, which are ranged on three sides of the fosse; and every one of these passages should be sixty feet wide.

Battista. I confess my ignorance in these matters, and think I have no reason to be ashamed of it, as the Art of War is not my profession. The disposition however, which you have made, pleases me very much; and I have but two questions to ask relating to it, which I beg the favour of you to resolve: the first is, why you make the ways and passages about the lodgements so broad? The second (which perplexes me the most) is, in what manner the spaces you allow for the lodgements are to be occupied?

Fabrizio. The reason why I have made all the passages sixty feet wide, is that a whole battalion at a time, drawn up in order of battle, may pass through them: for I told you before, if you remember, that every battalion takes up a space of fifty or sixty feet in width. It is necessary also, that the interval betwixt the lodgements and the fosse should be two hundred feet wide, in order to draw up the battalions there in a proper mariner upon occasion, to manage the artillery, to make room for booty or prisoners taken from the enemy, and for throwing up new banks and ditches, if it should be requisite. It is likewise proper to have the lodgements at a good distance from the fosse, that they may be more out of the reach of fireworks, and other offensive things, which an enemy might otherwise throw in amongst them.

In answer to your second question, I must tell you, it is not my intention that every space which I have laid out for lodgements should be wholly covered by one great tent only, but that it should be divided and occupied in such a manner as may best suit the convenience of those for whose use it is designed; and have more or fewer tents in it as they please, provided they did not exceed the limits prescribed them.

But in order to lay out these lodgements, there should always be able and experienced engineers, quartermasters, and builders, ready to mark out a camp, and distinguish the several passages and divisions of it with stakes and cordage, as soon as the general has fixed upon a proper situation for it: and to prevent confusion, the front of the camp should always look the same way, that so every man may know near what passage, and in which quarter, he may find his tent. This rule being constantly observed, the camp will be a sort of a moving town, which carries, the same streets, the same houses, and the same aspect with it wherever it goes; a convenience which those must not expect, who make choice of such situations only as are naturally strong and advantageous; because they must always change the form of their camp according; to the nature of the ground.

The Romans (as I said before) made their camps strong in any situation, by throwing up a ditch and rampart about them, and leaving a vacant space betwixt their lodgements and the ditch, which was generally twelve feet wide, and fix deep; though they sometimes made it both wider and deeper, especially if they either designed to continue long in the lame place, or expected to be attacked. For my own part, I would not fortify a camp with a palisade, except I intended to winter in it; but content myself with a rampart and a ditch, not of less width or depth than what has been just now mentioned, but greater, if occasion required: besides which, I would have an half moon at every angle of the camp, with some pieces of artillery in it, to take the enemy in flank, if the trenches should be attacked.

In this exercise of encamping and decamping, the army should frequently be employed, in order to make the several officers ready and expert in laying out the distinct lodgements in a proper manner, and to teach the soldiers to know their respective quarters; nor is there any great difficulty in it, as I shall shew elsewhere; for I will now proceed to say something concerning the guards that are necessary in a camp, because if that point is not duly attended to, all the rest of our labour and care will be to no purpose.

Battista. Before you do that, I wish you would inform me what is to be done when you would encamp near an enemy, for surely there cannot be time enough, upon such an occasion, to dispose things in this regular order, without exposing yourself to great, danger.

Fabrizio. No general will ever encamp very near an enemy, except he is in a condition to give them battle whenever they please: and if the enemy be likewise disposed to engage, the danger cannot be more than ordinary; because he may draw out two thirds of his army, and leave the other to form his camp. The Romans, in such cases, committed the care of throwing up entrenchments, and laying out their camp, to the *triarii*, and caused the *principes* and *hastati* only to stand to their arms: for as the *triarii*, were the last line of their army that was to engage, they might leave their work if the enemy advanced, and draw up under arms in their proper station. So that if you would imitate the Romans in the like case, you should leave the care of laying out and fortifying your camp to the battalions in the rear of your army, which referable the *triarii* in those of the Romans.

But to return to what I was going to say concerning the guards of a camp. I do not remember to have read that the ancients used to keep any guards or sentinels on the outside of their entrenchments in the night-time, as we do at present. The reason of which I take to be, that they thought their armies were exposed to much danger by making use of them; as perhaps they might either betray or desert them of their own accord, or be surprised or corrupted by the enemy: and therefore they did not think fit to put any confidence in them. Upon these considerations, they trusted wholly to the guards and centinels that were stationed within their entrenchments; which were keep with such order and exactness, that the least failure in that duty was punished with death.

I shall not trouble you however, with a long and circumstantial detail of the order and method which they observed in this matter, because you very likely have read it in their histories, or if you have not, you may meet with it there whenever you please. For the sake of brevity then, I will only tell you what I would do myself upon such occasions. I would cause one third of my army to continue under arms every night: and one fourth of this to be upon guard along the entrenchments and other proper places of the camp allowing a double guard at every angle of it; one part of which should constantly remain there, and the other be patrolling all night from that angle to the next, and back again: and this method should be observed in the daytime also, if the enemy lay near me. As for giving out a parole, or watchword, and changing it every night, and other such circumstances belonging to guards and sentinels, I shall lay nothing of them, because they are known by everyone.

But there is one thing of the utmost importance, the practice of which will be attended with much advantage, and the neglect of it with great prejudice; and that is, to observe strictly who lies out of the camp at night, and what strangers come into it: which is a very easy matter to be done by such as observe the manner and order of encamping I have recommended; because every lodgement having a certain number of men belonging to it, you may presently see if there be more or fewer in it than there should be: if any are absent without leave, they should be punished as deserters; and if there are more than there ought to be, you should diligently enquire who they are? what business they have there? and of other circumstances relating to them.

This precaution will make it very difficult, if not impossible, for the enemy to hold any secret correspondence with your officers, or to penetrate into your designs: and if the Romans had not carefully attended to this point, Claudius Nero could not have left his camp in Lucania, and gone privately into the territories of Picenum, and returned from thence to his former quarters, whilst Hannibal knew nothing of the matter all the while, though the two camps lay very near each other.(*Vide* Livy, Lib. Xxvii.)

But it is not sufficient barely to give out good and wholesome orders for this purpose, if the observance of them is not enforced with the utmost severity: for there is no case whatsoever in which the most exact and implicit obedience is so necessary as in the government of an army: and therefore the laws that are established for the maintenance of it ought to be rigorous and severe, and the general a man of inflexible resolution in supporting them. The Romans punished with death, not only those that failed in their duty when they were upon guard, but all such as either abandoned their post in time of battle, or carried anything by stealth out of the camp, or pretended they had performed some exploit in action which they had not done, or engaged without the orders of their general, or threw away their arms out of fear: and when it happened that a *cohort* or a whole legion had behaved ill, they made them cast lots, and put every tenth man to death, which was called *decimation*: this was done to avoid shedding too much blood, and that though they did not all suffer, every man might be under an apprehension that the lot might fall upon him.

But where there are severe punishments, there should likewise be proportionable rewards, to excite men to behave themselves well by motives both of hope and fear; and therefore they always rewarded those that had distinguished themselves by any meritorious action; especially such as had either saved the life of a fellow-citizen in battle, or been the first in scaling the walls of an enemy's town, or storming their camp, or had wounded, or killed, or dismounted an enemy. In this manner every man's desert was properly taken notice of, and recompensed by the consuls, and publicly honoured: and those that obtained any reward for services of this kind (besides the reputation and glory which they acquired amongst their brother soldiers) were received by their friends and relations with all manner of rejoicings and congratulations, when they returned from the wars.

It is no wonder then that a people, who are so exact in rewarding merit, and punishing offenders, should extend their Empire to such a degree as they did: and certainly they are highly worthy of imitation in these respects. Give me leave therefore to be a little more explicit in describing one of their punishments.—When a delinquent stood convicted before his general, the latter gave him a slight stroke with a rod; after which, he might run away if he could: but as every soldier in the army had liberty to kill him, he no sooner began to run but they all fell upon him with their swords, or darts, or other weapons; so that he seldom escaped: and if he did, he was not allowed to return home, except under heavy penalties, and such a load of infamy, that it would have been much better for him to have died.

This custom is in some measure still kept up by the Swiss in their armies, (as at time of first publication), who always cause a convicted offender to be killed by the rest of the soldiers: and I think it is a very good one; for in order to prevent others from supporting or protecting an offender, it is certainly the best way to leave the punishment of him to themselves; because they will always look upon him with a different eye in that case, from what they would if he is to be punished by anybody else. This rule will also hold good in popular Governments, as we may learn from the example of Manlius Capitolinus, who being acceded by the Senate, was strenuously defended by the people, till they were left to judge him themselves: after which, they presently condemned him to die.

This then is a good method of punishing delinquents, and of causing justice to be executed upon them in security, without fear of exciting mutiny or sedition. But as neither the fear of laws, nor reverence to man alone, are sufficient to bridle an armed multitude, the ancients used to call in the aid of religion, and made their soldiers take a very strict oath to pay due obedience to military discipline with many awful ceremonies and great solemnity: besides which, they used all other methods to inspire them with a fear of the Gods; that so if they violated their oaths, they might have not only the asperity of human laws, but the vengeance of Heaven to apprehend.

Battista. Did the Romans ever suffer women or gaming in their camp, as we do at present?

Fabrizio. They prohibited both: nor was the restraint very grievous; for their soldiers were so constantly employed either in one sort of duty or other, that they had no time to think either of women or gaming, or any other of those vile avocations which commonly make soldiers idle and seditious.

Battista. They were in the right of it.—But pray tell me what order they observed when they were going to decamp.

Fabrizio. The general's trumpet was sounded three times: at the first sounding, they struck their tents and packed them up; at the second, they loaded their carriages; and at the third, they began their march in the order I have described before, with their legions in the middle of the army, and their baggage in the rear of every particular corps. For which purpose, it is necessary that one of the auxiliary regiments should move first with its own baggage, and a fourth part of the public impediments in its rear, which was placed in one or other of the four divisions in the western part of the camp that I spoke of not long ago: and therefore every legion should have its particular division assigned to its charge; that so when they are about to march, every one of them may know where to take its place.

Battista. Did the Romans use to make any other provisions in laying out their camps besides those which you have already mentioned?

Fabrizio. I must tell you again that they always kept to the same form in their encampments, which was their first and principal consideration. Besides this, they had two other great points in view: the first of which was a wholesome situation; and the next, to encamp where the enemy could neither surround, nor cut them off from water or provisions. To prevent sickness in their army therefore, they always avoided marshy grounds, and such as were exposed to noxious winds: of which they formed their judgement not so much from the quality of the place, as from the constitution and appearance of the people who lived thereabout: for if they either had sickly complexions, or were subject to asthmas, or dropsies, or any other endemic disorder, they would not encamp there.

As to the other point of not being liable to be surrounded by an enemy, they considered where their friends and where their enemy lay, and judged from thence of the probability or possibility of their being surrounded or not: upon which account, it is necessary that a general should be very well acquainted with the nature and situation of the country he is in, and that he should have others about him who are as knowing in these respects as himself. There are other precautions also to be used in order to prevent distempers and famine in an army; such as restraining all manner of excess and intemperance amongst the soldiers, by taking care that they sleep under cover, that your camp may be near trees that will afford them shade in the daytime, and wood enough for fuel to dress their victuals, and that they do not march when the heat of the sun is too intense.

For this reason, they should decamp before daylight in the summer, and take care not to march through ice and snow in the winter, except they have frequent opportunities of making good fires, and warm cloathing to guard them again the inclemency of the weather. It is necessary likewise to prevent them from drinking stagnated and fetid water: and if any of them happen to fall ill, you should give strict orders to the physicians and surgeons of the army to take great care of them: for bad indeed is the condition of a general, when he has a sickness amongst his men and an enemy to contend with at the same time. But nothing conduces so much to keep an army in good health and spirits as exercise: and therefore the ancients used to exercise their troops every day. Due exercise then is surely of great importance, as it preserves your health in the camp, and secures you victory in the field.

As to guarding against famine, it is only necessary to take timely care that the enemy may not be able to cut you off from provisions, but to consider from whence you may be conveniently supplied with them, and to see that those which you have are properly distributed and preserved. You should therefore always have a month's provisions at least beforehand, and afterwards oblige your neighbouring friends and allies to furnish you daily with a certain quantity: you ought likewise to establish magazines and storehouses in strong places, and above all to distribute your provisions duly and frugally amongst your men, giving them a reasonable proportion every day, and attending so strictly to this point that you may not by any means exhaust your stores, and run yourself aground: for though all other calamities in an army may be remedied in time, famine alone grows more and more grievous the longer it continues, and is sure to destroy you at last; nor will any enemy ever come to an engagement with you when he is sure to conquer you in such circumstances without it: for though a victory obtained in this manner may not be so honourable as one that is gained by dint of arms, it is certain however, and not attended with any *risque*.

An army then cannot possibly escape famine which wantonly and extravagantly wastes its provisions without foresight, or regard to rule or measure, or the circumstances of the times: for want of timely care will prevent its having supplies, and profusion consumes what it already has to no purpose: upon which confederation, the ancients took care their soldiers should eat no more than a daily and reasonable allowance, and that too only at stated times; for they never were suffered either to breakfast, or dine, or sup, but when their general did the same. How well these excellent rules are observed in our armies at present, I need not tell you; for everyone knows that our soldiers, instead of imitating the regularity and sobriety of the ancients, are a parcel of intemperate, licentious, and drunken fellows.

Battista. When our conversation first turned upon encampments, you said you would not confine yourself to two regiments only, but take four, the better to shew how a complete army should be encamped. But I should be glad to know in the first place, how you would quarter your army if it consisted of a greater or smaller number of men than that? and in the next, what number you would think sufficient to engage any enemy?

Fabrizio. To your first question, I answer, that if your army has five or six thousand, more or less than that number, in it, you have nothing to do but either to add or to diminish your rows of lodgements accordingly: and this you may do in what proportion you please. The Romans however had two different camps when they joined two consular armies together, the rear quarters of which (where the impediments and unarmed people were) faced each other. As to your second question, the common armies which the Romans brought into the field usually consisted of about twenty-four thousand men, and upon the most pressing occasions they never exceeded fifty thousand.

With this number they made head against two hundred thousand Gauls who invaded them after the conclusion of the first Carthaginian war: with the same number they opposed Hannibal: indeed, both the Romans and Greeks, depending chiefly upon their discipline and good conduct, always carried on their wars with small armies; whereas both the eastern and western nations had vast and almost innumerable hosts: the latter trusting wholly to their natural ferocity, and the former availing themselves of the implicit submission which their subjects shew to their princes.

But neither the Greeks nor Romans being remarkable either for natural ferocity, or implicit submission to their princes, were obliged to have recourse to good discipline; the power and efficacy of which were so great, that one of their small armies often defeated a prodigious multitude bf the fiercest and most obstinate people. In imitation then of the Greeks and Romans, I would not have about fifty thousand men in an army, but fewer if I might chuse: for more are apt to create discord and confusion, and not only become ungovernable themselves, but corrupt others that have been well-disciplined: Pyrrhus therefore used to say, that "with an army of fifteen thousand good soldiers he would fight the whole world."[1]

But let us now proceed to other matters. You have seen our army

---

1. "At the Siege of Alexia, the Gauls having drawn all their powers together to fight Caesar, after they had made a general muster of their forces, resolved in a council of war to dismiss a good part of that great multitude, that they might not fall into confusion." And indeed it stands to reason that the body of an army should consist of a moderate number, and retrained to certain bounds, both in regard to the difficulty of providing for them, and the difficulty of governing and keeping them in order: at least it is very easy to make it appear by example, that armies so monstrous in number have seldom done anything to the purpose. According to the saying of Cyrus in Xenophon, "it is not the number of men, but the number of good men, that gives the advantage;" the remainder serving rather to embarrass than assist: and Bajazet principally grounded his resolution of giving Tamerlane battle, contrary to the opinion of all his captains, upon this, that the numberless host his enemy had brought into the field, gave him assured hope of their falling into confusion. Scanderbeg, a good and expert judge in these matters, used to say, "that ten or twelve thousand faithful fighting men were sufficient for a good leader to secure his reputation on all military occasions." See *Montaigne*, book II. chap. xxxiv.

gain a battle, and the accidents which may occur in the time of action: you have likewise seen it upon a march, and been acquainted with the dangers and embarrassments it is subject to in those circumstances: and lastly, you have seen it regularly quartered in camp, where it ought to stay awhile, not only to enjoy a little rest after its fatigues, but to concert proper measures for bringing the campaign to a happy conclusion: for many things are to be considered and digested in camp, especially if either the enemy still keeps the field, or there are any towns belonging to them not yet reduced, or any in possession of people whose fidelity and affection you have reason to suspect; because in these cases you must make yourself master of the one, and secure the attachment of the other.

It is necessary therefore to shew in what manner, and by what means, these difficulties are to be surmounted with the same reputation with which we have hitherto carried on the war.—To descend to particulars then, I say, that if several different persons, or different states, should think of doing any particular thing which may tend to your advantage and their own prejudice, such as dismantling some of their towns, or banishing a great number of their inhabitants, you should encourage them in it in such a manner that none of them may suspect that it will prejudice their interest; by which you may amuse them so effectually, that instead of confederating together for their own safety, they will not think of giving each other the least assistance, and then you may suppress them all without any material opposition. But if this method will not succeed, you must order every one of them to execute what you desire on the same day; that so each state imagining that no other has any orders of the same kind, may be obliged to obey, because it has no support from its neighbours to depend upon; and thus you may succeed in your designs without any resistance or combination being formed against you.

If you should suspect the fidelity of any state, and would secure yourself by falling upon them unawares, in order to disguise your intentions the more effectually, it is the best way to pretend a perfect confidence in them, to consult them in some design which you seem to have upon others, and to desire their assistance, as if you had not the least doubt of their sincerity, or thought of molesting them; which will put them off their guard, and give you an opportunity of treating them as you please.——If you suspect any person in your army of giving the enemy intelligence of your designs, you cannot do better than avail yourself of his treachery, by seeming to trust him with some secret resolution which you intend to execute, whilst you carefully conceal your real design: by which, perhaps, you may discover the traitor, and least the enemy into an error that may possibly end in their destruction.

If, in order to relieve some friend, you would lessen your army so privately that the enemy may not be aware of it (as Claudius Nero did) you should not lessen the number of your lodgements, but leave the vacant tents standing, and the colours flying, making the same fires and keeping the same guards that you did before. In like manner, if you receive fresh supplies, and would not; have the enemy know that you have been reinforced, you must not increase the number of your tents; for nothing is of greater importance than to keep these and other such transactions as secret as possible. When Metellus commanded the Roman armies in Spain, a certain person took the liberty of asking him what he intended to do the next day; upon which, he told him that "if he thought the shirt upon his back knew that, he would immediately take it off and burn it."

Marcus Crassus being likewise importuned by one of his officers to let him know when he designed to decamp, asked him "if he thought he should be the only one in the camp that would not hear the sound of the trumpets."—In order to penetrate into the secret designs, and discover the condition of an enemy, some have sent ambassadors to them with skilful and experienced officers in their train, dressed like the rest of their attendants; who have taken an opportunity of viewing their army, and observing their strength and weakness in so minute a manner that it has been of much service.

Others have pretended to quarrel with and banish: some particular confidant, who has gone over to the enemy, and afterwards informed them of their designs. The intentions of an enemy are likewise sometimes discovered by the examination of the prisoners you take.—When Marius commanded in the war against the Cimbrians, and wanted to try the fidelity of the Gauls, who at that time inhabited Lombardy, and were in confederacy with the Romans, he wrote some letters to them which were left open, and others that were sealed; in the former of which, he desired they would not open those that were sealed till a certain day; but before that time he sent for them again, and finding they had been opened, he perceived there was no confidence to be put in that people.

Some princes have not immediately sent an army to oppose the enemy when their territories have been invaded, but made an incursion into their country, and thereby obliged them to return to defend themselves; a method which has often succeeded: for in such cases, your soldiers being elated with victory, and loaded with plunder, fight with spirit and confidence; whilst those of the enemy are dejected at the thoughts of being beaten instead of conquering: so that a diversion of this kind has frequently been attended with good consequences. But this you must not attempt, except your country is better fortified than that of the enemy: for if you do, you will certainly be ruined.

If a general is blocked up in his camp by an enemy, he should endeavour to set a treaty of accommodation on foot with them, and to obtain a truce for a few days; during which, they are apt to be so careless and remiss that he may possibly find an opportunity or slipping out of their hands. By these means, Sylla twice eluded the enemy; and in this manner Asdrubal got clear of Claudius Nero when he had surrounded him in Spain.

Besides these expedients, there are other methods likewise of extricating yourself from an enemy; as either by attacking them with one part of your forces only, that so while their attention is wholly turned upon that side, the rest of your army may find means to save themselves; or by some uncommon stratagem, the novelty of which may fill them with terror and astonishment at the same time, so that they cannot resolve how to act, or whether to act at all; as Hannibal did, when he was surrounded by Fabius Maximus: for having a great number of oxen in his camp, he fastened lighted torches to their horns in the night-time and let them loose to run about the country; at the strangeness of which spectacle Fabius was so perplexed that he could not prevent their retreat.—But above all things, a general ought to endeavour to divide the enemy's strength, either by making him suspicious of his counsellors and confidants, or obliging him to employ his forces in different places and detachments at the same time, which consequently must very much weaken his main army.

The first may be done by sparing the possessions of some particular men in whom he most confides, and not suffering their houses or estates to be damaged in a time of general plunder and devastation; or by returning their children and other relations when they are taken prisoners, without any ransom. Thus when Hannibal had ravaged and burnt all the towns and country round about Rome, he spared the estate of Fabius Maximus alone: Coriolanus likewise, returning at the head of an army to Rome, carefully preserved the possessions of the nobility, and burnt those of the plebeians.

When Metellus commanded the Roman army against Jugurtha, he tampered with the ambassadors who were sent to him by that prince, to deliver up their master prisoner to him, and kept up a correspondence with them for the same purpose after they had left him, till Jugurtha discovered it, and grew so jealous of his counsellors, that he put them all to death upon one pretence or other: and after Hannibal had taken refuge with Antiochus, the Roman ambassadors managed so artfully that Antiochus became suspicious of him, and would neither take his advice, nor trust him again in any matter whatsoever.—As to dividing the enemy's strength, there can be no better way of doing it than by making incursions into their country, for that will oblige them to abandon all other enterprises, and return home to defend their own.

This was the method which Fabius took when he had not only the Gauls, but the Tuscans, the Umbrians, and the Samnites to deal with at the same time. Titus Didius having but a small army in comparison of the enemy, and expecting to be reinforced by another legion from Rome, was apprized that the enemy had formed a design to cut it off upon its march: to prevent which, he not only caused a report to be spread through his camp that he would engage the enemy the next day, but suffered some prisoners he had taken to escape, who informed their general of the consul's intentions; which had such an effect, that he did not think fit to diminish his own forces by detaching any part of them to oppose the march of that legion; so that it joined the consul in safety: and though this stratagem indeed did not divide the enemy's army, yet it proved the means of reinforcing his own.

Some, in order to diminish the strength of an invader, have suffered him to enter their country, and take several towns: that so when he has weakened his main army by putting garrisons into them, they might fall upon him with a greater probability of success. Others, who have had a design upon one province, have made a feint of invading another: after which, turning their forces suddenly upon that where they were not at all expected, they have made themselves masters of it before the enemy could send any relief: for in such cases, the enemy, being uncertain whether you may not return to attack the province first threatened, is obliged to maintain his post, and not to leave one place to succour another: so that (as it often happens) he is not able to secure them both.

It is of great importance to prevent the spreading of mutiny or discord in an army: for which purpose, you should punish the ringleaders in an exemplary manner, but with such address that it may be done before they imagine you intend it. If they are at a distance from you, it is the best way to call both the innocent and the guilty together, left (if you summon the offenders alone) they should suspect your design, and either become contumacious, or take some other method to elude the punishment that is due to them: but if they are within your reach, you may avail yourself of those that are innocent, and punish the others by their assistance.

As to private discords amongst your soldiers, the only remedy is to expose them to some danger, for in such cases fear generally unites them: but what most commonly keeps an army united is the reputation of the general; that is, his courage and good conduct; for without these, neither high birth nor any sort of authority are sufficient. Now the chief thing incumbent upon a general, in order to maintain his reputation, is to pay well, and punish severely: for if he does not pay his men duly, he cannot punish them properly when they deserve it. Supposing, for instance, a soldier should be guilty of a robbery; how can you punish him for that when you give him no pay? And how can he help robbing when he has no other means of subsistence? But if you pay them well, and do not punish them severely when they offend, they will soon grow insolent and licentious: for then you will become despised, and lose your authority; after which, tumults and discords will naturally ensue in your army, which probably will end in the ruin of it.

The commanders of armies in former times had one difficulty to struggle with, from which our generals at present are in a great measure exempt; and that was the interpreting bad omens and auguries in such a manner, that instead of seeming adverse, they might appear to be favourable and propitious. For if a storm of thunder and lightning[2] fell upon the camp, or either the sun or moon was eclipsed, or there was an earthquake, or the general happened to get a fall in mounting or dismounting his horse, the soldiers looked upon it as an unhappy presage, and were so dismayed, that they made but a faint resistance against any enemy that attacked them.

Upon any accident of that kind therefore, they either endeavoured to account for it from natural causes, or interpreted it to their own

---

2. The words of the author are, "*perché se cadeva una saetta in uno esercito.*" Now the word *saetta* must here mean a stroke of lightning, most probably, or what the country people call a *thunder-bolt.* The old translation renders it thus: For if an arrow fell down in an army, &c. which I confess I do not understand.

purpose and advantage. When Julius Caesar landed in Africa, he happened to get a fall as soon as he set his foot on shore, upon which, he immediately cried out, "*Teneo te, O Africa, i.e.* Africa, I take possession of thee." Others have explained the reasons of earthquakes and eclipses to their soldiers. But such events have little or no effect in these times: for men are not so much given to superstition since the Christian Religion has enlightened their minds, and dispelled these vain fears: but if they should ever happen to return, we must imitate the example of the ancients upon such occasions.

If famine or any other kind of distress has reduced an enemy to despair, and they advance furiously to engage, you should keep close in your entrenchments, and avoid a battle, if possible; as the Lacedaemonians did when they were provoked to fight by the Messenians, and Julius Caesar by Afranius and Petreius.—When Fulvius the consul commanded the Roman army against the Cimbrians, he caused his cavalry to attack the enemy several days successively, and observing that they always quitted their camp to pursue his troops when they retreated, he at last placed a body of men in ambush behind their camp, who rushed into it, and made themselves masters of it the next time they sallied out to pursue his cavalry.

Some princes, when their dominions have been invaded, and their army has lain near that of the enemy, have sent out parties under the enemy's colours to plunder and lay waste their own territories: upon which, the enemy imagining them to be friends who were coming to their assistance, have gone out to join them; but upon discovering their mistake, have fallen into confusion, and given their adversary an opportunity of beating them. This stratagem was practised by Alexander of Epirus against the Illyrians, and Leptenes the Syracusan against the Carthaginians, and they both found their account in it.—Many have gained an advantage by pretending to run away in great fear, and leaving their camp full of wine and provisions, with which when the enemy have gorged themselves, the others have returned and fallen upon them whilst they were drunk or asleep.

In this manner Cyrus was deceived by Tomyris, and the Spaniards by Tiberius Gracchus. Others have mixed poison with the meat and drink they left behind them.—I told you a little before that I did not remember to have read that the ancients placed any centinels on the outside of the ditch that surrounded their camp in the night; and that I supposed it was to prevent the mischiefs they might occasion: for it has often happened that centinels, who have been stationed at outposts, even in the daytime, to observe the motions of an enemy, have been the ruin of an army; as they have sometimes been surprised and forced to make the signals for their friends to advance, who have thereby been drawn into a snare, and either killed or taken prisoners.

In order to deceive an enemy, it may not be amiss either to vary or omit some particular custom or signal that you have constantly made use of before, as a certain great general did of old; who having caused some of his advanced parties always to give him notice of the enemy's approach by fires in the night, and smoke in the daytime, thought proper to vary that custom at last, and ordered those parties to keep constant fires all the night long, and to make a smoke every day, but to extinguish them when they perceived the enemy in motion: upon which, the enemy advancing again, and not seeing the usual signals made to give notice of their approach, imagined they were not discovered, and pushed on so precipitately to the attack, that they fell into disorder, and were routed by their adversary, who was prepared to receive them.

Memnon the Rhodian, in order to draw the enemy out of a strong and advantageous situation of which they had possessed themselves, got one of his own men to pass over to them as a deserter, with intelligence that his army was in a mutiny, and that the greater part of it was going to leave him: to confirm which, he caused a great uproar and commotion to be counterfeited every now and then in his camp; by which the enemy were so imposed upon that they quitted their entrenchments to attack him, and were entirely defeated.——Great care is likewise to be taken not to reduce an enemy to utter despair. Julius Caesar was always very attentive to this point in his wars with the Germans, and used to open them a way to escape, after he began to perceive that when they were hard pressed, and could not run away, they would fight most desperately; thinking it better to pursue them when they fled, than to run the *risque* of not conquering when they defended themselves with such obstinacy.

Lucullus observing that a body of Macedonian horse, which he had in his army, were going over to the enemy, caused a charge to be sounded immediately, and ordered all the rest of his army to advance: upon which, the enemy supposing he designed to attack them, presently fell upon the Macedonians with such fury, that they were obliged to defend themselves, and fought bravely, instead of deserting him as they designed.

It is of great importance also to secure a town, when you suspect its loyalty, either before or after a victory.—Pompey suspecting the fidelity of the Catinenses, desired them to let him send the sick men whom he had in his army into their town, to be taken care of till they were well again: but instead of sick men, he sent a parcel of the stoutest and most resolute fellows he had in his army in disguise, who made themselves masters of the town and kept it for him.

Publius Valerius having been offended by the Epidaurians, and mistrusting their sincerity, caused a pardon to be proclaimed for all such as would come to accept of it at a certain temple without the gates of their town: upon which all the inhabitants repairing thither for that purpose, he shut the doors of the temple upon them, and suffered none to return to the town but such as he could confide in.—Alexander the Great, in order to secure Thrace when he was upon his march into Asia, took all the nobility and leading men of that province along with him, and allowing them pensions, left the common people to be governed by men of their own condition: by which, the nobility being content with their appointments, and the common people having no leading men to oppress, or instigate them to rebel, the whole province continued quiet.

But of all the methods that can be taken to gain the hearts of a people, none contribute so much as remarkable examples of continence and justice; like that of Scipio in Spain, when he returned a most beautiful young lady, safe and untouched, to her husband and relations; a circumstance which conduced more to the reduction of Spain, than any force of arms could ever have done.—Julius Caesar acquired such reputation for his justice in paying for the wood which he cut down to make palisades for his camps in Gaul, that it very much facilitated the conquest of that province. I think I have now nothing more to add to these particular documents, or the subject in general; except it be to say something concerning the nature of attacking and defending towns; which I will do as briefly and clearly as I can, if I have not already trespassed too much upon your patience.

Battista. You are so very complainant and obliging, Sir, that we shall desire you to indulge our curiosity in these points, without any apprehension of being thought troublesome to you; since you are so good to make a free offer of what we should otherwise have been ashamed to ask. We shall esteem it a very great favour therefore, as well as a pleasure, if you will be so kind to go on with the subject. But before you proceed to what you were speaking of, let us entreat you to inform us whether it is better to continue a war all the winter (according to the custom of these times) or to keep the field in the summer only, and put your troops into quarters before the winter comes on, as the ancients used to do.

Fabrizio. Indeed, Sir, if you had not asked this timely and pertinent question, I believe I should have forgot to have said anything of a matter which yet deserves much consideration and attention.—I must therefore beg leave to tell you again, that the ancients were wiser, and conducted their affairs with more prudence, than we do at present; but especially their wars: for though we are guilty of great errors in many other respects, we certainly are guilty of more and greater in this. Nothing can be more dangerous or indiscreet in a general than to carry on a war in winter-time: for in that case, the aggressor is sure to run a greater *risque* of being ruined than those who act upon the defensive. For as the main end and design of all the care and pains that are bestowed in keeping up good order and discipline, is to fit and prepare an army to engage an enemy in a proper manner, a general ought always to have that point in view; because a complete victory commonly puts an end to a war.

He therefore, who has an orderly and well-disciplined army under his command, will certainly have an advantage, over another general who has not, and be more likely to come off with victory Now it must be considered, that nothing is a greater impediment to good order and discipline than rough situations, and wet or cold weather: for in a bad situation you cannot range your forces according to your usual order, and hard weather will oblige you to divide them: in which case you cannot act with your whole force against an enemy, as they are cantoned in villages and towns, and fortresses, at a distance from each other, without any order or regularity, and in such a manner as necessity prescribes: so that all the pains you have taken to discipline your men, and make them observe good order, will signify nothing in such a season.

But it is not much to be wondered that the generals of our times carry on their wars in the winter: for as they are strangers to all sort of discipline and military knowledge, they are neither sensible of the losses and inconveniencies which must necessarily result from dividing their forces, nor do they trouble their heads in endeavouring to establish that discipline and good order amongst their men, which they never learnt themselves.—They ought to reflect, however, upon the numberless hardships and losses occasioned by a winter-campaign, and to remember that the defeat of the French near the Garigliano, in the year 1503. was owing, not so much to the bravery of the Spaniards as to the rigour of the season. For as I told you before, those that resolve to carry on a war in an enemy's country during the winter, must of necessity have the worst of it: because, if they keep their men all together in a camp, they must suffer much from rain and cold; and if they divide them into different cantonments, they must greatly weaken their army.

Whereas, those that wait for them at home may presently unite their forces, and not only chuse their time and place of attack, but keep their men safe and fresh under cover, till they have an opportunity of falling upon some of the enemy's quarters, who being divided and dispersed, cannot be supposed to make any great refinance. In this manner we may account for the defeat of the French, which I just now mentioned; and this will always be the fate of those who invade an enemy in the winter, that has any conduct or knowledge in military affairs. If a general therefore would plunge himself into such circumstances, that neither the number, discipline, good order, nor bravery of his troops, can be of any service to him, let him carry on a field war in the winter.

The Romans, however, in order to make the most of those qualifications which they took so much pains to acquire, always avoided winter-campaigns with as such care as they did rough, confined and inconvenient situations, or any other impediment that might prevent them from availing themselves of their valour and good discipline. This is all that I have to say at present in answer to your last question. Let us now proceed, if you please, to the method of attacking and defending towns, and the manner of building and fortifying them.

Book 7

In what manner towns and fortresses are to be built and fortified. Rules to be observed by those that are to defend a town that is threatened with a siege. Advice to such as are in want of provisions, when they are besieged; and to the besiegers. That appearances are not to be trusted to. How to draw a garrison out of a town that is besieged. That some towns may be corrupted; and others taken by surprise. That good guards should be kept at all times and places by the besieged. Different methods by which they may convey private intelligence to their friends. How to repair a breach, and defend it. Of Mines. That the besieged should take care to divide their forces as little as possible. That when a town or camp is surrounded on every side, it is sometimes necessary to expose it to an assault on one side. General rules to be observed in military discipline. The method of raising plenty of horses in any country. That a general ought sometimes to strike cut new inventions of his own. The conclusion.

Fabrizio. Towns and fortresses may be strong either by nature or art. Those are strong by nature that are either surrounded by rivers or morasses, or situated upon a rock or steep hill, like Monaco and Sanleo: for such as are situated upon hills that are not difficult of ascent, are looked upon as weak since the invention of mines and artillery: upon which account, those that build fortresses in these times often chuse a flat situation, and make it strong by art. For this purpose, their first care is to fortify their walls with angles, bastions, casemates, half moons, and ravelines; that so no enemy can approach them without being taken both in front and flank. If the walls are built very high, they will be too much exposed to artillery, if very low, they may easily be scaled: if you throw up a ditch on the outside of them to make a scalade more difficult, and the enemy should fill it up, (which may easily be done by a numerous army) they will presently become masters of them. In my opinion therefore, (with submission to better judges) the best way to prevent that would be to build the walls pretty high, and to throw up a ditch rather on the inside than on the outside of them.

This is the strongest method of fortifying a town: for it not only covers the besieged from the fire of the artillery, but makes it a very difficult matter for the besiegers either to scale the walls or fill up the ditch. Your walls then should be of a due height, and two yards thick at lead, to stand the fire of the enemy's batteries: there should likewise be towers all along them, at the distance of four hundred feet from each other.

The ditch on the inside ought to be no less than sixty feet wide and twenty-four deep, and all the earth that is dug out of it should be thrown up on that side which is next the town, and supported by a wall built in the ditch, and carried up the height of a man above the ground, which will make the ditch so much the deeper. In the bottom of the ditch I would have casemates[1] about four hundred feet from each other, to take those that might get down into it. The heavy artillery that is made life of for the defence of the town should be planted on the inside of the wall that supports the ditch: for as the other wall is to be a high one, you cannot make use of very large pieces there without much difficulty and inconvenience.

If the enemy attempts a scalade, the height of the first wall secures you: if they batter you with artillery, they must beat down that wall in the first place; and when it is beat down (as a wall always falls towards that side from whence it is battered) the ruins of it having no ditch to bury them in, the outside must naturally add to the depth of the ditch behind them: so that the enemy cannot well advance any further, being stopped there not only by those ruins, but the ditch on the inside of them, and the artillery planted on the other side of that ditch. The only expedient they have left upon such occasions, is to fill up the ditch, which is a very difficult matter on account of its great width and depth, the danger of approaching it from the bastions and other fortifications win which it is flanked, and the labour of climbing over the ruins with burdens of fascines upon their backs: so that I think a town fortified in this manner may be looked upon as impregnable.[2]

Battista. Would not the town be stronger do you think if there was another ditch on the outside of the wall?

---

1. Vaults of mason's work in the flank of a bastion next the curtain, to fire upon the enemy.
2. Not since the invention of bombs.

Fabrizio. Most certainly. But I meant that if there was to be one ditch only, it would be the best way to have it on the inside.

Battista. Would you chuse to have water in the ditches, or would you rather have them dry?

Fabrizio. People differ in their opinions of that matter: because ditches with water in them secure you against mines, and those that have none are harder to be filled up. But upon the whole, I should rather prefer dry ditches, because they are a better security than the other: for ditches with water in them have sometimes been frozen over in inch a manner in winter-time, that the towns they were designed to secure, have been taken without much difficulty; as it happened to Mirandola, when Pope Julius laid siege to it. But to guard against mines, I would make my ditches so deep, that if anyone should attempt to work under them, they must be prevented by water. I would likewise build a castle, or any kind of fortress, with the same sort of walls and ditches; which would make them very difficult, if not impossible to be taken.

In the next place, I would advise those that have the charge of defending a town that is going to be besieged, by no means to fuller any bullions or other works to be thrown up on the outside of the walls, or at a little distance from the town: and I would also advise those that build fortresses, not to make any place of retreat in them, whither the besieged may retire when the walls are either beat down or in possession of the enemy. The reason of my first caution is, that the governor of a town that is besieged, ought not to do a thing which will lessen his reputation at the very beginning of the siege: for the diminution of that will make all his orders but little regarded, and discourage the garrison.

But this will always be the case, if you build little forts out of the town you are to defend: because they are sure to fall into the enemy's hand, it being impossible in these times to maintain such inconsiderable places against a train of artillery: so that the loss of them will be the loss of your reputation, and therefore most probably of the town itself. When the Genoese rebelled against Lewis XII. King of France, they built some trifling redoubts upon the hills that lie round about Genoa, which being presently taken by the French, occasioned the loss of that city.

As to the second piece of advice, in relation to fortresses, I say, that nothing can expose a fortress to greater danger, than to have places of retreat into which the garrison may retire when they are hard pressed:

for if it was not for the hopes of finding safety in one post, after they have abandoned another, they would exert themselves with more obstinacy and resolution in defending the first; and when that is deferred, all the rest will soon fall into the enemy's hand.

Of this we have a recent and memorable instance in the loss of the citadel at Forli, when the Countess Catharine was besieged there by Caesar Borgia, son to Pope Alexander VI. at the head of a French army. That fortress was so full of such places of retreat, that a garrison might retire out of one into another, and out of that into many more successively upon occasion: for in the first place, there was the citadel; and in the next, a castle, separated from it by a ditch, with a drawbridge upon it, over which you might pass out of one into the other; and in this castle there were three divisions separated from one another by ditches full of water, with drawbridges over them. The duke therefore having made a breach in the wall of one of these divisions with his artillery, Giovanni da Cafala, who was the governor, instead of defending the breach, retreated into another division: upon which, the duke's forces immediately entered that division without opposition, and having got possession of the drawbridges, soon made themselves masters of all the rest.

The loss of that fortress then, which was thought inexpugnable, was owing to two great errors; the first in making so many conveniencies of retreating from one place to another; and the second, in that none of those places could command their bridges: so that the ill contrivance of the fortress, and the want of conduct in the garrison, defeated the magnanimous resolution of the countess, who had the courage to wait for an army there, which neither the King of Naples nor the Duke of Milan durst face: however, though her efforts did not succeed, she gained much reputation by so generous a stand, as appears from many copies of verses made in her praise upon that occasion.

If I was to build a fortress then, I would make the walls of it very strong, and fortify it with such ditches as I have just now described: but I would have no retreating places, nor anything in the inside but dwelling-houses, and those too so low, that the governor seeing every part of the walls at one glance of the eye from the middle of it, might know where to send relief immediately upon occasion, and the garrison be convinced that when the walls and ditch were lost, they had no other refuge left: but if I should by any means happen to be prevailed upon to make places of retreat, I would contrive them in such a manner, that every one of them should be able to command its own drawbridge, which I would build upon piles in the middle of the ditches that separated them from each other.

Battista. You say that small forts are not defensible in these times: but if I mistake not, I have heard others assert that the less any sort was, the better it might be defended.

Fabrizio. Their assertion is ill-grounded, because no place can be called strong at present where the besieged have not room to secure themselves by throwing up other ditches and ramparts when the enemy has got possession of the first: for such is the force of artillery, that whoever depends upon one wall and one ditch only will have reason to lament his error.

And since forts and bastions (provided they do not exceed the common dimensions, for then they may be deemed castles and fortresses) have no room for raising new works, they must presently be taken when they are assaulted. It is therefore the best way not to build any such forts at a distance from a town, but to fortify the entrance into it, and cover the gates with ravelines in such a manner that no person can either come in or go out of them in a right line; besides which, there should be a ditch betwixt the raveline and the gate, with a drawbridge upon it. It is a good way to have a portcullis likewise at a every gate to let in your men again after they have made a sally, and to hinder the enemy from entering with them if they should be pursued. This is the use of portcullises: (which the ancients called cataracts) for upon such occasions you could not receive any benefit either from the drawbridge or the gate, both of them being crowded with men.

Battista. I have seen portcullises in Germany made of wooden bars in the form of an iron grate; but those that are used in Italy are all made of whole planks: pray what is the reason of this difference? and which of them are most serviceable?

Fabrizio. I must tell you again, that the ancient military customs and institutions are almost abolished in every part of the world; but in Italy they seem to be totally extinct; and if we have any good thing to boast of, it is entirely borrowed from the Ultramontanes. You must have heard, and perhaps some of the company may remember, in how feeble and slight a manner we used to fortify our towns and castles before the coming of Charles VIII. King of France, into Italy in the year 1594. The merlons or spaces in the walls betwixt the embrasures were not above a foot thick; the embrasures themselves were made very narrow on the outside, and wide within, with many other defects which it would be too tedious to enumerate: for when the merlons are made so slight they are soon beat down, and embrasures of that construction are presently laid open.

But now we have learnt from the French to make our merlons strong and substantial: and though our embrasures are still wide within, and grow narrower and narrower to the middle of the wall, after which they begin to open again and grow wider and wider to the outside, the artillery cannot be so easily dismounted, nor the men driven from the parapets. The French have likewise many other improvements and inventions which our soldiers have never seen, and therefore cannot imitate: amongst these I must mention the portcullises you just now spoke of, made in the form of an iron grate, which, are much better than ours: for if you make use of one that is made of whole planks for the defence of a gate, when it is let down you shut yourself close up, and cannot annoy the enemy through it; so that they may either hew it down with axes, or set fire to it without any danger: but if it is made like a grate, you may easily defend it against them, either with spikes or firing shot through the interstices of the bars.

Battista. I have observed another Ultramontane invention which has been imitated of late in Italy, which is, to make the spokes of the wheels of our artillery-carriages incline obliquely from the fellies to the nave. Now I should be very glad to know the reason of this, because I always thought straight spokes had been stronger than any others.

Fabrizio. You must not look upon this deviation from common custom as either the effect of whim or caprice, or for the sake of ornament: for where strength is absolutely necessary but little account ought to be made of beauty. The true reason then of what you have observed, is that such wheels are safer and stronger than our own: for when the carriage is loaded it either goes even or inclines to one side: when it goes even, each wheel sustains an equal share of the weight, and is not too much oppressed by it: but when it inclines to either side, the weight lies wholly upon one of the wheels. If the spokes therefore are straight they are soon broken in that case; because if the wheel inclines, the spokes must incline also, and cannot support the weight that presses upon them. So that the French judge rightly in letting the spokes of their wheels obliquely to the nave: for when the carriage inclines to one side, and the weight bears directly upon them, instead of oblique they will then become straight in a line with it, and consequently better able to support the whole than they were to bear one half of the load when the carriage went even. But to return to our towns and fortresses:

The French have likewise another method of securing the gates of their towns, and of letting their men in and out of them with more ease and convenience when they are besieged, which I have not yet seen practiced in Italy. They erect two perpendicular piles or pillars at the end of the drawbridge on the outside of the ditch; upon each of which they balance a beam in such a manner that one half of it hangs over the bridge, and the other on the outside of it. Those parts of them which hang on the outside are joined together with cross bars like a grate, and at that end of each beam which hangs over the bridge they fix a chain and fasten it to the bridge: so that when they have a mind to shut up that end of the bridge they loose the chains and let the grate fall; and when they would open it they draw home the chains and heist the grate up again: by these means they can raise it up to such a height that either foot only, or horse, if it is necessary, may pass under, or may shut the passage up so close that nobody at all can get through; as the grate is raised and lowered like the port of an embrasure.

This I take to be a better contrivance than the portcullis; because the grate does not fall perpendicularly like a portcullis; and therefore is not so liable to be obstructed by an enemy. Those then that would fortify a town in a proper manner, should observe these directions: besides which, they should not suffer any lands to be tilled nor buildings to be erected within a mile at least of it: the whole country round it should be quite clear and open, free from all thickets, or banks, or plantations, or houses, which may hinder the prospect of the besieged, and afford shelter to an enemy in his approaches.—Remember likewise that a town, where the banks of its outside ditch are higher than the common surface of the earth, may be accounted very weak: for instead of doing you any good, they only serve to cover the enemy, and mask their batteries, which they may easily open upon you from thence.—But let us now proceed to shew what is to be done within a fortified town, for its greater security against an enemy.

I will not trespass so much upon your time and patience as to tell you that besides the directions already given, it is absolutely necessary to be well furnished with ammunition and provisions for the garrison; because everybody must know this, and that without such stores all other precautions and preparations are to no purpose. I shall only say in general, that there are two rules which should never be forgotten upon such occasions: the first is, to provide yourself with everything that you think you may want; and the next, to prevent the enemy from availing themselves of anything that may be of service to them in the country round about you: for which purpose, if there be any forage, or cattle, or anything else, that you cannot carry off into the town, you ought by all means to destroy it.

You ought likewise to take care that nothing be done in a tumultuous or disorderly manner; and that every man may know his station, and what part he is to act upon any occasion. It is necessary therefore to give strict orders that all the old men, women, children, and sick people, should keep close in their houses, in order to leave every passage clear and open for those that are young and fit for action; some of whom should always be under arms on the walls, others at the gates, and others at the principal passes in the town, to be ready upon any sudden emergency: there should be particular parties also which should not be confined to any certain station, but appointed to succour any quarter where there should be occasion for it: so that when such a disposition is made, it is hardly possible that any tumult should happen which can throw you into confusion.

There is another thing to be remembered both in besieging and defending a town; which is, that nothing encourages an enemy so much as their knowing that it has not been used to sieges: for it often happens that a town is lost through fear alone, without waiting for an assault. The besiegers therefore should endeavour by all means to appear as powerful and formidable as they can, and take every opportunity of making the most ostentatious display of their strength: the besieged, on the other hand, ought to post the stoutest of their men in places where they are attacked with the greatest fury, and such as are neither to be imposed upon by appearances, nor driven from their posts by anything but downright force of arms: for if the enemy fails in the first attempt, the besieged will take courage; and the enemy perceiving they are not to be dismayed by shew alone, must be obliged to have recourse to other methods.

The engines which the ancients made use of in the defence of a town were many; the chief of which were such a threw darts and huge stones to a great distance, and with astonishing force: they made use of several likewise in besieging towns, as the battering ram, the tortoise, and many others: instead of which, great guns are now used both by besiegers and those that are besieged. But to return.

A governor of a town must take care neither to be surprised by famine, nor forced by assault: as to famine, I told you before that he ought to lay in a plentiful stock of provisions and ammunition before the siege begins: but if the siege should prove a very long one, and they should fail, he must then devise some extraordinary method of procuring supplies from his friends and allies, especially if a river runs through the town, as the inhabitants of Casilinum did from the Romans: for when that place was so closely invested by Hannibal that they could send them no other provisions, they threw great quantifies of nuts into a river that ran through the middle of their town, which being carried down by the stream escaped the enemy's notice, and supplied the besieged with food for a considerable time.

The inhabitants of some towns which have been besieged, in order to make the enemy despair of reducing them by famine, have either thrown a great quantity of bread over their walls, or gorged an ox with corn, and then turned it out to fall into the enemy's hand; that so when they killed it, and found its stomach so full of corn, they might imagine they had abundance in the town.—On the other hand, some great generals have used as many artifices and expedients to distress a town. Fabius Maximus suffered the Campanians to sow their fields before he invested their city, in order to diminish their stores.

When Dionysius lay before Rhegium, he offered the people terms of accommodation, and during the treaty prevailed upon them to furnish him with a large quantity of provisions: but when he had thus lessened their stock and increased his own, he immediately blocked up the town so straitly on every side, that he soon obliged them to give it up. Alexander the Great having a design upon Leucadia, first made himself master of the neighbouring towns, and turned all the inhabitants into that place; which at last filled it so full of people, that he presently reduced it by famine.

As to assaults, I told you before that it is of the utmost importance to repel the first attack: for the Romans took many towns by suddenly assaulting them on every side, (which they called *aggredi urbem coronâ*) as Scipio did when he made himself maser of New Carthage in Spain. If such an assault therefore can be sustained, the enemy will find it a difficult matter to succeed afterwards: for though they should get into a town, the inhabitants may find some remedy, if they are not wanting to themselves; and it has often happened even in that case, that the assailants have either been all slain, or driven out again; especially when the inhabitants have got into garret windows, or upon the tops of houses and turrets, and fought them from thence. To prevent this, the assailants commonly either set open the gates to make way for the others to escape with safety, or gave orders loud enough to be heard by everyone, not to hurt anybody but such as were in arms, and to spare all those that would lay them down: and this has frequently been of great service upon such occasions.——It is an easy matter likewise to make yourself master of a town if you come suddenly and unexpectedly upon it; that is, if you are at such a distance from it with your army, that the inhabitants do not suspect you of any design of that kind, or imagine they shall have sufficient notice of your approach: so that if you can make a long and hasty march or two, and fall unawares upon it, you are almost sure to succeed.

I would willingly pass over some transactions in silence that have happened in our own times, as it would be disagreeable to talk of myself and my own exploits; and what to say of others I cannot well tell. Nevertheless, I cannot help proposing the example of Caesar Borgia (commonly called Duke Valentine) in this respect, as worthy of imitation: for when he lay with his army at Nocera, and pretended a design upon Camerino, he suddenly invaded the Duchy of Urbino, and made himself master of a state in one day without any difficulty, which another man could not have reduced without bellowing much time and expense upon it, if at all. It behoves those that are besieged likewise to beware of tricks and stratagems in the enemy, and therefore they ought not to trust to any appearance, though ever so usual and familiar to them, but to suspect there is some mischief lurking under it.

Domitius Calvinus laying siege to a town, used to march round it every day with a good part of his army: so that the besieged, imagining at last he did it only for exercise, began to grow remiss in their guards; which Domitius perceiving, made an assault upon the town, and carried it. Some generals who have had intelligence of troops that were upon their march to relieve a place they had inverted, have dressed a body of their own soldiers in the enemy's livery, and furnished them with the same colours, who being admitted into the town have presently made themselves masters of it. Cimon, the Athenian, set fire to a temple one night that stood without the gates of a town he designed to surprise: upon which, all the people running out of it to extinguish the flames, left the town to the mercy of the enemy.

Others, having met with a party of foragers who were sent out of a fortress, have put them all to the sword, and disguised some of their own men in their cloaths, who have afterwards given up the place to them.—Besides these artifices, the ancients used some others to draw the garrison out of a town they had a design upon. When Scipio commanded the Roman armies in Africa, he was very desirous to make himself master of some strong places which were well garrisoned by the Carthaginians: for which purpose, he made a feint of attainting them, but soon desisted from the attempt, and marched away again to a great distance, as if he was afraid of the enemy.

Hannibal therefore being deceived by appearances, immediately drew all the garrisons out of them, in order to pursue him with greater force, in hopes of entirely crushing him: but Scipio being informed of this, sent Massinissa with a sufficient number of men by another route, who presently got possession of them. Pyrrhus laying siege to the Capital of Illyria (now Sclavonia) where there was a very strong garrison, pretended at last to despair of reducing it, and turning his arms against other towns which were not so well defended, obliged the enemy to draw the greater part of the garrison out of the capital to relieve them: after which, he suddenly returned thither with his army, and took it without any difficulty.

Many have poisoned wells and springs, and diverted the course of rivers, to make themselves masters of a town; but have not always succeeded in that: others have endeavoured to dismay the inhabitants, by causing a report to be spread that they have lately gained some considerable advantage, and daily expect a powerful reinforcement. Some generals have made themselves masters of towns by holding a private correspondence with, and corrupting one party of the inhabitants; for which purpose they have made use of several methods: others have sent one of their chief confidants amongst them, who, under the pretence of desertion, has gained great credit in the town, and afterwards betrayed it, either by giving intelligence to his friend in what manner the guards were posted, or by preventing a gate being shut by the breaking down a carriage in it, or by some other means facilitating the entrance of the enemy.

Hannibal prevailed upon an officer to betray a garrison to him belonging; to the Romans, which was effected in this manner: the officer got leave to go a-hunting in the night, under a pretence that he durst not do it in the daytime, lest he should be taken by the enemy; and returning before morning, contrived matters so well that he got several of Hannibal's men admitted with him in disguise, who immediately killed the guards, and delivered up one of the gates to Hannibal. Some towns have been taken by suffering their garrison to make a sally upon the enemy, and then to pursue them to too great a distance when they pretended to fly before them: by which they have been drawn into an ambush and cut off. Many generals (and Hannibal among the rest) have let a besieged enemy get possession of their camp, in order to throw themselves betwixt them and the town, and to prevent their retreat.

Others have imposed upon them by pretending to raise the siege, as Phormio the Athenian did: for after he had lain some time before the city of Calcedon, and ravaged all the country round about it, the inhabitants sent ambassadors to him, whom he received with much courtesy, and made them so many fair promises, that having lulled them into security, he decamped and marched away to a distance from the city; but whilst they were weak enough to imagine they had got entirely quit of him, and had laid aside all, care. of their defence upon the strength of his promises, he suddenly returned, and falling upon them when they did not expect such a visit, presently took the city. The inhabitants of a besieged town ought likewise to secure themselves by all means against any of their own townsmen whole fidelity they have reason to suspect: but they may sometimes work upon them more effectually by kindnesses than severity and harsh treatment.

Marcellus knew that Lucius Bancius of Nola was inclined to favour Hannibal; yet he behaved to him with so much generosity, that instead of an enemy he became his firm friend. They should also be at least as much upon their guard when the enemy is at some distance as when he is near at hand; and to be particularly careful in guarding those places which they think are least exposed to danger: for many towns have been lost by being assaulted in a part which has been thought the most secure. The reason of this is, either because that part has been really strong of itself, and therefore neglected; or because the enemy has artfully made a shew of storming one part with great noise and alarm, whilst he was assaulting another in good order and silence.

The besieged therefore above all things should take the utmost care to have their walls always well guarded, but especially in the nighttime; and not only to post men there, but fierce and quick-nosed dogs also, to smell out an enemy at a distance, and to give an alarm by their barking: for dogs and geese too have sometimes been the preservation of a fortress, as they were of the Capitol at Rome when it was besieged by the Gauls. When the Spartans laid siege to Athens, Alcibiades ordered that whenever he should hoist a light in the night, every guard should do the same, upon pain of severe punishment in case of neglect.

Iphicrates the Athenian, finding a sentinel asleep at his post, immediately killed him, and said he had only left him as he found him.

Some who have been besieged have found out different methods of conveying intelligence to their friends; as in the first place, by writing letters to them in ciphers, when they durst not trust the messenger with a verbal errand, and concealing the letters in some manner or other. The nature of the ciphers hath been devised and agreed upon by the parties beforehand; and the methods of concealing them various. Some have written what they had to say in the scabbard of a sword: others have put their letters into paste, which they have baked and given to the bearer for food upon the road: others have concealed them in their private parts: and others again under the collar of the messenger's dog.

Some have written letters about common business, and interlined them with their main purpose written in a certain composition, which will not appear till they have been dipped in water, and held to a fire. This method has been very artfully practiced in our own times by a person, who having occasion to communicate a secret to some of his friends that lived in a town which was besieged, and not daring to trust any messenger with it, sent letters of excommunication written in the usual style, but interlined in the manner I have been speaking of; which being fixed to the doors of the churches were soon taken down, and the contents of them perfectly understood by those who knew from whom they came by some particular marks: and this is a very good way; for those that carry such letters cannot know the secret contents of them, nor can there be any danger of their being discovered by an enemy.

In short there are a thousand other methods of giving and receiving secret intelligence, which any man may either invent himself, or learn from others: but it is a much easier matter to convey intelligence to those that are besieged, than for them to send any to their friends; because none can be carried out of a town, except by such as pretend to be deserters; which is a very uncertain and hazardous method, especially if the enemy be vigilant and circumspect: whereas those that want to carry intelligence to the besieged have nothing more to do than to get into the enemy's camp (which they may do under almost any pretence) and take their opportunity of slipping from thence into the town.

But let us now proceed to the present method of repairing and defending a breach in the walls of a town.—If you should happen to be blocked up in a place where there is no ditch on the inside of the walls, in order to prevent the enemy from entering at a breach that may be made by their artillery, you must make a ditch behind that part which they are battering, at least sixty feet wide, and throw up all the earth that is dug out of it towards the town, to form a good rampart, and add to the depth of the ditch: and this you must carry on with such diligence, that when the wall is beat down, the ditch may be at least ten or twelve feet deep.

It is necessary likewise to flank the ditch with a casemate at each end of it, if you have time: and if the wall be substantial enough to hold out till these works are finished; you will be stronger on that side than in any other part of the town: for then you will have a complete ditch of that sort which I recommended above; but if the wall be so weak that you cannot have time to do all this, you must then depend upon your men, and exert your utmost vigour to defend the breach. This method was pursued by the Pisans when the Florentines laid siege to their city: and indeed they were very well able to do it; for their walls were so strong that they had time enough, and the soil upon which their city is built, is very proper for making ditches and ramparts: but if either of those conveniences had failed them, they must inevitably have been undone. It is the best way, however, as I said before, to have such ditches previously made all round the walls, for then you need not be afraid of any enemy.

The ancients sometimes made themselves masters of a town by mining: and this they did either by working a passage privately underground into the middle of the place, and entering their men that way, as the Romans did at Veii , or by undermining the walls only in such a manner as to make them tumble down. The latter method is now most in use; which is the reason that towns that stand high are accounted weaker than others, because more subject to be undermined: and when they are so, if the mines are filled with gunpowder, and alighted match put to a train that leads to them, they not only blow up the walls, but split the rocks upon which they are built, and tear a whole fortress to pieces at one.

The way to prevent this is to build upon a plain, and to make the ditch that surrounds your fortress so deep that an enemy cannot work under it without coming to water, which is the best defence against mines. But if you are in a town which stands upon a rock or hill, the only remedy is to dig several deep wells along the foot of the wall on the inside, which may serve to give vent to the powder when a mine is sprung. There is indeed another expedient, and a very good one too, which is to countermine the enemy, provided you can discover their mines; but that is a very difficult matter, if they take proper care to conceal them.

The governor of a town that is besieged ought likewise to take great care that he be not surprised whilst the garrison are reposing themselves; as after an assault, or when the guards are relieved, (which is generally at the break of day in the morning, and by twilight in the evening) but especially whilst they are at their meals: for at those time many towns have been surprised, and many sallies made which have proved fatal to the besiegers: upon which account, it is highly necessary to keep a strict guard always in every quarter and the greater part of the garrison under arms.

Another thing I must not forget to tell you, which is, that the chief difficulty in defending either a town or a camp is occasioned by your being obliged to divide your men: for as the enemy may assault you at any time, or any place he thinks proper, with all his forces at once, you must keep a constant guard at every place: so that when he attacks you with his whole strength, you can only defend yourself with part of your own.—The besieged are likewise often in danger of being totally ruined at one stroke; whereas the besiegers have nothing to fear but a repulse: upon which consideration, some who have been blocked up either in a town or in a camp, have made a sudden sally with all their forces, though they were inferior to the enemy, and utterly dispersed them; as Marcellus did at Nola, and Julius Caesar in Gaul; the latter of whom being attacked in his camp by a very powerful army, and finding he was neither able to defend himself there, nor fall upon the enemy with his whole strength, because he was forced to divide it to secure every part of his camp, threw open the entrenchments on one side, and facing about that way with all his men, exerted himself with such vigour and courage that he totally defeated the enemy.

The constancy and resolution of the besieged likewise often dismay and weary out the besiegers. In the wars betwixt Pompey and Caesar, their two armies lying near each other, and Caesar's being in great want of provisions, a piece of the bread which his men were forced to eat was brought to Pompey; who finding that it was made of herbs, gave strict orders that none of own soldiers should see it, lest they should be daunted when they perceived what an enemy they had to deal with. Nothing did the Romans so much honour in their wars with Hannibal as their unshaken firmness and constancy: for they never sued for peace, nor shewed the least signs of fear even in the lowed ebb of their fortune: on the contrary, when Hannibal was almost at their gates, they sold the ground upon which he was encamped at a much greater price than they would have asked for it at any other time; and were so inflexible in the prosecution of the enterprises they had in hand, that they would not raise the siege of Capua to defend Rome itself at a time when it was daily threatened with a siege.

I am sensible, that I have mentioned many things which some of you must have known before, and perhaps may have considered as well as myself: but this I did (as I told you) that you might more perfectly comprehend the nature of true military discipline and the Art of War, and for the instruction of such of the company who may not have had the opportunity of learning them.—And how, gentlemen, I think I have but little more to add to what I have laid upon this subject, except it be to lay down some general rules in military discipline, which yet you probably may think very obvious and common.

You must know then, that whatsoever is of service to the enemy, must be prejudicial to you; and every advantage you gain is detrimental to them.—He that is most careful to observe the motions and designs of the enemy, and takes most pains in exercising and disciplining his army, will be least exposed to danger, and has most reason to expect success in his undertakings.—Never come to an engagement till you have inspired your men with courage, and see them in good order and eager to fight; nor hazard a battle till they seem confident of victory.—It is better, if you can, to subdue an enemy by famine than the sword: for in battle, Fortune has often a much greater share than either prudence or valour.—No enterprise is more likely to succeed than one which is concealed from the enemy till it is ripe for execution.

Nothing is of greater importance in time of war than to know how to make the best use of a fair opportunity when it is offered.—Few men are brave by nature: but good discipline and experience make many so.—Good order and discipline in an army are more to be depended upon than courage alone.—If any of the enemy's troops desert them, and come over to you, it is a great acquisition, provided they prove faithful: for the loss of them will be more felt than that of those who are killed in battle; though deserters indeed will always be suspected by their new friends, and odious to their old ones.—In drawing up an army in order of battle, it is better to keep a sufficient reserve to support your front line upon occasion, than to extend it in such a manner as to make but one rank as it were of your army.—If a general perfectly knows his own strength and that of the enemy, he can hardly miscarry.

The goodness of your soldiers is of more consequence than the number of them: and sometimes the situation of the place is of greater advantage and security than the goodness of your soldiers.—Sudden and unexpected accidents often throw an army into confusion; but things that are familiar, and have come on by slow degrees, are little regarded: it is the best way therefore when you have a new enemy to deal with, to accustom your men to the fight of them as often as you can by flight skirmishes before you come to a general engagement with them.—He whose troops are in disorder whilst they are pursuing a routed enemy, will most probably lose the advantage he had gained before, and be routed in his turn.—Whoever has not taken proper care to furnish himself with a sufficient stock of provisions and ammunition, bids fair to be vanquished without striking a stroke.

He that is either stronger in infantry than cavalry, or in cavalry than infantry, must chuse his ground accordingly.—If you would know whether you have any spies in your camp in the daytime, you have nothing more to do than to order every man to his tent.—When you are aware that the enemy is acquainted with your designs, you must change them.—After you have consulted many about what you ought do, confer with very few concerning what you are actually resolved to do.—Whilst your men are in quarters, you must keep them in good order by fear and punishment; but when they are in the field, by hopes and rewards.—Wise generals never come to an engagement but when they are either compelled by downright necessity, or can do it with great advantage.

Take great care that the enemy may not be apprised of the order in which you design to draw up your army for battle: and above all things, make such a disposition that your first line may fall back with ease and convenience into the second, and both of them into the third upon occasion.—In time of action be sure not to call off any of your battalions to a different service from what they were destined to at first, lest you should occasion disorder and confusion in your army.— Unexpected accidents cannot well be prevented; but those that are foreseen may easily be obviated or remedied.—Men, arms, money, and provisions, are the sinews of war; but of these four, the two first are most necessary: for men and arms will always find money and provisions; but money and provisions cannot always raise men and arms.

A rich man without arms, must be a prey to a poor soldier well armed.—Accustom your men to abhor a soft and effeminate way of life, and to despise all manner of luxury, extravagance, and delicacy, either in their diet, or dress.

Let these general rules suffice at present as most necessary to be remembered, though I am sensible I might have introduced several other topics in the course of this conversation, which would have fallen in properly enough with our subject; for instance, I might have shewn in how many different dispositions the ancients drew up their armies, in what manner they cloathed their soldiers, and how they employed them at different times; with several other particulars, which I thought might be omitted, not only because you may have various other means of informing yourselves of these things, but because I did not propose to myself at first to enter into a minute detail of ancient military discipline, but only to point out the methods by which much better order and discipline might be established in our armies than there is any where to be found at present: upon which account, I thought I had no occasion to make any further mention of ancient rules and institutions than what was absolutely necessary for the introduction of such an establishment.

I know very well that I might likewise have taken an opportunity of enlarging more copiously upon the method of exercising and disciplining cavalry, and of discoursing upon the nature of sea-service: for those who write upon the Art of War tell us, there is a sea-army, and a land-army, an army of infantry, and an army of cavalry. Of naval affairs, however, I shall say nothing, because I do not pretend to have any knowledge of them, but leave that to the Genoese and Venetians, who have done such wonderful things by their experience in those matters: nor shall I say any more of cavalry, because (as I told you before) that part of our soldiery is the least corrupted: for if your infantry (in which the strength of an army chiefly consists) be well-disciplined, your cavalry must of necessity be so too.

I would advise everyone, however, who is desirous to raise and keep up a good body of cavalry, in the first place, to fill his country with stallions of the best breed that can be procured, and to encourage the farmers to rear colts as they do calves and mules; and in the next, (in order to promote the sale of them) to make everyone that keeps a mule keep a horse also; and to oblige him that will keep but one beast to make use of a horse: besides which, he should oblige all those that wear garments made of fine cloth to keep one horse at least. This method was taken by a certain prince in our own memory, and in a very little time he saw his country abound with excellent horses. As to anything else relating to cavalry, I must refer you to what I have said before upon that subject:, and the present established discipline.

But you may desire perhaps to know, before we part, what qualifications a general ought to be possessed of, and I will satisfy you in a few words; for I cannot make choice of a more proper man than such a one as is master of the qualifications I have already particularized and recommended: and [3] yet even those are not sufficient, except he has abilities to strike out something new of his own upon an emergency: for no man ever excelled in his professfion that could not do that; and if a ready and quick invention is necessary and honourable in any occupation, certainly it must be so in that of war above all others.

Thus we see that any invention or new expedient, how trifling so ever it was, is celebrated by historians. Alexander was admired only for causing a cap to be held up at the point of a lance as a signal for decamping (instead of sounding a trumpet as usual) in order to decamp in silence and unobserved. The same prince is likewise commended for ordering his men to kneel down on the left knee to receive the enemy upon a certain occasion, that so they might be able to sustain the attack with greater firmness: by which means, he not only gained

---

3. The ancients, in reckoning up the qualities of a good general, gave Fortune a place by itself, and distinguished it from Knowledge in the Art of War. "*Ego sic existimo, says Tully, in summo imperatore quatuor has res inesse oportere, scientiam rei militantis, virtutem, auctoritatem, felicitatem.*" He shews afterwards that these four qualities met eminently in Pompey. "*Reliquum est ut de fellicitate quam praestare de seipso nemo potest, meminisse, & commemorare de altero possumus; sicut aequum homini de potestate Deorum timide & pauca dicamus. Ego enim sic existimo: Maximo, Marcello, Scipioni, Mario, & caeteris Magnis Imperatoribus, not solum propter virtutem, sed etiam propter fortunam, saepius imperia mandata, atque exercitus esse commissos. Fuit enim perfecto quibusdam summis viris quaedam ad amplitudinem, & gloriam, & ad res magnas bene gerendas divinitus adjuncta fortuna.*" Pro lege Manil. cap. x. xvi. One might add another qualification that is requisite in a general, and a very necessary one too, *viz.* that he should be perfect in his bodily senses, such as seeing, hearing, &c. The great and decisive Battle of Yvry in France was lost by the short sightedness of one of the generals. The Viscount Tavannes being extremely short-sighted, had placed the several divisions of horse so close to one another, that there was not only no space left through which they might retire to rally in the rear of the army, after they had wheeled according to their orders: but even the very divisions themselves had no intervals, by means of which they might extend themselves when they moved. So that if they stirred ever so little, they jostled and crowded each other. An error, which not being observed by anybody, and therefore left without remedy, very much distressed the army of the League, and put it into great confusion. Nay indeed, it entirely occasioned the loss of the battle. See Davila's *Hist. of the Civil Wars of France*, book XI.

a victory, but such a degree of reputation that statues were erected to him in that attitude.

But as it is now high time to put an end to this conversation, I will conclude it with returning to the point from whence we set out; lest I should expose myself to the ridicule which is usually and justly bellowed upon such as make long digressions, and wander from their subject till they are lost.—If you remember, Cosimo, you seemed to wonder that I who professed to hold the ancients in such admiration, and so liberally bellowed my censure upon others for not imitating them in matters of the greatest consequence, have not copied their example myself in the Art of War, which is my profession, and in which I have spent so much of my time and studies. In answer to this, I told you that men who have any great design in view, ought in the first place to make due preparations, and qualify themselves in a proper manner to carry it into execution when they have a fair opportunity of so doing.

Now I must leave you to judge from the long conversation we have had today, whether I am master of sufficient abilities to reduce our present military discipline to the standard of the ancients, or not; and how often I must have revolved this matter in my mind: from whence you will be able to form a pretty good conjecture how much I have it at heart, and whether I would not actually have attempted to execute my design, if ever I had been favoured with a proper opportunity. For your further satisfaction, and my own justification, and to discharge my promise in some measure, I will shew you how difficult a matter it is in some respects, and how easy in others, to copy the ancients in this point at present.

I say then that nothing can be more easy, than to reduce military discipline to the standard of the ancients, if a prince or state be able to raise an army of fifteen or twenty thousand young men in their own dominions: on the other hand, nothing can be more difficult, if this power be wanting. Now to explain myself more fully, you must know that some generals have done great things, and gained much reputation, with armies ready formed and well-disciplined to their hands, as we might instance in several of the Roman citizens, and others who have commanded armies which they found ready disciplined, and therefore had nothing more to do but to keep them so, and to conduct them like able commanders.

Others, who have been no less renowned for their exploits, have not only been obliged to discipline their armies, but even to raise them out of the earth as it were, before they could face an enemy: and these certainly deserve a much greater degree of applause than those who had the command of veteran and well-disciplined troops. Amongst such, we may reckon Pelopidas, Epaminondas, Tullus Hostilius, Philip of Macedon, the father of Alexander the Great, Cyrus King of Persia, and Gracchus the Roman, who all had their armies to raise and discipline before they could least them into the field: and yet they were enabled to effect these things by their own abilities, and by having subjects of such a disposition, that they could discipline and train them up as they pleased.

But it would have been utterly impossible that any one of them, how great so ever his merit and qualifications might have been, should ever have performed anything memorable in a foreign country, the inhabitants of which were corrupt and adverse to all good order and subordination. It is not sufficient therefore in Italy to know how to command an army already raised and disciplined; a general must first raise and discipline it himself, before he puts himself at the head of it; but nobody can do that except a prince who is possessed of large territories, and has a great number of subjects, which I am not; nor did I ever yet, or ever can command any but foreign armies, composed of soldiers who owed me no natural obedience: and whether it is possible to establish such discipline as I have been recommending amongst troops of that kind, I submit to your consideration.

Do you think I could ever make these men carry heavier arms than they have been used to; and not only arms but provisions for two or three days, and a spade or mattock into the bargain? Could I ever make them dig, or keep them whole days together at their exercise, in order to fit them for the field? Could I keep them from gaming, drinking, whoring, swearing, and those other vices which are got to such a head amongst the soldiery of these times? How long must it be before I could establish such order, discipline, and obedience amongst them, that if there should happen to be a tree full of ripe fruit in the middle of the camp, not one of them should dare to touch it; of which sort we meet with several instances amongst the ancients? What rewards could I promise them of sufficient weight to make them love me? or what threats could I use to make them fear me, when they know that when the war is over I shall have nothing more to do with them?

How could I ever make those ashamed of anything, who have no shame in them? How can they respect me, when they hardly know my face? By what God or what saint must they swear? by him whom they worship, or those whom they blaspheme? What God they worship I know not; nor do I know what saint they do not blaspheme. How could I hope they would ever observe any promise, when I saw they did not pay the least regard to their word; or imagine they would reverence man, when they shew so much dishonour to God? What good impression then could I stamp upon so rotten and corrupt a mass?—If you object that the Swiss and Spaniards are good soldiers, I freely confess that I think them much better than the Italians; but if you have attended to what I have been saying, and consider the discipline of both those nations, you will find they fall very far short of the ancients in many respects.

The superiority of the Swiss is owing to their ancient institutions, and the want of cavalry, as I told you before; and that of the Spaniards, to necessity: for as they generally carry on their wars in foreign parts, they cannot hope to escape if they lose a battle, and therefore must either conquer or die. This it is that makes them resolute soldiers; but they are very deficient however in several other respects: for their chief, if not their only excellence, consists in standing firm to receive a charge from the push of a pike, or the point of a sword: and should any man attempt to instruct them in what they are still wanting, especially if he be a foreigner, he would find all his endeavours to no purpose.

As to the Italians, their princes have been so weak and pusillanimous for a long time, that they were not able to introduce any good military institution; and not being reduced to it by necessity like the Spaniards, they have attempted nothing of themselves; so that they are now become the scorn and derision or the world. The people indeed are not to be blamed for this, but their princes, who have been justly punished for it, and lost their dominions without being able to strike a stroke in their defence.

To confirm what I have said, let me desire you to recollect how many wars there have been in Italy since it was invaded by Charles VIII. of France: and though wars generally make men good soldiers, yet the longer these wars lasted, the worse were our officers and private men. This was owing to the nature of their military discipline and institutions, which have long been very bad, and still continue so: (as at time of first publication), and what is still worse, there is no person that is able to reform them. It is in vain therefore to think of ever retrieving the reputation of the Italian arms by any other method than what I have prescribed, and by the co-operation of some powerful princes in Italy: for then the ancient discipline might be introduced again amongst raw honest men who are their own subjects; but it never can amongst a parcel of corrupted debauched rascals and foreigners. No sculptor, how skilful so ever in his art, can hope to make a good statue out of a block of marble that has been mangled and spoiled before by some bungler; but he will be sure to succeed if he has a fresh block to work upon.

Before our Italian princes were scourged by the Ultramontanes, they thought it sufficient for a prince to write a handsome letter, or return a civil answer; to excel in drollery and repartee; to undermine and deceive; and to set themselves off with jewels and lace; to eat and sleep in greater magnificence and luxury than their neighbours; to spend their time in wanton dalliance and lascivious pleasures; to keep up a haughty kind of state; and grind the faces of their subjects; to indulge themselves in indolence and inactivity; to dispose of their military honours and preferments to pimps and Parasites; to neglect and despise merit of every kind; to browbeat those that endeavoured to point out anything that was salutary or praiseworthy; to have their words and sayings looked upon as oracles; not foreseeing, (weak and infatuated as they were) that by such a conduct they were making a rod for their own backs, and exposing themselves to the mercy of the first invader.

To this were owing the dreadful alarms, the disgraceful defeats, and the astonishing losses they sustained in the year one thousand four hundred and ninety-four: and hence it came to pass that three of the most powerful states in Italy were so often ravaged and laid waste in those times. But it is still more deplorable to see that those princes, who are yet left in possession of any dominions, are so far from taking warning from the downfall of others, that they pursue the same course, and live in the same sort of misrule and fatal security; not considering that princes in former times, who were desirous either to acquire new dominion, or at least to preserve their own, strictly observed all those rules which I have laid down and recommended in the course of this conversation, and that their chief endeavours were to inure their bodies to all manner of hardship and fatigue, and to fortify their minds against danger and the fear of death.

Thus Julius Caesar, Alexander of Macedon, and many other great men and heroic princes whom I have mentioned before, always fought at the head of their own armies, always marched with them on foot, and carried their own arms; and if any of them ever lost their power, they lost their life with it at the same time, and died with the same reputation and glory which they had always maintained whilst they lived. So that, how much so ever we condemn the inordinate thirst of dominion in some of them, we cannot reproach any of them with softness and effeminacy, or accuse them of having lived in so delicate or indolent a manner, as to enervate and make them unfit to reign over mankind. If then our princes would read and duly consider the lives and fortunes of these great men, one would think it impossible they should not alter their conduct, or that their dominions should long continue in the feeble and languishing condition they are in at present.

But as you complained of your militia in the beginning of this conversation, I must beg leave to tell you, that if you had formed it upon the model, and exercised it in the manner I have recommended, and it had not answered your expectation, you would then indeed have just reason for your complaint: but as you have neither formed nor disciplined it in that manner, you yourself are more properly to be blamed, if it has proved an abortion instead of a perfect birth. The Venetians, and the Duke of Ferrara also, made a good beginning, but they did not persevere: so that if they likewise miscarried, it is to be imputed to their own mismanagement, and not the detects of their men: for I will venture to affirm, that the first state in Italy that shall take up this method, and pursue it, will soon become matter of the whole province, and succeed as Philip of Macedon did; who having learnt from Epaminondas the Theban the right method of forming and disciplining an army, grew so powerful, whilst the other states of Greece were buried in indolence and luxury, and wholly taken up in plays and banquets, that he conquered them all in a few years, and left his son such a foundation to build upon, that he was able to subdue the whole world.

Whoever therefore despises this advice (whether he be a prince or governor of a Commonwealth) has but little regard for himself or his country: and for my own part, I cannot help complaining of Fortune, which should either not have suffered me to have known these things, or given me power to put them in execution; which is a thing I cannot hope for now I am so far advanced in years. For which reason, I have freely communicated my thoughts to you of this matter, as young men and well qualified not only to infill such advice into the ears of your princes, if you approve of it, but to assist them in carrying into execution whenever a proper opportunity shall offer: and let me conjure you not to despair of success, since this province seems destined to revive arts and sciences which have seemed long since dead; as we see it has already raised poetry, painting, and sculpture as it were from the grave.

As to myself indeed, I cannot expect to see so happy a change at my time of life: but if fortune had indulged me some years ago with a territory fit for such an undertaking, I think I should soon have convinced the world of the excellency of the ancient military discipline; for I would either have encreased my own dominions with glory, or at least not have lost them with infamy and disgrace.[4]

---

[4] "After all, (says Dr. Leland in a *Note upon his Life of Philip of Macedon*) a scrupulous regard to systematical rules, and pedantically reducing war to a science, sometimes proves a fatal enemy to that enthusiastic ardour, some spark of which must necessarily have a share in greatness of all kinds, and particularly in military greatness. Where the lively sense of honour, and the true patriot spirit which should animate a soldier, are wanting, it may serve to extinguish the sense of shame, and the fear of disgrace, by affording a fair pretence for justifying an instance of inactive conduct, or the declining an hazardous and dangerous enterprise. But when an exact knowledge of the military art is united with more elevated qualities, then it becomes really valuable. Of this, the present age hath an illustrious instance in a prince, who must be acknowledged to bear a strong and striking resemblance to the Macedonian, in all the bright and glorious parts of his character; to possess the same exalted genius, the same penetration, the same indefatigable vigour, the same firmness and greatness of mind, the same boldness in enterprise, the same taste for the polite arts, and the same regard to learning and its professors.

"Like Philip, in his most distressed condition, his abilities have been employed in bearing up with an unconquered spirit against the united power of many different enemies surrounding him with their formidable numbers. But as his difficulties have been infinitely greater; so his abilities in triumphing over them, have hitherto appeared unparalleled: the present age beholds them with astonishment; posterity must speak of them with delight and admiration." Such is the magnanimous prince whom we may justly call the greatest Hero (in the true sense of the word) that this or any other age has ever produced. As a soldier, a politician, a legislator, a philosopher, a poet, he leaves Julius Caesar, Alexander, Charles XII. of Sweden, &c. at a long interval behind him.

ALSO FROM LEONAUR
AVAILABLE IN SOFTCOVER OR HARDCOVER WITH DUST JACKET

"AMBULANCE 464" ENCORE DES BLESSÉS *by Julien H. Bryan*—The experiences of an American Volunteer with the French Army during the First World War

THE GREAT WAR IN THE MIDDLE EAST: 1 *by W. T. Massey*—The Desert Campaigns & How Jerusalem Was Won---two classic accounts in one volume.

THE GREAT WAR IN THE MIDDLE EAST: 2 *by W. T. Massey*—Allenby's Final Triumph.

SMITH-DORRIEN *by Horace Smith-Dorrien*—Isandlwhana to the Great War.

1914 *by Sir John French*—The Early Campaigns of the Great War by the British Commander.

GRENADIER *by E. R. M. Fryer*—The Recollections of an Officer of the Grenadier Guards throughout the Great War on the Western Front.

BATTLE, CAPTURE & ESCAPE *by George Pearson*—The Experiences of a Canadian Light Infantryman During the Great War.

DIGGERS AT WAR *by R. Hugh Knyvett & G. P. Cuttriss*—"Over There" With the Australians by R. Hugh Knyvett and Over the Top With the Third Australian Division by G. P. Cuttriss. Accounts of Australians During the Great War in the Middle East, at Gallipoli and on the Western Front.

HEAVY FIGHTING BEFORE US *by George Brenton Laurie*—The Letters of an Officer of the Royal Irish Rifles on the Western Front During the Great War.

THE CAMELIERS *by Oliver Hogue*—A Classic Account of the Australians of the Imperial Camel Corps During the First World War in the Middle East.

RED DUST *by Donald Black*—A Classic Account of Australian Light Horsemen in Palestine During the First World War.

THE LEAN, BROWN MEN *by Angus Buchanan*—Experiences in East Africa During the Great War with the 25th Royal Fusiliers—the Legion of Frontiersmen.

THE NIGERIAN REGIMENT IN EAST AFRICA *by W. D. Downes*—On Campaign During the Great War 1916-1918.

THE AUXILIA OF THE ROMAN IMPERIAL ARMY *by G.L. Cheeseman*

THE MILITARY SYSTEM OF THE ROMANS *by Albert Harkness*

AVAILABLE ONLINE AT **www.leonaur.com**
AND FROM ALL GOOD BOOK STORES

ALSO FROM LEONAUR
AVAILABLE IN SOFTCOVER OR HARDCOVER WITH DUST JACKET

THE ART OF WAR by Antoine Henri Jomini—Strategy & Tactics From the Age of Horse & Musket.

THE ART OF WAR by Sun Tzu and Pierre G. T. Beauregard—*The Art of War* by Sun Tzu and *Principles and Maxims of the Art of War* by Pierre G. T. Beauregard.

THE MILITARY RELIGIOUS ORDERS OF THE MIDDLE AGES by F. C. Woodhouse—The Knights Templar, Hospitaller and Others.

THE BENGAL NATIVE ARMY by F. G. Cardew—An Invaluable Reference Resource.

ARTILLERY THROUGH THE AGES—by Albert Manucy—A History of the DEvelopment and Use of Cannons, Mortars, Rockets & Projectiles from Earliest Times to the Nineteenth Century.

THE SWORD OF THE CROWN by Eric W. Sheppard—A History of the British Army to 1914.

THE 7TH (QUEEN'S OWN) HUSSARS: Volume 3—1818-1914 by C. R. B. Barrett—On Campaign During the Canadian Rebellion, the Indian Mutiny, the Sudan, Matabeleland, Mashonaland and the Boer War Volume 3: 1818-1914.

THE CAMPAIGN OF WATERLOO by Antoine Henri Jomini—A Political & Military History from the French perspective.

RIFLE & DRILL by S. Bertram Browne—The Enfield Rifle Musket, 1853 and the Drill of the British Soldier of the Mid-Victorian Period *A Companion to the New Rifle Musket* and *A Practical Guide to Squad and Setting-up Dtill*.

NAPOLEON'S MEN AND METHODS by Alexander L. Kielland—The Rise and Fall of the Emperor and His Men Who Fought by His Side.

THE WOMAN IN BATTLE by Loreta Janeta Velazquez—Soldier, Spy and Secret Service Agent for the Confederancy During the American Civil War.

THE BATTLE OF ORISKANY 1777 by Ellis H. Roberts—The Conflict for the Mowhawk Valley During the American War of Independenc.

PERSONAL RECOLLECTIONS OF JOAN OF ARC by Mark Twain.

CAESAR'S ARMY by Harry Pratt Judson—The Evolution, Composition, Tactics, Equipment & Battles of the Roman Army.

FREDERICK THE GREAT & THE SEVEN YEARS' WAR by F. W. Longman.

AVAILABLE ONLINE AT **www.leonaur.com**
AND FROM ALL GOOD BOOK STORES

www.ingramcontent.com/pod-product-compliance
Lightning Source LLC
Chambersburg PA
CBHW031620160426
43196CB00006B/214